INTENTIONALITY AND THE MYTHS OF THE GIVEN: BETWEEN PRAGMATISM AND PHENOMENOLOGY

STUDIES IN AMERICAN PHILOSOPHY

Series Editors: *Willem deVries*
Henry Jackman

FORTHCOMING TITLES

Richard Rorty, Liberalism and Cosmopolitanism
David E. McClean

www.pickeringchatto.com/sap

INTENTIONALITY AND THE MYTHS OF THE GIVEN: BETWEEN PRAGMATISM AND PHENOMENOLOGY

BY

Carl B. Sachs

PICKERING & CHATTO
2014

Published by Pickering & Chatto (Publishers) Limited
21 Bloomsbury Way, London WC1A 2TH

2252 Ridge Road, Brookfield, Vermont 05036–9704, USA

www.pickeringchatto.com

BRITISH LIBRARY CATALOGUING IN PUBLICATION DATA

Sachs, Carl B., author
Intentionality and myths of the given: between pragmatism and phenomenology. – (Studies in American philosophy)
1. Intentionality (Philosophy) 2. Sellars, Wilfrid 3. Lewis, Clarence Irving, 1883–1964. 4. Merleau-Ponty, Maurice, 1908–61
I. Title II. Series
128.2-dc23

ISBN-13: 9781848935075
Web-PDF ISBN: 9781781444788
ePUB ISBN: 9781781444795

This publication is printed on acid-free paper that conforms to the American
National Standard for the Permanence of Paper for Printed Library Materials.

Content Management Platform by Librios™
Typeset by Pickering & Chatto (Publishers) Limited
Printed and bound in the United Kingdom by CPI Books

CONTENTS

ACKNOWLEDGEMENTS

The concept behind this book was conceived a long time ago, and has developed over the last ten years. I first became interested in the general problem of whether normativity and naturalism could be reconciled. Was it possible, I thought, be both a Kantian and a Darwinian? My first exploration of that question led to a sustained interest in Nietzsche, which somehow became a dissertation. After finishing graduate school my research led me first to Dewey and then to Sellars. Merleau-Ponty, whom I encountered in a seminar led by Fred Olafson in my first year of graduate school, was never far from my concerns. The present work might be conceived as my *Habilitationschrift*, and I have many people to thank for their support and help in bringing it finally to full term.

First, my profoundest gratitude to my mentor in all things Sellarsian, Willem deVries. Bill patiently guided me through every stage of the process, including encouraging me to write a book in the first place, suggesting that I take it to Pickering & Chatto for their Studies in American Philosophy series, reading every chapter with exacting criticisms, and answering every frantic email. We have finally ended up agreeing to disagree on many issues, but I shudder to think how much worse the book would have been if not for his advice and criticisms. I would also like to extend my appreciation and thanks to Bill's co-editor in the Studies in American Philosophy series, Henry Jackman.

Second, a different kind of gratitude must go to Mark Lance and Bill Blattner at Georgetown University. They agreed to sponsor me as a Sponsored Researcher at Georgetown for 2013–14, discussed many ideas with me, and went out of their way to make me feel included in the department. Mark also read much of the manuscript and offered a tremendous amount of criticism and encouragement. Special thanks is also due to Wayne Davis, the chair of the GU philosophy department, for his role in making my position at GU possible.

Third, my philosophical community. As someone who works in the rich intersections of analytic philosophy, Continental philosophy, and pragmatism, I am blessed with a wide array of outstanding philosophical interlocutors around the world. Of them, four deserve special commendation: Maureen Eckert, Steve Levine, Pete Olen and Aaron Schiller. Maureen patiently listened to every idea I ever had and constantly pushed me to be both more creative and more rigorous. Steve introduced me to Sellars in 2007, and I vividly recall an afternoon spent with Steve wandering around Prague in May 2011 where we hashed out the central ideas that formed the nucleus of this book. Pete and I have corresponded regularly about both Lewis and Sellars and I have invariably been impressed with his forceful criticisms of my views, particularly as they bear on the history of philosophy. Aaron, with whom Bill and I co-founded the Sellars Society in 2012, introduced me to the work of McDowell when we were graduate students together. I am in the profoundest debt to all of them, and to many more as well.

Fourth, I would like to thank Stephanie Hutchison for the extraordinary effort and dedication she has shown in closely reading the manuscript for grammar and style, and for her immensely helpful criticisms on how to make the book more accessible to those not completely immersed in these issues.

Fifth, my heartfelt gratitude to Sophie Rudland, Commissioning Assistant at Pickering & Chatto for Economics and Philosophy, for her continual feedback and support, for gently keeping me on deadline (more or less), and for her role in guiding the miraculous transformation of the manuscript into a book.

Lastly, my parents, who generously agreed to support me while living in Washington, D.C. Without their uncompromising love and support, I would never have dared to become a philosopher and would never have dared to write this book. To my mother Kathie Beck Sachs, who has the heart of a poet, and my father Donald H. Sachs, who has the mind of a psychologist, this book is lovingly dedicated.

The following chapters and sections draw upon material from my previously published works:

Chapter 4, section 2: 'McDowell's Transcendental Empiricism' draws upon both C. Sachs, 'The Shape of a Good Question: McDowel, Evolution, and Transcendental Philosophy', *The Philosophical Forum*, 42:1 (2011), pp. 61–78, and C. Sachs, 'Resisting the Disenchantment of Nature: McDowell and the Question of Animal Minds', *Inquiry*, 55:2 (2012), pp. 131–47.

Chapter 5 and Chapter 6, section 1: 'Myths of the Given and Transcendental Friction' both draw upon C. Sachs, 'Discursive and Somatic Intentionality: Merleau-Ponty contra "Sellars or McDowell"', *International Journal of Philosophical Studies*, 22:2 (2014), pp. 199–227.

INTRODUCTION: WHY A NEW ACCOUNT OF INTENTIONALITY?

Looking back on what is now canonized as 'twentieth-century philosophy', it is tempting to think that 'the problematic of intentionality' is a persistent preoccupation, often implicit even where it is not made explicit. Many of the most prominent philosophers on both sides of the Atlantic devoted themselves to such questions as, what is the 'aboutness' of thought and perception? How can anything material or physical exhibit intentional states? Can intentional states be modeled or duplicated on a machine? What about animals and babies? The problem of intentionality made its appearance for the twentieth century with Franz Brentano, was refined and reformulated by major figures of both 'analytic' (Ryle, Chisholm, Sellars, Brandom, Dennett) and 'Continental' persuasions (Husserl, Heidegger, Merleau-Ponty), and has continued today as a central focus of discussion about 'naturalism' and its limits. While a few prominent philosophers (such as Richard Rorty) have denied that intentionality marks out anything ontologically, epistemologically, or methodologically distinctive, it is fair to say that most philosophers have been unable to fully dispense with the suspicion, or 'intuition', that there has got to be *something* to the notion of intentionality.

While I share this intuition, I would not seek to ground any argument as to the limits of 'naturalism' in an account of intentionality; on the contrary, I have no reason to deny that 'intentionality' cannot be fully 'naturalized' – provided a satisfactory account of intentionality and of naturalism. But I submit that our grasp on the notions of 'intentionality' and 'naturalism' is not yet firm enough – at least, not if the firmness of our grasp of these notions is measured by the degree of consensus about what exactly it is that is contentious. In the following pages I attempt to explicate and defend a new account of intentionality that is, while not 'naturalistic' in a straightforward sense, at least fully naturalizable, in a sense to be carefully specified.

Methodological Preliminaries

The present work is indebted to Immanuel Kant on numerous fronts, and I would gladly label myself a 'Kantian naturalist' if the appellation did not immediately provoke the complaint that it is a *contradictio in adjecto*. Not only do I take for granted the plausibility of 'the transcendental standpoint' for philosophical reflection, but I also construe the transcendental task in terms of *cognitive semantics*.[1] Cognitive semantics, in the part that I am concerned with here, identifies the minimally necessary conditions that must be satisfied in order for an utterance (spoken or written) to count as an assertion, as expressing a thought or judgment, at all. Cognitive semantics is distinct from epistemology insofar as the latter is concerned with notions such as justification, warrant, evidence, goodness of reasoning, and so on. Compared with epistemology, cognitive semantics is 'up-stream': it is concerned with what must be the case for anything to even be the object of deployment of normative notions. In the Sellarsian idiom, now made popular by Robert Brandom and John McDowell, cognitive semantics inquires into the minimal conditions necessary for anything to count as a move in the game of giving and asking for reasons – including, importantly, the criteria for determining what can count as a player of that game. As a transcendental inquiry, cognitive semantics is an *a priori* inquiry into the most basic kinds of conceptual and perceptual capacities necessary for judgment, in that it is a kind of high-level functional analysis that can get off the ground from the armchair. (However, in the long run, cognitive semantics must be matched adequately with empirical facts in order to be validated fully). Cognitive semantics therefore occupies the intersection of epistemology, philosophy of mind, and philosophy of language. In what follows I shall construe the adequate account of intentionality in terms of what is required by cognitive semantics.

Specifically, the argument turns on what I call *bifurcated intentionality*: we need two different concepts of intentionality in order to have a fully adequate conception.[2] These two concepts are discursive intentionality, the capacity to engage in linguistic semantic contents within a shared linguistic community, and somatic intentionality, the capacity to engage with the ambient environment through a system of bodily relations. These two capacities are individually necessary and jointly sufficient for all reasoning with empirical content, and thus are essentially bound up with perception and action. (It is logically possible that a disembodied mind – one that had only discursive but not somatic intentionality – would be able to reason over purely formal domains. It could not have any substantive empirical content or any *a posteriori* knowledge).

Though the present work is heavily invested in the history of philosophy, it is not conceived, first and foremost, as a contribution to the history of philosophy. Let me be clear: I regard the history of philosophy as a valuable end in itself, and often the very project of philosophical reflection is carried out through our attempts to clarify and understand what Plato, or Descartes, or Kant, really thought about any particular topic or interconnected set of topics. And I do aim at correctly understanding what C. I. Lewis, Wilfrid Sellars and Maurice Merleau-Ponty really thought about perception, intentionality, conceptuality, mindedness, experience, and action. Nevertheless, if at the end of the day scholars find fault with my interpretations, I hope that they would nevertheless appreciate the novelty of the distinctive theory of intentionality that emerges from those interpretations.

For this reason, however, one may wonder why I bother to couch my account in the historical context used here. Why not simply present the positive account and leave the history to the historians? For one thing, I think that philosophy and the history of philosophy should be in better conversation than they are at present; for another, I think that we can better understand why we have the philosophical options that we have by reconstructing how the views were adopted and evaluated by those who held them. I take seriously Sellars's remark that 'The history of philosophy is the *lingua franca* which makes communication between philosophers, at least of different points of view, possible. Philosophy without the history of philosophy, if not empty or blind, is at least dumb'.[3] We must do philosophy historically if we are to embody within our philosophical practice our understanding that none of the concepts with which we are concerned reside in some Platonic heaven. I would ask those interested in the positive theory of intentionality developed here to take seriously the role that historical interpretation plays in that development, and those interested in the interpretations of historical figures to take seriously how those interpretations can be used in promoting substantive philosophical views. For this reason the book is somewhat heavy on quotations, so that those who are not familiar with the relevant texts can see exactly why they are being invoked to the extent that they are, and that those who are familiar with the relevant texts can appreciate their richness from a somewhat different perspective. (Due to the specific philosophical views at issue here, I have elected not to broaden the historical focus to include Kant or Hegel; though some may feel that this restriction is unforgivable, I hope that this will not be the majority opinion).

A similar commentary is called for with regard to the societally-marked distinction between 'analytic philosophy' and 'Continental philosophy', and the terms 'pragmatism' and 'phenomenology' as used here. It is my fervent hope that we will see soon see treatments on *The Rise and Fall of the Analytic/Continental Distinction*; while I am not entirely sure that this distinction ought to be 'overcome', the very idea of there being such a distinction has done far more harm than good to professionalized philosophy. For one thing, I do not regard either 'analytic philosophy' or 'Continental philosophy' as a natural kind, in that I doubt that there are any substantive philosophical views found in one camp that are not found in the other. This is not to say that there are no profound substantive differences between particular analytic and Continental philosophers. On the contrary, I shall argue that, on the construal of intentionality urged here, Lewis and Sellars share a serious blind-spot that is best revealed by the contrast with Merleau-Ponty. It is to say only that there are no substantive differences between all the philosophers classified as 'analytic', on the one hand, and all the philosophers classified as 'Continental', on the other. The differences, though not illusory, concern metaphilosophical views, rhetorical tropes, and the kind of training necessary to read the primary texts as a secondary language. At any rate, I am interested here with using specific philosophers associated with 'analytic philosophy' (Lewis, Sellars) and with 'Continental philosophy' (Merleau-Ponty) in order to say something new and interesting about an important philosophical problem.

In my view, similar considerations apply to the words 'pragmatism' and 'phenomenology', though I am more comfortable with these terms because are there are family resemblances. However, despite John Dewey's formative impact on my thinking about the role of embodiment in experience, I shall have nothing to say here about the so-called 'classical pragmatists' (canonically, Peirce, James, and Dewey), although I have a great deal to say about the so-called 'analytic pragmatists' or 'neo-pragmatists' Lewis, Sellars, and Brandom. I think that more sustained attention to Lewis and Sellars will help show what is mistaken about the very idea of an 'eclipse narrative' (according to which pragmatism went into eclipse after Dewey's death until it was revived in the 1980s by Rorty, Richard and Putnam).[4] I focus on Lewis and Sellars here because of what they contribute to our thinking about the social nature of conceptuality, intentionality, and normativity. If one were to insist that this is not pragmatism, I would point to the numerous borrowings and convergences between them and 'classical pragmatism'; if another were to agree with me but ask why I do not write about Peirce, James, and Dewey instead, I would say that there is much to be said for intellectual division of labor. Likewise, with respect to phenomenology, my chosen focus on Merleau-Ponty (with some attention to Dreyfus and Todes) should not be taken to mean that I neglect Husserl, Heidegger, or Sartre out of principle, misguided or otherwise.

The Plan of the Book

This book consists of six substantive chapters and a conclusion. Chapter 1 presents the need for a new conception of intentionality, based on John Haugeland's taxonomy of the positions and on what I call 'the demand for transcendental friction'. Chapter 2 shows how Lewis's attempt to satisfy the demand led him to distinguish between epistemological and semantic issues. In making sense of Lewis here, I propose a new distinction between the Myth of the epistemic Given and the Myth of the semantic Given. In those terms, I argue that C. I. Lewis is explicit in rejecting the former but that he implicitly accepts the latter. In presenting this claim I also argue that this was Lewis's consistent view in both *Mind and the World Order* and *An Analysis of Knowledge and Valuation*, and that Lewis appeared to change his views because he was obliged to make the distinction between epistemology and semantics more explicit due to pressure from the logical empiricists with whom he was in conversation.

Chapter 3 examines Sellars's criticisms of Lewis, and shows that Sellars understood Lewis to be committing the semantic Myth, not the epistemic Myth. The stage is set by situating Sellars's criticisms of Lewis in terms of Sellars's attempt to reconcile Lewis's views with those of Sellars's father, Roy Wood Sellars. Accordingly I devote some time to the debate between Lewis and Sellars *peré* before turning to Sellars *fils*. In context, Sellars's account of conceptual content – even empirical conceptual content – as wholly constituted by its functional role in an inferential system is crucial to his cognitive semantical criticism of Lewis. Yet Sellars also noticed the need for a suitable reinterpretation of nonconceptual states of consciousness, though his view is not without substantial difficulties. On that basis I turn in Chapter 4 to explaining why Brandom and McDowell reject nonconceptual content and what they attempt to replace it with. Doing so shows that neither Brandom nor McDowell have a wholly satisfactory view of what constrains the application of conceptual content. Yet there is surely something right in the thought that 'the senses do not judge'. I argue that the acceptability of this commitment turns on whether 'judgment' is the only kind of intentional content.

Chapter 5 turns to phenomenology and shows that Merleau-Ponty's phenomenology of lived embodiment provides us with the theory of somatic intentionality necessary to complement the account of discursive intentionality drawn from Lewis, Sellars, and Brandom. The account of somatic intentionality yields a kind of 'givenness' that is not Mythic – a 'perceptuo-practical Given' – and that getting clear on this concept affects our conception of 'nonconceptual content'. (In the Appendix I argue that there is a phenomenological version of the Myth of the Given, but that Merleau-Ponty's own phenomenology does not commit itself to the Myth). Putting somatic intentionality together with discursive intentionality completes the account of bifurcated intentionality. Finally, in Chapter 6 I show how the account of intentionality resolves a key problem of cognitive semantics by specifying precisely how somatic intentionality constrains discursive intentionality. I also compare and contrast bifurcated intentionality with similar proposals made by recent philosophers. Chapter 6 ends by showing how bifurcated intentionality bears on eliminativism about original intentionality and on the prospects for 'naturalizing' intentionality generally. The Conclusion notes some implications for further research.

1 INTENTIONALITY AND THE PROBLEM OF
TRANSCENDENTAL FRICTION

Original Intentionality and the Naturalist Challenge

In his insightful (and delightful) 'The Intentionality All-Stars', John Hauge-land examines the problem of how there can be original intentionality within a naturalistic world-view. How, he asks, can any part of the natural world bear an intentional relation to any other part? 'How can there be norms among the atoms in the void?'.[1] I use 'original intentionality' here in Haugeland's sense: 'original' contrasts with 'derived', with the kind of intentional, semantic content that sentences and signs have. Since not all semantic content can be derived, the argument goes, there must be original intentionality. Put otherwise, origi-nal intentionality does not mean a particular *kind* of intentionality but rather ground-level, 'original' *cases* of intentionality that need to be understood in order for other cases of intentional content to be understood.

This is not to say that any particular item has its own intrinsic semantic con-tent independent of all other semantic contents – that, I will show below, is an episode of the Myth of the semantic Given. Rather, it is to say that the entire rela-tional *system* of semantic contents does not have its content conferred upon it by something else; intentional content is a holistic property of the system, not of any specific part of the system. Nor does "original" here mean ineffable, private, inexplicable, or unexplained. Like Haugeland, I am interested in explaining the place of original intentionality within the broader framework of a naturalistic world-view (subject to caveats about 'natural'). In that sense, what is original under one set of considerations (the order of understanding) can be a result or product when viewed naturalistically (the order of being). The question is, how to regard original intentionality as something other than a Lever of Archimedes, how to explicate what original intentionality is, and how to explain the place of original intentionality *in rerum natura*.

On Haugeland's analysis, those who are interested in explaining original intentionality can be divided into three camps, which he calls neo-Cartesianism, neo-behaviourism, and neo-pragmatism. The neo-Cartesians (e.g., Jerry Fodor) seek to explain intentionality in terms of the pattern of relations amongst internal mental states, whereas the neo-behaviourists and neo-pragmatists broaden the scope. The neo-behaviourists (e.g., Willard V. O. Quine, Daniel Dennett) focus on ascriptions of intentional contents by virtue of patterns of interactions between organisms and their environments, particularly in perception and action. By contrast, the neo-pragmatists (e.g., Wilfrid Sellars, Robert Brandom) explicate intentionality in terms of social norms. All three positions purport to account for original intentionality, and to that extent are rivals. But Haugeland allows a position between neo-behaviourism and neo-pragmatism, and more interestingly, for the possibility of being both a neo-behaviourist and a neo-pragmatist:

> we might imagine a neo-behaviorist and a neo-pragmatist agreeing that animals and people share a certain primitive sort of intentionality (second-base position), and yet also that a qualitatively 'higher' intentionality is possible only for conformists with a culture and language (third-base position). Questions could be raised, of course, about what the two sorts of intentionality have to do with one another – why, in particular, both are sorts of *intentionality* – but perhaps there would be enough similarities to justify the common term.[2]

The position taken up here answers Haugeland's challenge by showing just how one can be both a neo-behaviourist and neo-pragmatist about original intentionality by distinguishing between the different *kinds* of intentionality. The key difference between Haugeland's suggestion and my developed view is that I draw extensively on Maurice Merleau-Ponty's first-person-standpoint descriptions of perception and action, rather than on the third-person-standpoint of the neo-behaviourists. The benefits of construing one kind of original intentionality as both non-social and non-linguistic will be made clear.

Hence, my approach is what I call *bifurcated intentionality*: that there are two basically different kinds of intentionality, both of which are 'original' in the relevant sense. The first is what I call *discursive* intentionality: the kind of intentionality that we use to characterize the 'aboutness' or 'of-ness' of thoughts, beliefs, desires, and more generally, anything with propositional content. The second is what I call *somatic* intentionality: the kind of intentionality that we use to characterize the lived bodily engagements with and comportments towards the world as enactively perceived and practically grasped. I aim to show that both discursive and somatic intentionality must be considered as *equally original* with regard to the philosophical work they are called upon to perform, because discursive intentionality (the intentionality of propositional discourse) and somatic intentionality (the intentionality of embodied perception) are *individually* necessary and *jointly* sufficient for judgements with empirical content:as empirical content or objective purport. To motivate this view, I shall show just why it is that we need both discursive and somatic intentionality, how to remove the obstacles that have prevented us from accommodating both kinds, what further distinctions are needed in order to render the view intellectually satisfactory, and what further consequences this view has for philosophizing about mindedness and experience.

The Naturalistic Challenge to Intentionality

This work is animated by a commitment to what I call transcendental naturalism: the view that transcendentally-specified roles must have empirically-specifiable role-players.[3] I aim to use 'transcendental' in a minimal sense, avoiding transcendental arguments or substantive metaphysical doctrines with 'transcendental' in the name. By 'transcendental', I mean the activity of identifying those items in a basic inventory of our cognitive capacities: what conceptual and perceptual roles must be filled in order for a cognitive system to count as having a mind similar to the kinds of minds that we have, and thereby to have the kinds of experiences that we have (however loosely and contextually characterized is the 'we' in this usage). Within this loose construal, philosophical methods as different as Lewis's 'reflective analysis', Sellars's comparison of the manifest and scientific images, and Merleau-Ponty's phenomenological descriptions of embodied perception will all count as different implementations of transcendental philosophy.

But transcendental philosophy is not, I think, sufficient: we can, on the other hand, interpret the insights and discoveries of the natural (and social) sciences as providing specifications of the role-players for various transcendentally-specified roles. So I take 'intentionality' to be a transcendental notion, rather than a straightforwardly empirical one – but with the caveat that the theory of intentionality that we arrive at should be, at the end of the day, at the very least fully consistent with the natural sciences– it should not commit us to positing the existence of any entities that are not required for any other explanatory purposes. Rather than hastily attempt to 'naturalize intentionality', I want to inquire more carefully into what sort of thing intentionality is, such that it could be naturalized (or perhaps not). To see the value of doing so, consider the following line of thought:

(1) The concept of original intentionality requires that the basic units of thought are sentence- and term-shaped representations;

(2) If original intentionality is real, then it must be empirically identifiable;

(3) Hence the most plausible candidate for being the bearer of original intentionality is the primate (perhaps even human) brain;

(4) But cognitive neuroscience shows that brains do not represent their environments in sentence-shaped representations – there are no propositions in the prefrontal cortex;

(5) So, there is no such thing as original intentionality.

As Alex Rosenberg confidently summarizes this view:

> The illusion of original intentionality has its origin in the fact that while the brain
> stores information in nonpropositional data structures of some kind, it extracts and
> deploys the information in temporally extended processes, such as noises and marks –
> eventually speech and writing – and it is these together with the conscious states that
> they result in that generate the illusion of propositional content.[4]

I am uncertain what to say about (5) save that I find this conclusion so 'counter-intuitive' that I would be hard-pressed to locate a common ground with those who think that (5) is correct. Yet I find no problem with either (2) or (4); the problem lies entirely with (1) and (3). Against (1), I urge a distinction between two different kinds of intentionality, discursive and somatic, so that the identifica-tion of intentional content with propositional content does not go unquestioned. Against (2), the two basic kinds of original intentionality are 'at home' in *lin-guistic communities* and in *embodied animals*, respectively. This allows that intentionality may be 'naturalized', with the crucial proviso that we do not have at present a sufficiently fine-grained comprehension of the intricate causal interplay between brains, bodies, and environments that would be needed to fully specify how discursive and somatic intentionality are causally instantiated. (Whether it is possible or probable that we may eventually have such a comprehension is beyond the scope of the present investigation). In other words, Rosenberg-style elimina-tivism about intentionality does not follow from neuroscience alone; it follows from neuroscience conjoined with a specific picture of what intentionality must be like. It is that picture which I aim to dislodge by offering a series of minor cor-rections to those who have preceded me in this enterprise.

One constraint on the account of intentionality to be developed here is that it must avoid what is called, following Sellars, 'The Myth of the Given'. Yet here at once a whole net of problems arise as to what is supposedly Given, just why the Given is supposedly a Myth, how the Myth of the Given should be avoided, and whether our commitment to avoiding the Myth entails that we ought eschew 'nonconceptual content'. The interpretation of the Myth of the Given is compounded by according undue emphasis to Sellars's 'Empiricism and the Phi-losophy of Mind', at the expense of the comprehensiveness of Sellars' philosophy as a whole, even though Sellars himself insists at the outset:

> This framework [the Given] has been a common feature of most of the major systems
> of philosophy, including, to use a Kantian turn of phrase, both 'dogmatic rationalism'
> and 'skeptical empiricism'. It has, indeed, been so pervasive that few, if any, philoso-
> phers have been altogether free of it; certainly not Kant, and, I would argue, not even
> Hegel, that great foe of 'immediacy'. Often what is attacked under its name are only
> specific varieties of 'given.' Intuited first principles and synthetic necessary connec-
> tions were the first to come under attack. And many who today attack 'the whole idea
> of givenness' – and they are an increasing number – are really only attacking sense
> data. For they transfer to other items, say physical objects or relations of appearing,

the characteristic features of the 'given.' If, however, I begin my argument with an attack on sense-datum theories, it is only as a first step in a general critique of the entire framework of givenness.[5]

Accordingly, I want to be bear in mind 'a general critique of the entire framework of givenness' through the current project. Our understanding of the Myth has been hampered in two different ways. Firstly, critics of the Myth (and even a few defenders) have emphasized the empiricist version of the Myth at the expense of rationalistic, Kantian, and even Hegelian versions.[6] These versions of the Myth differ according to what is said to be given: sense-data, universals, real connections, the typology and structure of mental representations, and so on. That is, the Myth has a much wider *scope* than usually understood. Secondly, the Myth has been construed as merely an epistemological thesis rather than, as I argue here, also a cognitive-semantic thesis. While this is understandable, it matters because Lewis (as I shall argue in Chapter 2) does *not* commit the Myth *if* the Myth is just an epistemological mistake – nor, importantly, does Sellars himself think that Lewis' error was an epistemological one. Rather, I will argue, Sellars' criticisms of Lewis' notion of 'the given' is not epistemological, but *cognitive-semantic* – a kind of reflective inquiry closely related to what Hegel called 'logic' and to what Wittgenstein called 'grammar'.

In its most general form, the Myth of the Given is the idea that a fully adequate cognitive semantics can identify cognitive-semantic contents simply as such, independent of the role(s) that they play in perception, thought, and action. Thus construed, the Myth of the Given constrains any account we can construct of what is necessary for any being to count as sapient (to be able to play the game of giving and asking for reasons) as well as sapient-and-sentient (to be able to play the game of giving and asking for reasons with regard to perception and action). The *traditional* defender of the Given holds that the Given is not a Myth by arguing that there are contents of cognitive experience that do not require awareness of any other cognitive-semantic contents in order to be known as those contents. Those who hold that the Given is a Myth argue that all cognitive access to cognitive-semantic contents is itself mediated by their role in perception, thought, and action; consequently, identification of anything as Given either covertly depends on our ability to deploy cognitive-semantic contents generally, or that the purported contents do not actually play any cognitive-semantic role. One central problem, for those who think that the Given is a Myth after all, is whether avoiding the Myth requires adjuring from any commitment to 'nonconceptual content', much-vexed notion as that is. If so, we shall need to know under what specifications nonconceptual content would be consistent with that criticism, and under what specifications the commitment to nonconceptual content would be an instance of the Myth.

The challenge thereby posed is this: how can one accept nonconceptual content without committing the Myth? Is it coherent that nonconceptual content could be a kind of intentional content, or must all intentional content be conceptually structured? The concept of nonconceptual content in recent analytic philosophy of perception has a complicated history.[7] Consequently, several scholars have urged that the very debate between conceptualism and nonconceptualism rests on undiagnosed equivocations. Though I agree with that line of thought, I am unsure that the present diagnoses of those equivocations have gotten it entirely right. To see why, consider the following supremely condensed summary of the debate based on recent contributions by Richard Heck, Jeff Speaks, T. M. Crowther, and Josefa Toribio.[8]

Heck argues that the key idea behind 'nonconceptual content' is that there is a kind of mental content that is *representational* but nonconceptual by virtue of failing to satisfy Gareth Evans's Generality Constraint: that a subject cannot conceive of a *is* F if she cannot also entertain the thought that a *is* G and that b *is* F. However, Speaks and Crowther both argue that this is an insufficient characterization of nonconceptual content based on the arguments brought forth by both nonconceptualists (Peacocke, Evans, Heck, Kelly) and conceptualists (McDowell). Based on both Speaks and Crowther, Toribio puts the contrast between 'content nonconceptualism' and 'state nonconceptualism' – capturing both Speaks's distinction between 'absolute nonconceptual content' and 'relative nonconceptual content' and also Crowther's distinction between 'compositional content' and 'possessional content'. According to Toribio, content nonconceptualism holds that 'for any perceptual experience E with content C, C is nonconceptual$_c$ if C is essentially different in kind to the content of belief',[9] whereas state nonconceptualism holds that 'for any perceptual experience E with content C, any subject S and any time t, E is nonconceptual$_s$ if it is not the case that in order for S to undergo E, S must possess at t the concepts that a correct characterization of C would involve'.[10] One note of caution: since Crowther distinguishes between compositional and possessional conceptualism *and* conceptualism, one could hold both compositional nonconceptualism and possessional conceptualism or both compositional conceptualism and possessional nonconceptualism.

In these terms, I take 'nonconceptual content' to be personal-level representational cognitive-semantic content that does not conform to the Generality Constraint. Each of these points deserves separate elucidation: NCC is personal-level, not a feature of subpersonal neurocomputational processing; it is representational, not a mere sensory quale; it is cognitive-semantic, and not 'mental' in the sense of a psychological state. The last point becomes particularly important because I will treat normative inferential semantics, as developed by Lewis, Sellars, and Brandom, as a way of specifying why the Generality Constraint holds of conceptual content. In addition to what kind of concept of NCC is, we also need to know how we have any cognitive grip on this concept. In the dominant literature, NCC is posited (or denied) in order to explain the psychology of perception; it is a psychological, hence empirical, concept. However, I am interested here in the role of NCC as a transcendental concept – as what must be at work in any adequate explication of the cognitive machinery of any being with a finite mind like ours. The key differences to be explored in what follows turn on what is necessary to account for our grasp of NCC as a transcendental concept: whereas for Lewis transcendental argument grounded in the explication of cognitive experience is both necessary and sufficient, Sellars holds that the transcendental status of the concept of NCC must be supplemented with a *genealogy* of the origins of the concept (hence his well-known 'Myth of Jones') that accounts for 'sheer receptivity' in terms of causal explanation of perceptual episodes. By contrast, Merleau-Ponty holds that the transcendental status of the concept of NCC must be underpinned by *phenomenological description* of motor intentionality in embodied perception, both normal and pathological. The importance of transcendental content nonconceptualism will become especially clear in Chapter 5, where I contrast my views with those of Robert Hanna and Jay Rosenberg. As I will show there, everything turns on whether we are willing to accept Merleau-Ponty's conception of *non-apperceptive* or *pre-subjective* consciousness as having its own kind of *intentional* content.

The Demand for Transcendental Friction

Thus far I have only raised the possibility of bifurcated intentionality and some of the problems that must be faced in order to make the view acceptable. What I have not done, however, is suggest any reasons why one would want to adopt such a view. Though there are perhaps several distinct reasons, the most salient in my view is that it satisfies what I call *the demand for transcendental friction*: that it must be possible, by reflecting on our most basic conceptual and perceptual capacities and incapacities, to guarantee that we are in cognitive contact with a world we discover and do not create. Here I will first briefly sketch how I understand C. I. Lewis and Sellars as trying to satisfy the demand for transcendental friction. I will then turn to John McDowell's account of experience and argue that his distinction between discursive and intuitional conceptual content cannot satisfy the demand. (Importantly, McDowell rejects the Lewis-Sellars thesis that the demand could not be satisfied if all content were conceptual; his entire project is an attempt to satisfy the demand through conceptualism.)

Generally speaking, we can understand Lewis's project, at least with regard to *Mind and the World Order* (hereafter *MWO*) as a reflective analysis of cognitive experience.[11] By 'a reflective analysis of cognitive experience', I mean that Lewis makes explicit, for the purposes of clarification and improvement, the implicit features of our own practices of classification and predication concerning the objects, properties, and relations that we experience. Central to this inquiry is the nature of *objective purport*: how is it that our experiences can so much as seem to be a taking in of things being thus and so. To clarify the structure of objective purport, Lewis distinguishes between the two necessary conditions of objective purport: that there must be *conceptual interpretation* and there must be *the given*.[12] Conceptual interpretation and the given are individually necessary and jointly sufficient for objective purport, or to use a coextensive term, empirical content.

In order to understand the exact role of the given for Lewis' project, consider his transcendental arguments for the individual necessity of both the given and concepts. On the one hand, a being that had nothing given to it would have nothing for its judgements to be about; they would lack all content, in the sense that while the judgements could very well form an internally consistent, norm-governed inferential nexus, there would be no possibility of *applying* this conceptual framework, and so no way of *using* it. Such a being could not have the kind of cognitive experience that we manifestly have. On the other hand, a being that only had a pure given in experience, and lacked concepts, could only experience an undifferentiated flux. Indeed, on Lewis's pragmatist conception of concepts as essentially connected with action, a being entirely bereft of concepts would be an entirely *passive* being, unable to even distinguish between past and future, self and world. This kind of being, too, could not possibly have the kind of cognitive experience that we manifestly have. On the basis of these arguments, Lewis concludes that any analysis of our cognitive experience must account both for the basic structure of our implicit-yet-explicable, fallible-but-corrigible categories at work in our practical dealings with things, and for the application of these categories to a reality that is not itself merely constituted by those categories. This is why concepts and the given are individually necessary and jointly sufficient to characterize the kind of cognitive experience that we are able to recognize as having objective purport for beings like us.

To distinguish between the achievement of objective purport and its conditions, Lewis draws a distinction between 'thick experience of the world of things' and 'thin experience of immediacy'.[13] Whereas 'thick experience' is of a world of objects and their properties and relations, persisting through space and time, 'thin experience' is the minimal sensory apprehensions to which concepts are applied in order to yield objective purport. In (roughly) Kantian terms, thick experience is the experience resulting from the synthesis of the sensibility (the given) and the understanding (concepts), whereas thin experience is sensibility considered independent of the understanding. The need for sensibility to function as a constraint on conceptual application is made clear by Lewis's definition of the given as that element *in* experience which is unalterable by thought. It guarantees that there is transcendental friction: that our concepts are constrained by something external to and independent of them. In other words, the given functions as a 'tribunal of experience'.[14] The problem, of course, is how to understand this. If we understand experience in the thick sense, where conceptual interpretations are already fully engaged, then the concepts are not being constrained by something external to them. Yet if we understand experience in the thin sense, which threatens to recede into the specious present, then it seems mysterious as to how the given can have enough determinacy to it for it to function as a tribunal for our conceptual interpretations of it at all. Lewis's contrast here shows us the Demand can be satisfied only if some experienceable content is both sufficiently distinct from concepts to serve as a constraint, and not just more of the same, and yet sufficiently proto- or quasi-normative in basic structure to *be* a constraint.

The tensions in Lewis's conception of the given are only heighted as Lewis tries to specify more precisely what he means by it. For example, Lewis proposes two different characterizations of the given: (a) that it has a specific feeling-quality; (b) that it is inalterable by thought.[15] By 'inalterable by thought', Lewis means that the given is constant under imaginative variation – I can alter, in my imagination, my judgement that I am looking at a coffee-mug as I write (is it a coffee-cup façade? a hologram? a hallucination?) – but what I cannot alter by any such variations is the sheer awareness of *something* to which those categories *apply*. (That we cannot say exactly *what* the given is – that it is, in other words, ineffable – is a point that Lewis not only concedes but emphasizes, at least in MWO). This awareness is not even that of an *object*, since objects per se are only brought into the purview of conscious experience insofar as the given is conceptually interpreted.

Lewis himself stresses, rightly, that the constancy-under-imaginative variation conception of the given is of far greater philosophical importance than Lewis's identification of the given with 'qualia', because constancy-under-variation shows that the given is sufficiently *independent* from the categories to be *external* to them, in the way necessary to satisfy the Demand. Indeed, to identify the given with qualia – as Lewis eventually did – spoils the entire attempt to vindicate transcendental friction. With this move, the given is identified only by virtue of its phenomenal properties – a move that Lewis makes because he is unable to disentangle conceptuality from intentionality, and so the nonconceptual becomes the non-intentional and *a fortiori* non-representational. But then it becomes mysterious as to how anything merely phenomenalistic, as qualia evidently are, could generate any real friction on our cognitive activities. In general terms, this problem then exercised all those who came after Lewis – Goodman, White, Quine, Firth – and especially Sellars, who was not fully engaged in these debates as they unfolded but who has much to contribute to what we should learn from those debates.

Much like Lewis, Sellars is both rarely far from Kant and rarely uncritical. In his *Science and Metaphysics* (hereafter *S&M*), subtitled "Variations on Kantian

Themes", Sellars, Wilfrid departs from Kant in many crucial respects – leaving many to wonder ever since how the appearance of Kant in Sellars's text could ever be confused with Kant -in-himself.[16] One of the most substantive and far-reaching of these departures is Sellars's revision of the Kantian concept/intuition distinction, which Sellars argues rests on an ambiguity that Kant simply conceals by conflating it with the general/particular distinction. For it is just not the case that all and only conceptual representations are generals; there are conceptual representations of particulars as well. And once we take full cognizance of this (rather obvious) fact, we will see, Sellars argues, that 'intuition', in the Kantian sense, is ambiguous between 'representation of particulars' to which we are (ostensibly) 'immediately' related – e.g. '*this* cup here now'- and sense-impressions proper.

Given Sellars's conception of intentional content as entirely constituted by functional role in an inferential system, intentional content is not *directly* related the world, although the entry and exit transitions are caused by the impingements of worldly objects on our cognitive systems. And yet there must be a point of 'contact' or 'friction' between us and the world – in other words, there must be 'sheer receptivity', or a kind of mental state that is not intermingled with the 'spontaneity' of discursive intentionality. This is required in part by the Demand itself, and in part by a satisfactory interpretation of what Kant was aiming at, insofar as meeting the Demand is something with which Kant was concerned. In Sellars's terms, we can satisfy the Demand only by distinguishing the sheer receptivity of sense from the guidedness of intuitions. The latter, as this-such complexes, are already displays of the productive imagination; they lack the independence from conceptual capacities generally which would be needed for genuine friction. This is why we need the sheer receptivity of sense, which is 'sheer' in that nothing of spontaneity – understanding, conceptuality, apperception, rationality – has yet entered onto the scene. We need sheer receptivity, with no spontaneity as yet combined with it, in order to guarantee the right sort of external constraint that, in turn will terminate the dialectic that leads from Hegel's insights to Bradley, Blanshard, Bosquanet, or for that matter, Lewis's philosophical mentor, Josiah Royce.

As Sellars is not exceedingly clear as to how sensations perform their 'guiding' role, the following tentative remarks on the role of sensations in Sellars's epistemology will have to suffice. Sellars requires that we think that "having a sensation of a red triangle is a fact *sui generis*, neither epistemic nor physical, having its own logical grammar'.[17] That is, sensations must be *non-physical causes*. They must be causes because they have no *epistemic* or *rational* character: the mere having of a sensation is not itself within the space of reasons, and they are necessary but insufficient for language-entry transitions (perceptual reports). Indeed, to treat the mere having of a sensation as itself playing any epistemic or semantic role is simply the empiricist version of the Myth of the Given. But though sensations are merely causal, they cannot be physical – they are *states of consciousness*, conceptually distinct from the triggering of external neuroceptors. This is why Sellars was eventually led, in the Carus Lectures, to insist that the absence of 'sensa' from the scientific image was a serious oversight.[18] Only if sensa are both non-epistemic but only causal, and yet non-physical but only states of *consciousness,* can we adequately explain the difference between perception and judgement, which is needed to satisfy the Demand – precisely what was lost in the dialectic that led to nineteenth-century idealism. The crucial difference between Lewis's qualia and Sellars's sensa is that sensa play only a causal-functional role and have no semantic content, since semantic content is explained entirely in normative-functional terms. By contrast, as I will show in Chapter 2, Lewis's qualia are not causal antecedents of empirical content, but partially constitutive of empirical semantic content.

To summarize a complicated line of thought from *Science and Metaphysics*, then: Sellars's thought is that we can satisfy the Demand by recognizing that the noumenal world, the things in themselves, gets a vote in what we say about it by causing sensations – the moment of sheer receptivity – which are then taken up in judgements about the world, the semantic content of which is, of course, dependent on the rest of the conceptual framework, and the phenomenal objects are what are referred to from 'within' that conceptual framework. The question is, how is this gap from causes to reasons bridged? Suppose we think of a process with three arrows:[19]

Physical objects → sensings of sense contents → noninferential beliefs → inferential belief

It seems obvious that the first arrow is a merely causal arrow. Physical objects cause our sensations by virtue of how photons and molecules affect the neuroceptors in our retinas, cochlea and epithelial surfaces. And it seems obvious that the third arrow is a rational arrow — noninferential beliefs serves as reasons or justifications for inferential beliefs ("I see that the streets are wet, so I have good reason to believe that it was probably raining earlier"). But what is the second arrow? Is it causal? Rational? (Both? Neither?) Sellars's metaphor of "guidance," borrowed from Wittgenstein, is both insightful and unhelpful; it tells us where to look for transcendental friction but not what it actually is. Hence it should come as no surprise that post-Sellarsian philosophers such as Rorty, Brandom, and McDowell find the notion of sheer receptivity to be utterly unworkable. But if the given is a myth, and sheer receptivity is unworkable, then we might worry that the Demand cannot be satisfied.

The problem of transcendental friction has also been central to McDowell's attempt to dislodge us from the oscillation between the Myth of the Given and coherentism as 'frictionless spinning in a void'.[20] Since publishing *Mind and World*, McDowell has made increasingly explicit that he shares Sellars's conviction that Kant's concept of 'intuition' needs rehabilitation and clarification. Unlike Sellars, however, he sees no need for 'sheer receptivity with regard to transcendental philosophy – a point that proved central to McDowell's criticism of Sellars in the 1998 Woodbridge Lectures.[21] Insofar as sheer receptivity is *posited*, McDowell argues, it belongs with other causal posits in the realm of law, not in the explication of the standpoint of experience in which we do transcendental philosophy. In the terms deployed in those lectures, sensations are 'below the line' that separates characterizations that belong to the space of reasons from characterizations that belong to the realm of law. Instead, McDowell thinks that is necessary and sufficient to distinguish between perceptual experience as the passive actualization of conceptual capacities in sensory consciousness and judgement as the free exercise of those very same capacities.[22]

So experience can constrain judgement because experience already involves conceptual content, though since it is passively actualized rather than freely exercised, it is not under the control of the subject. In this way the subject can be reassured that what she experiences is sufficiently independent from what she judges that her judgements are constrained, and indeed, *normatively* constrained – experience can be a genuine tribunal because concepts are already at work within it.

McDowell's 'Avoiding the Myth of the Given' recasts this account in terms of the distinction between 'discursive conceptual content' and 'intuitional conceptual content', and that making this distinction will satisfy our Demand.[23] As I will show in detail in Chapter 4, McDowell now regards intuitional content as actually conceptual because it is potentially propositional. Though this modification makes clear that experience does not itself have *propositional* form, even this modified version of McDowell's view does not, contrary to his intention, satisfy the Demand. If intuitional conceptual contents are stipulated to have the right sort of form to be suitable for discursive articulation, though they are not discursively articulated, then we have satisfied one aspect of the Demand at the expense of the other.

Recall that the Demand requires that some experienceable content have *both* the requisite quasi- or proto-normative structure to constrain the application of conceptual contents *and* that it be sufficiently distinct from conceptual contents to be a genuinely *external* constraint, and not just 'more of the same' (as arguably was the problem with nineteenth-century idealism). McDowell's attempt to dislodge the oscillation between the Myth of the Given and coherentism is his version of the need to satisfy both constraints at once. But it is not clear that he can do so in a satisfactory way, because intuitional conceptual contents have the structure that they have – the structure that is supposed to constrain application of discursive conceptual contents – because they have, in fact, the exact same structure, the structure of conceptual content – that differs only by virtue of the *mode* in which that content is present (as discursively articulated or as intuitionally articulable).[24] But since experience and judgement have the exact same content, and differ only in mode, McDowell cannot satisfy the Demand, because the Demand requires that conceptual content itself be constrained by something external to it.

The preceding compressed sketch, to be expanded upon significantly in Chapters 2–4, shows that the demand for transcendental friction is a central, animating concern of Lewis, Sellars, and McDowell, but that none of them can satisfy it. Should we then conclude that the Demand itself is fundamentally misconceived? That conclusion would be, I suggest, premature. Before dismissing the Demand altogether, we should reconsider the terms in which the Demand is conceived, and perhaps in the process discover why those terms prevented it from being satisfied. I thereby suggest that the very heart of the entire problem is *not* the Demand itself, but rather in the next move: in the assumption that rational conceptuality is the paradigm of intentional activity – consider how this might have come about through the history of reception of Kant's notion of 'spontaneity' – and then it will seem that only that which is passive can provide friction. But passivity cannot provide friction, since sheer passivity lacks the requisite structure to offer the constraint that friction requires. What we ought to learn from the history of Lewis's, Sellars's, and McDowell's instructive failures to meet the demand for transcendental friction is this: if nothing passive (transcendentally considered) can give us the friction we need, we should re-think that assumption that only the conceptual is intentional. What we ought to, instead, is find a way to accept that there is a kind of proto- or quasi-normativity, a kind of nonconceptual (at least non-discursive) intentionality, that can indeed satisfy the demand for transcendental friction. It is only the assumption that the conceptual is the intentional – an assumption shared by Lewis, Sellars, and McDowell – which has prevented us from noticing that we needed to find it. Put otherwise, if we can see our way clear to accepting the bifurcated account of intentionality – that there is both discursive intentionality and somatic intentionality – we will indeed be able to satisfy the Demand. Putting this audacious claim on the gold standard of textual and conceptual analysis is the goal of Chapter 5 and 6, and of the book as a whole. With the new conception of intentionality defended here, we will have the right sort of 'hybrid position' that Haugeland suggested but did not explore, and that in turn will shed new light on whether Rosenberg's eliminativist challenge to intentionality can be refuted.

2 THE EPISTEMIC GIVEN AND THE SEMANTIC GIVEN IN C. I. LEWIS

Once widely known to have been one of the most prominent epistemologists of the first half of the twentieth century, today C. I. Lewis has largely faded into obscurity. This is highly unfortunate, because much of the landscape of analytic philosophy that we today take for granted, such as the debates about the analytic/synthetic distinction or about the intelligibility of 'the Given', took shape as White, Goodman, Quine, Firth, and Sellars argued amongst themselves in the wake of Lewis. In her recent history of American pragmatism, Cheryl Misak gives considerable priority to Lewis, noting that, 'Indeed, Sellars perfectly exemplifies the spirit of the Peirce-Lewis brand of pragmatism ... but his intellectual relationship to Lewis is another one of those gaps in scholarship that seems to plague Lewis's reputation'.[1] I hope to remedy this omission by re-examining Lewis's contribution to epistemology and philosophy of mind and of language, the extent to which it is vulnerable to Sellarsian criticisms, and the extent to which, for all its flaws, Lewis's view attempts to capture something of the utmost importance for a correct understanding of intentionality.

To take one prominent example of how difficult the issues are, Robert Hanna provocatively claims that there is no such thing as the Myth of the Given, and that the error lies not just in Sellars, but rather in Lewis's continuation of a Hegelian error:

> [The Myth of the Given] began in Hegel's misinterpretation of Kant, when Hegel wrongly claims that Kant is a subjective or phenomenal idealist. Then Hegel's misinterpretation was re-transmitted via late nineteenth-century and early twentieth-century Oxford neo-Hegelians and neo-Kantians, together with C. I. Lewis at Harvard, who passed it on to Wilfrid Sellars, who studied Kant at both Oxford and at Harvard. C. I. Lewis's influence on Kant studies in particular was directly and widely felt in North America in the second half of the twentieth century via the writings of Lewis White Beck and Sellars. Beck and Sellars were both Lewis's PhD students at Harvard. On the other side of the Atlantic, in 1936, Lewis's *Mind and the World Order* was the first contemporary philosophical text ever to be taught at Oxford, in a seminar run by J. L. Austin and Isaiah Berlin. Not altogether coincidentally, the second chapter of *Mind and the World Order* is entitled 'The Given'. Sellars in fact attended this Oxford

seminar, started a D. Phil. dissertation on Kant with T. D. Weldon the same year, and later transferred to Harvard. Then Hegel's misinterpretation of Kant was again re-transmitted at the University of Pittsburgh, where Sellars taught and was enormously influential. ... But in point of fact, in my opinion, what is being rejected by McDowell under the rubric of 'non-conceptual content' is nothing more and nothing less than *Hegel's misinterpretation of Kant's philosophy of cognition*.[2]

Contra Hanna, whose defense of nonconceptualism I nevertheless find highly congenial (see Chapter 5), I take the Myth of the Given seriously. Moreover, Lewis introduces the Given precisely in order to avoid the excessive conceptu-alism of late nineteenth-century idealism; Lewis studied under Royce, whom he admired greatly, but was also deeply influenced by the new realists, such as Ralph Perry, who convinced Lewis that absolute idealism was an untenable posi-tion.[3] Moreover, as I shall argue here, Lewis's implicit commitment to the Myth of the Given does not depend on the flawed interpretation of Lewis as a phe-nomenalist that Hanna tacitly endorses. At pain of excessive contextualization: Rorty famously remarks that Sellars described his own project as 'an attempt to usher analytic philosophy out of its Humean and into its Kantian stage'.[4] But this way of seeing Sellars's project wrongly neglects the Kantian pragmatism of C. I. Lewis to which Sellars is responding. For Lewis had already staked a Kantian position within 'analytic philosophy' *avant la lettre*, and Sellars himself moves beyond Kant towards Hegel, thereby taking analytic philosophy well along the path towards its rendezvous with Hegelian thought that has since become in-and-for-itself with Brandom and McDowell.[5]

A natural starting-point here is to examine Lewis and Sellars on the problem of 'the given'. Whereas Lewis argued that no account of our cognitive experience can ignore the nonconceptual element of experience, what he calls simply 'the given' or 'givenness', Sellars is well-known for his famous (though less-than-clear) critique of 'the Myth of the Given'. But is the given really a myth? To what extent is Lewis vulnerable to Sellarsian criticisms? How might Lewis be defended from Sellars's criticisms, if at all? Are there any insights in Lewis that survive Sellars's criticism? To answer these questions, I distinguish between the *epistemic* given and the *semantic* given. The epistemic given has both epistemic efficacy (it plays a justificatory role in our inferences) and epistemic independence (it does not depend on any other justified assertions).[6] Analogously, the semantic given is both efficacious and independent with regard to *cognitive semantics*, which differs from epistemology by being concerned with having the right form and content to be playable in that game, whereas epistemology deals with assessment of warrant, evidence, justification, and so on. The shift in emphasis from epis-temology to cognitive semantics announced in the Introduction is justified by how it both resolves ambiguities in interpreting Lewis and in how it clarifies Sellars's criticisms of Lewis.

In those terms, I shall argue that both Lewis and Sellars reject the epistemic given, but that while Lewis accepts the semantic given, Sellars criticizes Lewis for accepting the semantic given. Specifically, in both *Mind and the World Order* (hereafter *MWO*) and *Analysis of Knowledge and Valuation* (hereafter *AKV*), Lewis was both a critic of the epistemic given and a defender of the semantic given. I will first show how Lewis criticizes the epistemic given (emphasizing *MWO*), then turn to the defense of the semantic given (emphasizing *AKV*). I conclude by showing in detail just how and why Lewis accepts the semantic given, such that his position is vulnerable to Sellarsian objections.

Lewis's Kantian-Pragmatist Rejection of the Epistemic Given

When Lewis is remembered at all today, it is primarily as an antiquated defender of phenomenalism and foundationalism. In what follows, I rely upon recent scholarship that emphasizes Lewis's 'Kantian pragmatism' and rejection of epistemological foundationalism, as he construed it. Lewis embraces a thoroughly fallibilistic conception of knowledge, a keen sense of the powers and limits of logic, and a realization that pragmatism requires what he calls 'the pragmatic conception of the *a priori*'.[7] Like Kant, Lewis examines cognitive experience: the kind of experience that has objective purport, which so much as seems to be a taking-in that things are thus and so. (Lewis acknowledges that there are non-cognitive experiences, but that he is not interested in examining them. In his sense of non-cognitive, Lewis means mere aesthetic 'havings' or enjoying; moral evaluations (the 'V' in *AKV*) are, in his sense, cognitive as well as affective.) Accordingly, we need to examine the basic structure of cognitive experience, to survey the basic kinds of cognitive experience that we have, and to articulate the principal similarities and differences between those kinds.

In doing so, Lewis embraces the Kantian thesis that concepts are brought to bear in experience by the active mind, but without construing this point in favor of idealism. To avoid idealism, there must be a nonconceptual element of experience: 'The two elements to be distinguished in knowledge are the concept, which is the product of the activity of thought, and the sensuously given, which is independent of such activity'[8], as a result of which 'empirical truth, or knowledge of the objective, arises through conceptual interpretation of the given'.[9] The given and its interpretation are individually necessary and jointly sufficient for any candidate for empirical knowledge; if either the given or conceptual interpretation were absent, we could not so much as entertain thoughts that seem to be about the world, and whose truth-conditions depend on how the world is. As Hookway correctly observes, Lewis's distinction between the given and the concept is not motivated by a concern with 'the structure of justification' but with 'the nature of cognitive experience'.[10] Lewis is a coherentist about the structure of justification and a fallibilist about the dynamics of justification; contra Lawrence Bonjour, the given does not play a direct epistemic role, though it does play a semantic role.[11]

Moreover, the given is necessary for the very distinction between fact and fiction, for '[i]f there be no datum given to the mind, then knowledge must be contentless and arbitrary, there would be nothing which it must be true to'.[12] If experience were conceptual 'all the way down', none of our thoughts could have objective purport – they would simply not bear on the world. Our thoughts would be, at best, part of a self-contained axiomatic system with no bearing on states of affairs. Hence objective purport has, as its necessary conditions of possibility, both that something is given within experience and that what is given is interpreted through some set of concepts or other.

But what exactly is the place of the given in our cognitive semantics? Lewis informs us that the given is present in experience as that which is distinct from conceptual interpretation. When I look at a pen, to use Lewis's own example, I can mentally subtract from this experience all the concepts that are actualized in my awareness of the pen as a pen, as a writing instrument, or even as a physical object. What remains after all concepts have been subtracted is that which would be the same for myself, an infant, or someone from a radically different culture who had never before seen a pen – the unconceptualized sense-qualities alone are the given, external to and independent of all conceptualizing, interpretative schemata. Since the given is independent of all conceptualization, our awareness of it is simply of awareness of that element in experience which cannot be altered by thought or imagination. Lewis is quick to note that this makes the given impossible to describe:

> While we can thus isolate the element of the given by these criteria of its unalterability and its character as sensuous feel or quality, we cannot describe any particular given *as such*, because in describing it, in whatever fashion, we qualify it by bringing it under some category or other, select from it, emphasize aspects of it, and relate it in particular and avoidable ways ... in a sense the given is ineffable, always. It is that which remains untouched and unaltered, however it is construed by thought.[13]

The given is ineffable because *any* description necessarily involves interpretation, even if it is only the selection of what to designate as the given at all. To a certain degree, the given can only be defined ostensively as that which all kinds of sensory consciousness have in common, whether they are genuine perceptions, hallucinations, or dreams, since it is only conceptual interpretation which classifies any episode of sensory consciousness as falling into one of those categories. It is the given *as interpreted* which yields the contrast between 'the thick experience of the world of things' and 'the thin given of immediacy', though the former 'constitutes the datum for philosophic reflection'.[14]

This point must be underscored to avoid misinterpretation: the philosopher does not begin with the given, or by taking the given as given, but by reflecting upon the thick experience of the world of things, examining the necessary conditions of there being such a world, and producing the concept of the given through her reflection on the nature of experience. On this basis, the reflective philosopher demonstrates that there could not be a thick world of experience if there were not something given to us in experience, independent of all conceptual interpretation and incapable of alteration by it.

The relation between the thin given of immediacy and the thick experience of the world of things is not like the relation between objects observed in space and time and theoretical posits based on those observations; it is the product of transcendental reflection on the role of concepts in experience. More specifically, Lewis's transcendental argument for the given is that if there were no given, then there could not be any experience of the sort we manifestly have; if there were no given, we would be *purely* discursive beings who never *apply* or *use* concepts in perception or action. Indeed, given Lewis's pragmatist insistence on the tight connection between knowledge and action, a purely discursive being – a being to whom nothing was given – could not even be said to know anything at all. Such a being would be, however, nothing at all like the kind of being that we manifestly are – hence there must be something purely given which is conceptually interpreted to produce the world of thick experience, including our self-experience. Since the concept of the given is grounded in a transcendental argument, Lewis has not yet provided any reasons for thinking that his notion of the given is Mythic.

The exteriority or independence of the given from all categories deserves emphasis; Lewis goes so far as to say that 'a distinction between the subjective and the objective ... is irrelevant to givenness as such'.[15] If the given is classified as objective, then it is a perceptible thing or property; if the given is classified as subjective, then it is modification of the sensory consciousness of the perceiver (an illusion or dream). But since the given is prior to all classification, it is immune to normal epistemic worries – one cannot even begin to worry whether an experience has been correctly classified until it has been classified. Though Lewis is a fallibilist about what is predicated of the given, the given itself, as completely antepredicative, is immune to doubt. However, the given is not immune to doubt because it is an infallible object of experience; it is immune to doubt because the given is not an object of experience at all, and doubt is only intelligible with regard to objects of experience. Appreciating this point is important to understand why it is mistaken to treat Lewis as a foundationalist about knowledge *per se*.

Famously, Lewis identifies the given with what he calls 'qualia'. The given is characterized by two different features: its specific sensory quality and its unalterability by thought. (Importantly, however, only the latter is necessary and sufficient for something to count as given). The identification of the given with qualia permits Lewis to be more precise in how he thinks of the kind of constraint that the given plays for conceptual interpretation. The constraint is not epistemic but one of cognitive semantics:

> no such concept would have a meaning if we could not, through the terms in which the meaning is explicated, get back eventually to concepts which are correlated for us with specific and identifiable qualities of sense. It is thus that we surmount our individual limitations.[16]

It is a necessary condition on the possibility of objective purport that each and every individual be able to correlate, for him or herself, the specific sensations and images that he or she associates with a concept, and the concept itself. The concept is essentially public; the given is essentially private. The reason why two different people can use the word 'dog' to mean roughly the same thing cannot depend on roughly the same range of sensations and images associated with the word, because they almost certainly will not. But unless I can associate a term with some range of sensations and images, it will have no empirical content for me. Thus the givenness of qualia is not an epistemic characterization but a necessary posit of cognitive semantics, because the givenness of qualia is posited as a necessary condition on the possibility of empirical content. Without qualia, thought could have no content that even seems to be about the world.

The given must be interpreted by concepts in order to yield the thick world of cognitively significant objects and properties. Here Lewis holds an inferentialist view of conceptual content: the content of any concept is 'constituted by that pattern which is set up by the expression of one concept in terms of others'.[17] In Brandomian terms, Lewis holds 'weak inferentialism' about empirical concepts – inferential articulation is necessary but not sufficient for determining the content of empirical concepts, since a nonconceptual element, the given, is necessary in addition to the conceptual. (It is precisely this point that is the focus of Sellars's criticisms, as we shall see in Chapter 3. However, in Chapter 6 I show that bifurcated intentionality revives weak inferentialism against Sellarsian and Brandomian criticisms.)

To the inferentialism about concepts, Lewis adds a pragmatic twist. Objects do not tell us which categories they belong to; rather, our biologically and culturally acquired cognitive needs and interests guide the interpretation of what is given. In all of this there is an ineliminable tentativeness to classification, what he calls 'the hazarding of something by the mind and its retention or rejection according to the success or non-success of what is based upon it'.[18] *Contra* Kant, there is something essentially experimental and provisional about all cognitive experience.

What concepts do, briefly put, is make experience – experience in the 'thick' sense of objects, properties, and relations – possible. There is no cognitive experience without concepts:

[A]ll concepts, and not simply those we should call 'categories', function as criteria of reality. Every criterion of classification is criterion of reality of some sort. There is no such thing as reality in general; to be real, a thing must be a particular sort of thing.[19]

The transcendentally-specified role of concepts is to explicate the cognitive experience of everyday life and action ('thick experience') in terms of the conceptually mediated interpretation of sensations and images that are transcendentally posited as immediately presented ('thin experience'). Thus, the role of the given is not to determine what is real or what is known, but to indicate how our knowledge of reality must be constrained in order to count as having objective purport. Thought with empirical content requires that the given be classified, conceptualized, or interpreted – even interpreted as real or unreal.

The transcendental character of Lewis's cognitive semantics allows us to compare Lewis with Kant's famous claim that 'thoughts without content are empty, intuitions without concepts are blind'.[20] The immediacy of the given is a necessary condition for knowledge of presented objects, but neither a sufficient condition nor an instance of it. If the awareness of the given is *immediate*, then presumably we are not aware of the given *as given*. The philosopher's awareness of the given is not immediate but *mediated* – that is, mediated by the reflective method of epistemology itself. As Christopher Hookway puts this extremely important point:

we do not have immediate reflective knowledge of which elements of cognition are immediate or given. The claim that the given is *immediate* means, presumably, that the given element in cognition is not itself the result of inferences or other cognitive activities. That something is given is not mediated through other cognitive operations, although the *knowledge* that something is given may indeed be so mediated.[21]

Uninterpreted qualia contain no assertions; they cannot be meaningful or meaningless, true or false, justified or unjustified – and hence are 'blind' insofar as they entail no predictions and, most importantly, guide no actions. Conversely, 'thoughts without content are empty' because, in the absence of qualia, we cannot distinguish between thoughts about the world and statements in a consistent, self-contained axiomatic system, because qualia are necessary for any possible *verification* of objective judgements. Empirical judgements would be indistinguishable from logico-mathematical judgements if we could not specify the possible sense experiences that would verify them.

Hence, the conditions of objective purport require that both the given and concepts are brought into play, and the interpretation itself is not given. Though the categories constitute the basic rules for interpretation, they are transcendental, not transcendent, since the categories are themselves nothing more than our social, shared ways of acting.[22] Hence the pragmatic re-casting of transcendental inquiry prevents Lewis's cognitive semantics from the ghost of solipsism that haunts transcendental idealism. Since it is the given as interpreted that is the object of cognitive experience, and the interpretation requires social and shared categories, all objects are necessarily public *because* all concepts are necessarily public. In taking pragmatism seriously, we finally and decisively reject 'the delusion that fixed and eternal categories of human thought, on the one side, are confronted with equally fixed and given 'things' on the other side'.[23] There is a given, but it is neither conceptual nor objectual – it is what we posit as being interpreted by concepts to account for our consciousness of objects, properties, and relations.

Crucially, Lewis's commitment to the given in his explication of our cognitive vocabulary must be reconciled with his epistemic fallibilism, as indicated by his rejection of

> the erroneous conclusion that there is a kind of conceptual apprehension – of simple qualities or essences – which terminates directly in the given; it may even be supposed that other knowledge rises out of this by some kind of complication and thus that direct awareness is the simplest and the basic type of knowledge.[24]

In other words, we should reject the mistaken view that the given can be assigned an epistemic role independently of the epistemic roles assigned to objects of possible experience. But that rejection is consistent with holding that it is because we have first recognized the epistemic roles assigned to objects of possible experience that we can subsequently posit the given as a necessary condition for assigning epistemic roles to anything at all. For all his Kantianism, Lewis nevertheless accepts the Hegelian dictum that all immediacy is mediated.

Without concepts, there is no experience *of* anything, not even 'of reality', since 'reality' is itself a category.[25] Hence the given is not real; to be real *is* to belong to some category or other. From this it should not be inferred that the given is unreal, for to say that something is not real, when properly explicated, only indicates that the explicitly specified item does not belong to some implicitly specified category. Something that belongs to no categories at all, cannot have anything said about it, because a category just is a template for classification and predication. Since the given, without conceptual interpretation, lacks all epistemic status, it cannot be epistemically efficacious and thereby cannot be the epistemic given.

Despite his rejection of the epistemic given, Lewis has often been interpreted as a defender of phenomenalism – even though Lewis understood himself as *rejecting* phenomenalism, since he rejects the following assumption:

> the object is 'known as' some complex of presented or presentable qualities, and is thus analyzable into 'simple' qualities which are capable of being presented and identified in a momentary experience and are essence or the denotations of certain simple concepts.[26]

Phenomenalism as Lewis understands it would not only conflict with his rejection of the epistemic given and his commitment to inferential semantics, but also because genuine knowledge of any kind requires transcending what is immediately given to the mind at any particular moment. At the same time, Lewis admits that phenomenalism correctly recognizes that 'without the correlation of concept and qualia, no experience could verify or fail to verify anything at all.'[27]

The error of phenomenalism lies in conflating the requirements of cognitive semantics with those of epistemology, and the interpretation of Lewis as a phenomenalist – even by Sellars *peré* and Sellars *fils* – rests on failing to recognize Lewis's sensitivity to this distinction. The central claim of Lewis's cognitive semantics (and a claim that bifurcated intentionality aims to defend, albeit not in the precise form that Lewis casts it) is this: only because there is a nonconceptual element within experience can any experience, even possible experience, play a cognitive function.

Lewis's Commitment to the Semantic Given

Thus far I have argued that Lewis's conception of the given is not vulnerable to Sellarsian criticism of the Myth of the Given. But that is only half of the story, and it relies on the (admittedly reasonable) interpretation of the Myth as a criticism of the *epistemic* given. Lewis's given does not play a directly epistemic role, and so Lewis is innocent of committing himself to the Myth in that sense. However, what Lewis is committed to – as MWO strongly implies and AKV extensively explicates – is what I call the *semantic given*: the thesis that cognitive significance, objective purport, requires something with a *semantic* status, or a kind of *meaning*, independent of and yet bearing on the meaning of objectively valid judgements. Here I will explain why I attribute the semantic given to Lewis, and on that basis explain how Lewis committed himself to the semantic given by virtue of being tempted by a certain vision of language

One clear example of the semantic given in MWO lies in the connection between conceptual interpretation and qualia, as for example when Lewis insists that '[t]he intelligibility of experience consists precisely in this; that between the specific quality of what is given and the pattern of its context in possible experience there is some degree of stable correlation.'[28] Elsewhere Lewis is even more explicit about the fundamentally semantic role of qualia:

> immediate qualia constitute the ultimate denotation in experience of our concepts, and the specific character of the given plays its indispensable role in any verification. It is difficult, if not impossible, to express the content of the given without importing what is not given; and our awareness of it has not been called 'knowledge', because with respect to it there can be no error. Nevertheless it functions as an absolute που στω [*pou sto*] for the knowledge of nature.[29]

Since immediate qualia are necessary for conceptual denotation at all, their basic role is semantic – they are the Archimedean lever, not for *knowledge*, but for *meaning*.

The central difficulty that Lewis confronts here is this: exactly *how* do qualia constrain the application of concepts? Lewis clearly recognizes that qualia must have some minimally detectible regularity and structure in order to yield the necessary constraint; an undifferentiated flux of experience, where all structure and order comes from the conceptual order, cannot constrain that order. This is precisely why Lewis must accept that we can recognize relations of sameness and difference with regard to the qualia themselves: 'the *same* property may be validly predicated on the basis of *different* presented qualia, and *different* properties may be signalized by the *same* presented qualia'.[30]

And yet here the decisive step towards a Mythic conception of the Given has been taken, for the following reason: there must be universals and particulars *at the level of qualia themselves* in order for us to recognize sameness and difference with regard to those qualia. If the universal/particular distinction did not obtain with regard to one's own sensory apprehensions, then no classification of qualia as 'same' and 'different' would be possible. But, if we were to accept the broadly Kantian point that the universal/particular distinction is itself only properly at home with regard to classification of *objects* and *judgements*, then concepts must already be involved. In that sense, Lewis has simply imported into his description of sensory consciousness per se a distinction that is only intelligible when concepts are at work. In short, Lewis can account for how sensory consciousness constrains conceptual application only by importing features of the conceptual order into his account of sensory consciousness.

Any account of sensory consciousness as external to conceptual application must, therefore, escape the two horns of what I call the Lewisian Dilemma: *either* (1) sensory consciousness is described as having *no* structure at all – an undifferentiated flux of experience – in which case it cannot *constrain* the application of concepts *to* experience, or (2) sensory consciousness is described as having the same *kind* of structure as concepts and judgements have, in which case the constraint is not genuinely *external* to the conceptual order. Lewis, having seen how (1) plays out in Bergson (and perhaps James), wisely avoids it, but at the cost of committing himself, *malgré lui*, to (2).

Far from being resolved, the Lewisian Dilemma is exacerbated in the transition from MWO to AKV. Though MWO does deal extensively with cognitive semantics, it does not explicitly distinguish between cognitive semantics and epistemology; rather Lewis was obliged to clarify his semantics under pressure from the logical positivists, thereby distinguishing between epistemology and cognitive semantics. Hence AKV deals not only with questions of value, but also clarifies the epistemology developed in MWO and further explicates the underlying cognitive semantics. As in MWO, Lewis maintains here that all knowledge has an eventual empirical significance in that all which is knowable or even significantly thinkable must have reference to meanings which are sense-representable. Our empirical knowledge rises as a structure of enormous complexity, most parts of which are stabilized in measure by their mutual support, but all of which rest, at bottom, on direct findings of sense. Unless there should be some statements, or rather something apprehensible and statable, whose truth is determined by given experience and not determinable in any other way, there would be no non-analytic affirmation whose truth could be determined at all, and no such thing as empirical knowledge.[31]

Sense-representable meanings are a necessary condition for the possibility of non-analytic truths, i.e. truths that are *not* based on linguistic meaning (i.e. intension) alone. And as with MWO, Lewis maintains in AKV that 'there is such a thing as experience, the content of which we do not invent and cannot have as we will but merely find. And that this given is an element in perception but not the whole of perceptual cognition'.[32] Lewis is well-aware, however, of the extraordinary difficulties he imposes on himself in describing what he frankly admits to be ineffable but indispensable for empirical knowledge and indeed for empirical contentfulness generally.

AKV marks an advance over MWO by explicating Lewis's cognitive semantics in terms of three different kinds of empirical statements: expressive statements, terminating judgements, and non-terminating judgements. Expressive statements directly express what is immediately apprehended; '[a]pprehensions of the given which such expressive statements formulate, are not judgements; and they are not here classed as knowledge, because they are not subject to any possible error'.[33] 'Knowledge' and 'doubt' are co-constituted categories – if something cannot be doubted, then it cannot be known, though it can be 'certain'. Yet immediate apprehensions of sense are not properly regarded as known:

> if it [knowledge] be given this broader meaning which would include apprehension of the immediate, it must then be remembered that one cannot, at the same time, require that knowledge in general shall possess a signification of something beyond the cognitive experience itself or that it should stand in contrast with some possible kind of error or mistake. Apprehension of the given, by itself, will meet neither of these requirements.[34]

In other words, the given cannot be classified as known precisely because it neither transcends the present moment nor is vulnerable to skeptical worries. If the given is functioning here as a 'foundation', it is not an epistemic foundation since the foundation is not itself an instance or kind of knowledge. Rather, as with MWO, Lewis is committed to a semantic foundationalism. The key difference lies in how Lewis's refined typology of statements allows him to make the semantic foundationalism more explicit than in MWO.

Unlike expressive statements, which concern only what is actually presented in immediate experience, terminating judgements concern *possible* experience. The general form of a terminating judgement is 'S being given, if A then E'[35] , where S is the presented sensory intake, A is some proposed action, and E is the expected sensory experience. Hence S and E are variables that take expressive statements as their values. Consider the experience of looking at a glass of wine, reaching for it, taking a sip, and putting it back down. 'There is a glass of wine in my visual field' is itself too 'thick' to count as an expressive statement, since the description of the wine-glass and its contents implicitly contains descriptions of unobserved conditions, counterfactuals, and so on. The expressive statement, properly pared down, would be, 'there is such-and-such transparent shape in my visual field, and the bottom half of the shape is filled with a red liquid'. Since the expressive statement is merely a description of what is immediately given, it has no epistemic character – it is neither true nor false. By contrast, terminating judgements have an epistemic character, because

> unlike statements of the given, what such terminating judgements express is to be classed as knowledge: the prediction in question calls for verification, and is subject to possible error ... non-terminating judgements assert objective reality ... non-termi-nating judgements which assert objective reality; some state of affairs as actual ... no limited set of particular predictions of empirical eventualities can completely exhaust the significance of such an objective statement.[36]

By contrast with terminating judgements, non-terminating judgements are objective beliefs, e.g. 'there is about half a glass of wine left'.

Terminating judgements play a crucial role in Lewis's cognitive semantics of objectively valid judgement: 'the statement of the objective belief must be translat-able into terms of passages of possible experience ... that is, it must be translatable into the predictive statements of terminating judgements'.[37] But the terminating judgement is not explicated entirely in terms of expressive judgements; they are connected by the *action*. Lewis gives us a semantic version of the transcendental argument for why our cognitive grasp on such notions as objecthood, tempo-rality, and the world all transcendentally presuppose activity, and that a purely passive contemplative mind could have no cognitive experiences of the sort that we manifestly do.[38][39] Terminating judgements have an epistemic character because they are *predictions*: given such-and-such apprehension of the immediately given, if I were to perform such-and-such action, I would then apprehend differently. If the prediction is not borne out by experience, then the terminating judgement is false. Hence, a thesis of cognitive semantics, a statement has objective purport if and only if it is analyzable into a set of statements, each of which is a conditional in which an expressive statement occurs in both antecedent and consequent.

Though Lewis's epistemology explicitly rejects the epistemic given, his cog-nitive semantics implicitly accepts the semantic given because the correlations between non-terminating and terminating judgements must be analytic. Con-sider a sentence such as the following:

(1) There is wine in my glass if and only if (2a) I am visually presented with a transparent, partially reflective container partly occupied by a reddish liquid and (2b) if I were to take a sip of the liquid (2c) I would be gustatorily presented with taste-qualia that I learned to associate with wine on previous occasions.

The acceptability of (1), the objective or non-terminating judgement, depends on seeing it as equivalent in intension to (2a)-(2c), where (2a) is the given situation (2b) is the proposed action, and (2c) is the possible new experience. Importantly, both (2a) and (2c) are expressive statements; it is (2b), the proposed action, that links them together. Taken together (2a)-(2c) verify (1). But on Lewis's account, the intelligibility of the statement depends upon our ability to grasp, immediately and without further explication or argument, that what comes before and after 'if and only if' are equivalent in intension – there is no deeper explanation or analysis. The semantic given lies in the biconditional as a whole: it is both semantically efficacious – it stipulates the conditions under which objective judgements are meaningful – and semantically independent – the equivalence of intensions stipulated by the biconditional cannot be further grounded in any other semantic properties or relations.

Lewis thus rejects the epistemic given and accepts the semantic given on the following lines. On the one hand, immediate apprehensions of the given, whether conceived of as qualia (in MWO) or as expressive statements (AKV) cannot satisfy the conditions of knowledge; they lack the requisite intensional semantic form of knowledge-claims, since they cannot be true or false. On the other, nothing can have objective purport, as a matter of cognitive semantics, without its being the case that it can be, at least in principle, fully explicated in a form that mentions what is immediate, given, or expressed, because without that immediate or nonconceptual element, the judgement could not be verified by any possible sense-presentation; it would be *meaningless*.

One serious difficulty that has plagued Lewis's reputation concerns the degree of his commitment to foundationalism. As noted already, Lewis has long been interpreted as an epistemological foundationalist. The foundationalist interpretation has been recently bolstered by Bonjour, who defends foundationalism, especially that of AKV, against coherentism, whereas Hookway presents Lewis, at least with regard to MWO, as committed to epistemological coherentism. For these reasons, some scholars have argued that AKV differs markedly from MWO, perhaps as a result of how Lewis was pressured by the logical positivists to indicate how his view differed from theirs. Thus, for example, Christopher Gowans correctly notices that, contra the received view of Lewis, he actually rejects foundationalism in MWO, but that he came to accept it in AKV.[40] By contrast, both Eric Dayton and Sandra Rosenthal argue that Lewis's views did not change significantly over the course of his career.[41] The proposed distinction between the epistemic given and the semantic given resolves both whether Lewis is committed to foundationalism and also the complicated question as to how much Lewis's views changed between MWO and AKV.

On the interpretation offered here, Hookway, Gowans, Dayton, and Rosenthal all correctly note that Lewis rejects epistemological foundationalism in MWO, insofar as he rejects the epistemic given. However, Gowans holds that Lewis reverses his position and embraces foundationalism in AKV. This is mistaken because Gowans does not notice that (i) Lewis's commitment to the given in AKV is fundamentally *semantic* rather than *epistemic*; (ii) Lewis's explicit commitment to the semantic given in AKV is already implicit in the cognitive semantics of MWO; (iii) AKV does not repudiate the rejection of the epistemic given central to MWO. Conversely, although Dayton and Rosenthal correctly point out that Lewis's views changed very little from MWO to AKV, they do not distinguish between the epistemic given and the semantic given and so misconstrue Lewis's criticism of foundationalism and phenomenalism. The one major change in Lewis's cognitive semantics from MWO to AKV is the exact status of the given.[42] In MWO, Lewis insists that the given is, strictly speaking, 'ineffable', since any description of it involves concepts and so cannot be the pure given itself. In AKV, the ineffable given has been replaced by infallible (certain) expressive statements. Due to this shift in the cognitive semantics, what appeared as a raft of cognitively significant statements floating on the sea of the ineffable now appears as having a solid foundation. In this sense, though Lewis consistently held epistemological coherentism, AKV makes explicit a commitment to semantic foundationalism that is implicit in MWO. Once we notice the distinction between the epistemic and the semantic, and that Lewis was (however consistently or inconsistently) both an epistemic coherentist and a semantic foundationalist, the debate over the difference between MWO and AKV is resolved.

Similar complexities abound in deciphering Lewis's exact place in the history of pragmatism. Though Lewis has been largely written out of the pragmatist canon, there are signs that Lewis's reputation is undergoing a much-deserved renaissance. Murray Murphey subtitles his excellent intellectual biography of Lewis 'the last great pragmatist', which may be an overstatement, as it underestimates what Sellars and others since have contributed to pragmatism.[43] Contributing to this direction of interpretation, Hookway, Misak and Rosenthal also establish Lewis's systematic and complicated relations to pragmatism, especially to Peirce and to James. Whereas Hookway concludes that Lewis was 'too much of a Kantian and too little of a pragmatist',[44] Misak stresses how Peircean Lewis was. The beginning of the correct view, I think, would locate Lewis's conceptualistic pragmatism within the broader currents of pragmatist thought through his review of Dewey's *The Quest for Certainty*, where he writes:

> If it is difficult to deny what Professor Dewey positively says, it is nevertheless possible to feel that something has been left unsaid which is important. In particular, it may be remarked that the author is preoccupied with the forward-looking function of knowledge to the neglect of its backward-looking ground or premises.[45]

In other words, while Lewis shares Dewey's pragmatist rejection of the Quest for Certainty as a *terminus ad quem*, he nevertheless retains the Quest for Certainty as a *terminus a quo*, provided that the latter is construed in terms of the methodological priority of cognitive semantics over epistemology that is more narrowly construed. This is why Lewis is both a coherentist and fallibilist about justification in the strict sense *and* a foundationalist about cognitive significance, given his analysis of the semantics of cognitive experience.

Lewis on Language and Meaning: Why Lewis Accepted The Semantic Given

At this point, I have argued that Lewis is committed to what I have called the semantic given, but I have not yet shown exactly what motivates Lewis to accept the semantic given. This issue becomes important in part because one might plausibly think that Lewis's acceptance of the semantic given is a retreat from the deeper insights of the pragmatist tradition, and also because Sellars's criticisms of Lewis turn on the semantic given. Here I will show that Lewis's implicit commitment to the semantic given spoils what would otherwise be Lewis's anticipation of the discursive/somatic distinction central to bifurcated intentionality. His distinction between what he calls 'linguistic meaning' and 'sense meaning' both anticipates what I am calling bifurcated intentionality and undermines that anticipation through a tacit acceptance of the intelligibility of what I call, following Ludwig Wittgenstein, an 'Augustinian' vision of language – which is to say, the Myth of the semantic Given in one of its deeper and more pervasive manifestations.[46]

To situate Lewis's tacit acceptance of the 'Augustinian' picture of language, we must turn from Lewis' account of empirical knowledge to his semantics *tout court*. One difficulty that confronts the contemporary reader of Lewis' philosophy of language is that he predates the 'linguistic turn' in analytic philosophy and does not think that analysis of linguistic forms is the right way to analyze meanings. Instead he proceeds by distinguishing what he calls 'the modes of meaning': intension, comprehension, denotation, and signification. Of particular interest here is intension, which Lewis tends to (somewhat confusingly) identify with 'meaning', of which he says, 'formally considered, the intension of a term is to be identified with the conjunction of all other terms each of which must be applicable to anything to which the given term would be correctly applicable'.[47] This puts the emphasis squarely the normativity of meaning: the meaning of a term, in the 'intension' sense of meaning, lies in *correctness* of application. And to speak of correctness here requires, in turn, a grasp of the *criteria* whereby correct (and incorrect) application is determined. Though Lewis recognizes that intensions are closely bound up with linguistic expression, he thinks it would a serious error to identify intensions *per se* with language. Instead he insists on distinguishing between two modes of intensional meaning, linguistic meaning and sense meaning.

This distinction between the two modes of intensional meaning lies at the very heart of Lewis's theoretical philosophy – his conception of analyticity (hence also of modality), his account of the pragmatic difference of degree between the *a priori* and the *a posteriori*, the nature of empirical knowledge, and his rejection of synthetic *a priori* judgements.[48] By linguistic meaning, Lewis means the pattern of relations between linguistic expressions, as when dictionaries define a word in terms of other words. Whereas linguistic meanings are 'the pattern of definitive and other analytic relationships holding between linguistic expressions', sense meanings are 'the criterion in mind by which what is meant is to be recognized'.[49] These must be distinguished from language *per se*; sense meanings are independent of language, and yet without them, no linguistic meaning would even be possible.

In contrast to the emphasis on linguistic forms that has prevailed in twentieth-century analytic philosophy, Lewis regards sense meanings as the fundamental cognitive semantic phenomenon to be examined and explained. Though linguistic meanings are necessary for ordinary human life, and close analysis of them necessary for certain philosophical purposes, Lewis nevertheless holds that:

> In order that linguistic expressions should function for guidance of such ways of action, there must be, correlated with words in our minds, a meaning which cannot literally be disclosed by any use of words or any inspection of words and their relations.[50]

Lewis's line of thought seems to be that linguistic meaning is only the kind of meaning that one finds by seeing how a word is defined in a dictionary. But simply knowing how to define a word through other words – setting up or noticing the patterns of relations among words – would not tell one how to use the *definiendum* unless one already knew how to use the words in the *definiens*. In Lewis's account, that means knowing which sense meanings are correlated with the linguistic meanings of the terms in the *definiens*. Hence sense meanings are fundamental: 'If there were no meanings in the mode of sense meaning, there would be no meaning at all'.[51] Sense meanings must be distinguished from immediate apprehensions of the given: all statements, even analytic statements, involve sense meanings, whereas only empirical judgements involve immediate apprehensions of the given. However, the doctrine of sense meaning is central to Lewis's account of empirical judgements, as Murphey nicely puts it, 'a nonterminating judgement implies a specific set of terminating judgements, and that the terminating judgements of that set exhibit the sense meaning of the nonterminating judgement'.[52]

In other words, Lewis thinks, intensions do and must mediate between perceptual input and motor output, but mere linguistic meaning cannot play that role, because linguistic meaning is specified entirely in terms of how words are related to one another. Linguistic meaning, as Lewis conceives of it, cannot play the mediating role between perception and action that some account of meaning must play. Though Lewis gives several arguments for this claim, the one I want to consider here is a transcendental argument that turns on Lewis's genuine insights into the role of embodiment in human cognitive semantics.

What would be the case if there were no sense meanings? What would a being possessed exclusively of linguistic meanings be like? For being like these – what Lewis calls 'disembodied spirits in an empirical vacuum',[53] nothing could be sensually apprehended (since it is an empirical vacuum) nor could there be any sensuous apprehension (since the beings are disembodied). Perhaps these beings communicate; perhaps they would not. But they would neither perceive nor act, hence have nothing to talk about except their own thought-processes; they could have no need for sense meanings, since they could not link perception to action, having neither. Lewis assumes that linguistic meanings cannot be *directly* related to the world by themselves, because he understands linguistic meanings in terms of dictionary definitions. For this reason, he concludes that for beings without sense meanings, their linguistic meanings cannot be about anything besides other linguistic meanings.

But then we see that *it simply does not matter* whether or not these discursive spirits communicate with each other or not, since in either case, they have nothing to talk about which grounds their discourse in extra-linguistic reality. It is the mediating role of sense meanings between perception and action that connects linguistic expressions to the world as experienced; in the absence of an integrated functional totality of perceptual uptake, sense meanings, and volitional actions, there is nothing left for words to mean (except, perhaps, themselves). For this reason, Lewis concludes that if there were no sense meanings, there could not be anything even so much as conceivable to us of the kinds of experience we manifestly have; sense meaning is a transcendental condition of our experience.[54]

In addition to the transcendental argument, Lewis points out that restricting meaning to language deprives us of the resources necessary to recognize the deep continuity between lingual and nonlingual animals:

> the need to entertain fixed meanings goes deeper still [than the need to communicate] and must characterize the mentality of any creature capable of consciously affecting its own relation to environment, even if that creature should live without fellows and find no use for language.[55]

Conversely, any attempt to build an account of meaning on the basis of language must either flatly deny that non-linguistic animals and pre-linguistic babies are able to entertain any meanings at all, or else adopt a different account of the kinds of meanings that animals and babies are able to entertain while distinguishing between those kinds of meanings and the rich, full-blooded meanings that come on the scene only with the acquisition of language. Likewise, any attempt to construe meaning by analogy with abstract deductive systems would be no more insightful than doing so by analogy with chess. *Contra* Sellars, as we shall see, Lewis thinks that it is the symbols *as associated with meanings* that even so much as count as symbols in the first place, and not just as marks or noises, and that the associations are merely conventional – though the meanings themselves are not.

Although these considerations indicate why Lewis holds that there must be something other than linguistic meanings, as Lewis conceives of them, this alone does not tell us how to conceive of sense meanings. (Nor, as Chapter 3 will make clear, does this argument establish that Lewis conceives of linguistic meanings correctly). The key to sense meanings is the idea of 'criteria in mind': the sense meaning of a term or statement is constituted by the criteria that would be held in mind in order to determine whether the term or statement correctly applies to some presented or presentable experience. It is this which must be conventionally associated with some mark or noise in order for that mark or noise to count as a symbol or utterance at all, and not a mere *flatus vocis*.

Though Lewis is critical of several core Kantian notions, such as the conceivability of things in themselves or the possibility of synthetic *a priori* judgements, he does think that Kant understands correctly how to think about the entanglement between the sensory and the rational: they are related by means of the schematism: 'a sense meaning, when precise and explicit, is a schema; a rule or prescribed routine and imagined result of which will determine applicability of the expression in question'.[56] On this point, Rosenthal helpfully points out that sense meanings are explicit schemata insofar as the former are made precise and explicit, usually by means of linguistic meanings; a sense meaning is a habit for generating the corresponding rule. As she puts it,

> what is 'fixed' for Lewis is precisely that which determines the nature of and governs the range of the inexhaustible variety of specific schemata. Thus, what is 'fixed' is the rule of generation of explicit schemata, and this, for Lewis, is the concrete disposition or habit. ... the series of possible schemata is 'fixed' prior to the imposition of a linguistic structure, not by an eternal ontological structure, but rather by the concrete, biologically based, disposition or habit as the rule of generation of explicit schemata ... meanings emerge from organism-environment interaction as precise triadic relational structures unified by habit as a rule of organization and as a rule of generation of specific schemata.[57]

Two remarkable aspects of Rosenthal's interpretation of Lewis deserve comment. The first is that she correctly points out that Lewis's conception of meaning is neither psychologistic nor Platonistic – two objections that were often raised against Lewis. Instead, the account of sense meaning is fully naturalistic, in the broad and generous sense of 'naturalism' that typifies American pragmatic naturalism at its best and in which purposive, intelligent behaviour is irreducible to law-governed physico-chemical regularities. In this sense, Lewis has clearly anticipated what I call here 'somatic intentionality': the kind of cognitive semantic content manifested in our various ways of bodily engagement with motivationally salient objects in the ambient environment. For this reason, Lewis's commitment to two modes of intensional meaning, linguistic meaning and sense meaning, is clearly related to my account of two kinds of intentional content, the discursive and the somatic. Lest one think that I am simply conflating intensions and intentions, I am intentionally adopting what Hanna calls 'the Brentano/Chisholm thesis' that 'the notions of intensionality and intentionality are irreducible, interderivable, and mutually indispensable'.[58]

The second comment on Rosenthal's interpretation is that it shows how Lewis's notion of sense meaning is a version of the Myth of the Given. To see this, consider how Lewis's vision of the relation between linguistic meaning and sense meaning approximates the 'Augustinian' picture of language presented at the opening of Wittgenstein's *Philosophical Investigations*:

> 'When grown-ups named some object and at the same time turned towards it, I perceived this, and I grasped that the thing was signified by the sound they uttered, since they meant to point *it* out. ... In this way, little by little, I learnt to understand what things the words, which I heard uttered in their respective places in various sentences, signified' ... These words, it seems to me, give us a particular picture of the essence of human language. It is this: the words in language name objects – sentences are combinations of such names – In this picture of language we find the roots of the following idea: Every word has a meaning. This meaning is correlated with the word. It is the object for which the word stands.[59]

The problem at work here in the 'Augustinian' picture of language is nicely exposed by Braver's exposition:

> Once engaged speaking or writing has come to a halt, 'the dead line on paper' does not seem up to the job of meaning something, demanding 'a further dimension' to jolt the detached limb into motion, like Galvani's electrically stimulated frog's leg. Nothing of the same nature as further sounds or marks can do the trick – if it could, we would just stick with the words in the first place – thus making meaning queer: something gaseous, ethereal, shadowy.[60]

In other words, the very idea that meanings are something distinct from their linguistic expressions – that marks or noises must somehow be supplemented by something else, their 'meaning', in order to mean anything at all – is sustained by the detached, disengaged attitude taken towards language in the first place. In the Augustinian picture, the meanings are fixed ahead of linguistic expression, and learning a language is just a matter of learning the conventional associations between meanings on the one hand and noises and marks on the other. In other words, the Augustinian picture of language completely *mystifies* the acquisition of language, by treating the child as already having something like a language – e.g. sense meanings – prior to learning the language, i.e. associating sense meanings with linguistic meanings. Along similar lines, Zack points out that by construing the given as 'pre-linguistically identifiable but ineffable', Lewis is 'open to the charge of confusing the situations in which languages are learned or perhaps deliberately constructed in special fields, with the ordinary ease of the linguistically competent practitioner'.[61]

What is 'Augustinian' about Lewis, in Wittgenstein's sense of an 'Augustinian' vision of language, is *not* that Lewis thinks of words as names. Rather the deeper point is that Lewis shares the 'Augustinian' vision of language in which meaning is fixed independently of and prior to linguistic expression – 'the imposition of a linguistic structure', as Rosenthal revealingly put it. This is why Lewis can regard the association between linguistic meaning and sense meaning as conventional, while still holding that sense meaning is not conventional, and why he can hold that inspection of linguistic forms *per se* will not illuminate the nature of analyticity or of the *a priori*. But why think that there is some kind of intensional, semantic-like structure already at work on to which language is an 'imposition'? Lewis takes this stance because it is the only way he can see to resolve the Lewisian Dilemma. What is astonishing about Lewis is how he succeeded in *translating* the 'Augustinian' picture of language into the non-Platonic and non-psychologistic pragmatist idiom of purposive behavioural dispositions, and without rationalist or empiricist epistemologies, but without disrupting the grip that the Augustinian picture has on his thinking about meaning at a deeper level. Ironically, Lewis complained that the Platonic treatment of meaning 'substitutes adoration of a mystery for explanation of a fact',[62] but then Lewis is hoisted by his own petard – not because he posits Platonic ideas to explain meaning, but because he retains a place in his picture of meaning that the concept of Platonic ideas occupied in older elaborations of that basic picture. Simply putting purposive behavioural dispositions in that place prevents Lewis from seeing the problem all the way to its roots.

The upshot of this criticism is that I fully agree with recent scholarship that stresses the Kantian and realistic strands of Lewis' conceptualistic pragmatism, his fallibilism, and his coherentism. The dominant interpretation of Lewis as a phenomenalist and epistemological foundationalist has done much damage; it has obscured Lewis's own complex relation with American pragmatism, it has made almost unintelligible Lewis's search for a *via media* between Royce's idealism and Perry's realism, and it has prevented a correct appreciation of Lewis's influence on Quine, Sellars, and Goodman (among others). Yet for all that, there is an element of insight in the old interpretation: Lewis does indeed commit himself to the Myth of the Given, not in his epistemology, but in his tacit acceptance of the 'Augustinian' vision of language, as displayed in the incorrigible authority accorded to introspective access to correlations between conceptual meanings and qualia, and in the thought that we can identify sense meaning apart from linguistic meanings. Far from it being the case that 'those who, like Wilfrid Sellars, have assailed the 'myth of the given' have been bewitched by language, as Lewis was not' it is Lewis who is bewitched by a particular picture of what language is.[63]

As is well-known by now, it is the criticism of 'the myth of the given' by Sellars, and more specifically, how that criticism was received by Rorty and Brandom, that led the so-called 'neo-pragmatists' to reject the very notion of experience. Since it must be emphasized that Sellars himself did not go so far as Rorty and Brandom, and indeed thought that the concept of experience must be (somehow) rescued from the Myth of the Given, Sellars thereby indicates a proximity to Lewis that merits investigation. For like Lewis and unlike Brandom, Sellars does not want to eliminate the concept of experience, but to understand the nature of experience, and how perceptual experience can serve as a basis (in one sense) for empirical knowledge. Sellars's criticisms of Lewis leave us with the problem of how to retain what is basically right in Lewis's distinction between linguistic meaning and sense meaning while rejecting, root and branch, the Augustinian picture of language that Sellars, closely following Wittgenstein, did so much to criticize. It is in answer to that question that I will draw the distinction between discursive and somatic intentionality. For the time being, however, we must turn to Sellars's criticism of Lewis's distinction between linguistic meaning and sense meaning and see how that criticism serves as part of the motivation for Sellars's own account of nonconceptual content – the steps that Sellars took from Lewis's conceptual pragmatism to his own, complex Kantian-Hegelian pragmatism.

3 DISCURSIVE INTENTIONALITY AND 'NONCONCEPTUAL CONTENT' IN SELLARS

In light of the worries raised in the last chapter about Lewis's tacit commitment to an 'Augustinian' picture of language, I aim to show here how Sellars's deeply Wittgensteinian understanding of linguistic practice both informs his criticisms of Lewis's commitment to sense-meanings and his non-Wittgensteinian account of episodes of nonconceptual consciousness as explanatory posits.[1] Throughout, Sellars's conception of discursive intentionality is defended against Lewis's, and the implications are explored for how Sellars and Lewis differ on the pragmatic *a priori*. Of particular importance here are the precise grounds on which Sellars charges Lewis with the myth of the semantic given and why the Sellarsian alternative is desirable. Here I will develop the distinction between Lewis's conceptualistic pragmatism and Sellars's 'transcendental naturalism'. As deVries puts it, 'It is a principle of Sellars's transcendental naturalism that transcendental structures must be reflected in causal structures, even if there is no reduction of the transcendental to the causal'.[2] The contrast with Lewis will clarify just why Sellars is committed to 'transcendental naturalism', how the 'must' in deVries's interpretation should be understood, and how we can distinguish 'reflected in' and 'reduced to'.

Here I begin with a historical overview of the relation between Lewis and Sellars, with some discussion of the exchanges between Lewis and Sellars's father, Roy Wood Sellars, in order to better appreciate how transcendental naturalism functions as a *via media* between conceptualistic pragmatism (Lewis) and physical realism (RWS). (Throughout this chapter I use 'RWS' or 'Sellars *père*' to indicate 'Roy Wood Sellars' and 'WSS' or 'Sellars *fils*' to indicate 'Wilfrid S. Sellars' when discussing them together. When 'Sellars' is used, it is to indicate Sellars *fils* alone). I will then reconstruct the details of Sellars's criticisms of Lewis, with particular emphasis on their differing uses of analyticity and apriority and Sellars's rejection of the distinction between linguistic meaning and sense meaning. Sellars's transcendental naturalism comes through in his treatment of sensations; on the one hand there are transcendental considerations for why there must be nonconceptual content, while on the other hand, the role of nonconceptual content must be played by something with the right kinds of causal relations.

The resurgence of conceptualism with Brandom and McDowell (Chapter 4) turns on regarding Sellars's attempted rehabilitation of nonconceptual content as itself the last vestige of the Myth, though in turning to Merleau-Ponty (Chapter 5) I shall show how the criticism of 'nonconceptual content' turns on an ambiguity that, once clarified, shows how there is a defensible conception of 'nonconceptual content' that is not vulnerable to conceptualist criticisms.

Conceptualistic Pragmatism and Physical Realism

Though many historical influences bear on the development of Sellars's mature philosophical position, one much-neglected line of influence – though I do not insist that it is the most important one – is the debate between C. I. Lewis and Roy Wood Sellars. This debate between conceptualistic pragmatism and 'physical realism' (as RWS sometimes called his view, though he also called it 'critical realism') bears directly on Sellars's philosophy because of his attempt to arrive at a *via media* between Lewis and RWS. Specifically, Sellars accepts both Lewis's pragmatic inferentialism about conceptual content and RWS's denial that sensations play any epistemic, but only a causal, role in perception.

Here, I will first reconstruct RWS's basic position and criticisms of Lewis, as well as Lewis's response to these objections, before turning to WSS's *via media*. The debate takes place across five key registers: metaphilosophical, methodological, epistemological, metaphysical, and cognitive-semantical. (For reasons of space I neglect here the ethical and religious registers). Metaphilosophically, the debate concerns the continuity or discontinuity between science and philosophy; metaphysically, it concerns realism vs. idealism or phenomenalism; methodologically, it concerns whether epistemology is independent of metaphysics; cognitive-semantically, it concerns whether there is an identifiable 'stratum' of discourse more fundamental than our discourse about things and properties. I shall argue that on the cognitive-semantical point, RWS misunderstands Lewis's position – as Lewis's response to the objections indicates – but that on the broader issues at stake, the debate is not so clear and cannot be resolved so decisively.

RWS refers to his position alternatively as 'critical realism', 'natural realism', or 'physical realism', consisting of non-reductive naturalism (in metaphysics) and non-phenomenalistic empiricism (in epistemology). The goal of the overall position is to reconcile empiricism and naturalism by showing that empiricism can be disentangled from phenomenalism by accounting for sensations in causal-functionalist terms as 'guides to perceiving'.[3] RWS's naturalism – what he sometimes calls 'evolutionary naturalism' – is emergentistic and identifies different 'levels of causality', such as physical, chemical, biological, and psychological. In his review of Dewey's *Experience and Nature* RWS agrees with Dewey that experience is itself natural but worries that Dewey fails to appreciate that experience, as a property of living organisms, is only a small part of the natural world, and cannot be isomorphic with it.[4] The ultimate aim of *The Philosophy of Physical Realism* is to defend a version of naturalism that works as a fully adequate metaphysical and epistemological position with profound ethical significance:

> Thrown back upon himself and with no further hope of special cosmic succor, man may face the possibilities of human life with greater courage, imagination, and audacity. It may be that we can combine the insights of those two great naturalists, Spinoza and Nietzsche, uniting the passion for life of the one with the cosmic calm of the other.[5]

Though it is unclear how much of this ethical significance carries over in WSS, its role in RWS's philosophy must be recognized. It also plays a significant role not only in RWS's criticisms of Dewey but also of Lewis.

Generally speaking, RWS praises Lewis for the clarity and rigor he brings to pragmatism but also criticizes *Mind and the World Order* for its phenomenalism. Since this objection has been usually regarded as carrying some plausibility, and since I find it mistaken (for reasons given in Chapter 2), it is important to examine both how RWS misinterpreted it and what survives in his criticism once the misinterpretation is corrected. If 'phenomenalism' means that one identifies physical objects with 'permanent possibilities of sensation', in Mill's phrase, then the phenomenalist would say that statements about physical objects are really about those possibilities of sensation. To resolve the ambiguities surrounding the term 'about' (or the related 'means'), I will restate the phenomenalist thesis in terms of *real* and *apparent* reference: phenomenalism holds that the subsentential expressions occurring in physical-object expressions that *seem* to refer to physical objects *actually* refer to the same items referred to by subsentential expressions in phenomenalistic expressions. Thus, in sentences such as 'This book weighs two pounds' – which seems to attribute a physical property ('weighing two pounds') to a physical object ('this book') – both 'this book' and 'weighs two pounds' actually refer to, or denote, a range of combinations of visual, tactile, and proprioceptive sensations. But if we interpret phenomenalism in those terms – which has the hermeneutic virtue of capturing what RWS seems to mean by 'phenomenalism', whatever its philosophical merits – C. I. Lewis *cannot* count as a phenomenalist. RWS's criticism neglects the resources in Lewis's work for interpreting him as a critical realist in epistemology, much like both RWS and WSS themselves. But if that is right, then the proper terms of the debate between Lewis and RWS, and WSS's *via media* between them, must lie elsewhere.

In *The Philosophy of Physical Realism*, RWS poses what he sees as the fundamental question: does empirical knowledge concern what transcends our experience of it, or is empirical knowledge restricted to what is immediately apprehended within experience? In other words, the debate between realism and phenomenalism (or idealism) turns on the question, are the properties and

relations ascribed to objects-as-known intrinsic to the mind-independent object
as such, or are those properties and relations ascribed only to the mind-dependent presentations comprising the course of experience. What is distinctive about
RWS is his view that resolution of this debate requires a correct understanding of the status of sensations. Are sensations *epistemic* intermediaries or merely
causal intermediaries? More specifically, are sensations the termini of perceptual
acts, or do we perceive physical objects *through* sensations, so that sensations
are causal (but not epistemic) intermediaries between us and physical objects?
Though he takes Lewis to ultimately side with phenomenalistic empiricists on
this question, there is little in Lewis to commend this particular interpretation.

The details of RWS's criticism of Lewis turn on his remark that Lewis's
MWO 'seems to me excellent in all but its treatment of what I would call categorial meanings'.[6] To motivate his criticism of Lewis, RWS stresses the distinction
between what he calls 'classificatory' and 'attributive' judgements. He notes that
according to Lewis:

> The class-concepts are *a priori* with respect to the presentations. We can deduce the
> implications of our concepts and test them out ... classificatory judgements presup-
> pose attributive judgements about things. *We do not classify presentations but things.*
> His mistake, as I see it, lies in his refusal to take perceiving as intending something
> manifested by presentations.[7]

By 'attributive judgements', RWS means the assignment of properties to an
object, whereas 'classificatory judgements' indicate what *kind* of thing something
is. So it would be 'attributive' to say, 'this thing is small, black, and rectangular',
since here one attributes properties to an object, but 'classificatory' to say, 'this
thing is a phone', since here one classifies the object under a category. We can
only classify objects as falling under kinds once there are definite objects to be
classified; the application of attributive terms is logically prior to the application
of sortal terms.

As RWS sees it, Lewis is basically right about classificatory judgements but
neglects that classificatory judgements depend on attributive judgements. On
this interpretation, since Lewis neglects this dependence, he is forced to treat
the thing-property discourse of attributive judgements as a kind of classification
– that is, the classification of qualia. RWS's argument here appears to go as follows: if one assimilates attributive judgements to classificatory judgements, then
all properties will be treated as categories into which things fit rather than as
inhering in the things themselves. But when all properties are treated this way,
what is left over belonging to the thing? RWS's point here is that the concepts
of 'thing' and 'property' are interdependent notions; if all properties are treated
as classifications, then there is no physical object left over them for them to classify. What is left is merely the bare presentation which is classified as physical, as
black, as small, as rectangular, as a cell-phone, and so on.

Hence, on RWS's view, the concept of the given is produced only by neglecting the difference between classificatory and attributive judgements. And this is an error because there is no isolatable stratum of discourse logically prior to the discourse that attributes properties to things. The thing-language is the fundamental stratum of discourse, and so there is no vocabulary for talking about free-standing and identifiable 'presentations' that are themselves classified in order to generate our knowledge of objects. If there were, then our statements about physical objects would refer to our presentations, rather than it being the case that our presentations figure only in *causal explanations* of our direct perception of physical objects.

With regard to the categories employed in classificatory judgements, RWS maintains that:

> the task of the epistemologist is to *exhibit* the categories he finds to be employed in cognitive acts. He can work here hand in hand with the psychologist and the logician. It is, to me, undeniable that such categories as self, external thing, cause, relation, activity, operation are features of our cognitive experience from the level of perceiving upward ... the categories express, and are reflections of, the felt attitudes of the organism toward its environment.[8]

If Lewis would object to any of this, it is only to a certain interpretation of 'the felt attitudes of the organism in its environment.' Although Lewis happily endorses Royce's pragmatist dictum that categories are modes of action, he was wary of identifying the modes of action with any particular set of biological or psychological occurrent or dispositional properties, lest we lose our grip on appreciating the normative dimension of our concepts. Otherwise Lewis would accept RWS's point that epistemology is essentially an explication of the concepts that are implicit in actual cognitive experience.

Having made this point, however, RWS proceeds to fault Lewis for being insufficiently respectful of the fact that our actual cognitive experience, including our ordinary empirical discourse about that experience, is not about immediate apprehensions of sense but about physical objects:

> It is independent and enduring things which we suppose ourselves to perceive, and not presentations ... we should begin our reflection with natural realism and hold to the realism. When I ordinarily assert that I bite into a peach, I do not mean that I am biting into a presentation, a sensory datum.[9]

At this point, however, RWS has mischaracterized his opponent, and this leads him to misunderstand Lewis's view. Presumably not even the most dedicated proponent of sense-data theory would say that 'I am biting into a peach' has the same *referent* as 'I am experiencing a correlation of a biting-presentation and a peach-presentation'. What she would say is that I *know* that I am biting into a peach *because* I am being presented with peach-presentations – because I am sensing peach-ly, perhaps (and sensing biting-ly). The question is not, 'do we perceive object or qualia?' but rather 'what role, if any, do qualia play in explicating the semantics of empirical knowledge?' Whereas Lewis holds that qualia play a necessary cognitive-semantic role in explicating the sense of empirical judgements, RWS (and WSS following him) holds that there is no cognitive-semantic role for sensations to play, only a causal-explanatory one.

While this demonstrates that RWS's interpretation of Lewis as a phenomenalist simply misinterprets Lewis, RWS does observe a more subtle and much more important difference between critical realism and conceptualistic pragmatism:

> the critical realist argues that knowing is, in intention, the interpretation of *physical things* as these in some measure appear, or are manifested, in sensory presentation and that, in critical knowing, we achieve a complex content which is regarded as revealing the independent, physical thing. On this basis, we can justify Lewis' predictive hypotheticals by giving their ground and, at the same time, satisfy the categorical meanings of antecedent reality which the pragmatist is aware of but which he rejects on the *negative ground* that no theory of knowledge has yet done justice to it.[10]

Here RWS has a deep insight into Lewis that is, unfortunately, obscured because RWS conflates two different issues: (i) the interpretation of Lewis's predictive hypotheticals and (ii) the 'ground' of those hypotheticals. For it is one thing to claim, as RWS does, that the hypotheticals themselves commit Lewis to a phenomenalistic empiricism; it is quite another to claim that Lewis neglects to account for the hypotheticals, even if Lewis is not committed to phenomenalism with respect to the hypotheticals themselves. By the 'predictive hypotheticals', RWS appears to have in mind Lewis's claim that empirical judgements about objects strictly imply subjunctive conditionals that relate sense-presentations to actions. But in light of Lewis's own distinctions between the various 'modes of meaning', everything depends on what 'means the same thing' means, especially with regard to Lewis's insistence on the distinction between intensions and extensions. As I argued in Chapter 2, at least by the time he writes *AKV* Lewis is concerned to show that non-terminating (objective) judgements and terminating (phenomenal) judgements 'mean the same thing' not in terms of identity of reference (extensions) but in terms of equivalence of sense (intensions). If Lewis were talking about identity of reference, then he would indeed to be committed to saying that statements about physical objects refer to sensations or presentations and so would be committed to phenomenalism as defined above. In other words, RWS misinterprets Lewis as making a claim about reference, whereas he is in fact making a claim about sense.

In responding to RWS in *AKV*, Lewis makes precisely this point in considering the objections that RWS posed to *MWO* in *The Philosophy of Physical*

Realism (hereafter *PPR*) – the allegation that Lewis's pragmatism cannot avoid becoming phenomenalistic.[11] In making this objection, Lewis claims, the physical realist regards the conceptualistic pragmatist 'as asserting that the fact or event of there being a tree out there before me means that I have a certain content of perception now in my mind'.[12] It should be pointed out that a defender of physical realism would object that Lewis's use of the external existence of trees perceived is not strictly relevant to the issue, since physical realism concerns the mind-independent reality of the cosmic order and our knowledge of that order. In those terms, one might think that Lewis would be addressing RWS's concerns if he were talking about the composition of distant stars, extinct species, atomic nuclei, or other things whose existence is posited rather than observed. However, in defense of Lewis, this objection is irrelevant, because the distinction between observed and posited entities makes no difference in the cognitive semantics of the empirical judgements involved. All empirical judgements are treated in the same way – in terms of subjunctive conditionals where presentations ('expressive statements', in the language of *AKV*) occur in the antecedent and consequent, because Lewis is concerned with the conditions of sense, and not with reference. Though there may be good reasons for distinguishing between observable physical objects and posited physical objects at the level of cognitive semantics, neither Lewis nor RWS do so.

Whereas RWS stresses how close Lewis's position approximates Berkeley's phenomenalism, Lewis stresses the key difference: his position

> *would* be thus subjectivistic if the sense of meaning in question were that of identifying the content of experience which evidences what is believed with the existence and character of the external reality of which it is accepted as being evidence.[13]

In those terms, Lewis acknowledges, Berkeley was subjectivistic and phenomenalistic. The reason why Lewis regards himself as entitled to distinguish his position from phenomenalism is that Lewis treats cognitive semantics as independent of ontology: 'two statements may have such equivalence of intension though the terms in which they are expressed may have quite different reference.'[14] Berkeley was a subjectivist precisely because he did conflate intension and denotation, and therefore analyzed sentences like 'there is a tree over there' such that the term 'tree' denoted, or referred to, a mind-dependent entity.

Lewis complains that such objections 'spring from the erroneous assumption that logical equivalence of statements argues existential identity of things referred to in them, and that what evidences an objective reality or verifies it must somehow be included in a metaphysical nature of it'.[15] Put otherwise, the translatability of non-terminating judgements into some set of terminating judgements does not entail that any of the terms mentioned in the former refer to the same objects as the terms mentioned in the latter. This is because Lewis understands equivalence of intension in terms of *logical inference*: two sentences have the same intension if everything inferable from the one is inferable from the other. But inferential relations between judgements are just orthogonal to the representational roles played by subsentential elements. Lewis is correct because equivalence of intension between non-terminating statements (statements about physical objects) and terminating statements (statements about the relation between actual sense-presentations, actions, and possible sense-presentations) does not entail that the physical-object terms that occur in non-terminating judgements are really referring to the sense-presentations whose referring terms occur in the expressive statements comprising the antecedent and consequent of the terminating judgements. In short, Lewis maintains that equivalence of sense between whole expressions does not entail identity of reference between any of their subsentential components, because inferential role does not determine referential role.

With respect to cognitive semantics, Lewis ably defends himself from RWS's objection that Lewis is implicitly committed to phenomenalism. Yet this does not entirely settle the matter in Lewis's favor, because of the broader issues at work here between them, and in particular, the relation between epistemology and metaphysics. RWS motivates his critical realism by starting off with a defense of non-reductive naturalism that allows him to explain perceiving and knowing *in rerum natura*. This assumes a certain philosophical methodology: one starts off with metaphysics and then accounts for epistemic activities in terms of the underlying metaphysics. Thus, the problem of knowledge can only be solved, RWS would argue, by first noticing that the knower-known relation is a special instance of the organism-environment relation, which in turn is a causal transaction in the natural order, albeit of a distinct kind. Hence the metaphysics must drive the epistemology. (Call this the 'Spinozistic' prioritization).

Against this, Lewis argues for a 'Kantian' prioritization in which the distinctive task of epistemology does not depend on metaphysics at all, let alone on the results of the natural sciences. Instead Lewis invokes the distinction between the *ratio essendi* (the order of being) and the *ratio cognoscendi* (the order of knowing) to explain why epistemology, as the explication of the *ratio cognoscendi*, need take no notice of what is discovered by natural science: 'It is particularly desirable to observe that there are two characteristic modes of 'explanation' – by the *ratio essendi* and by the *ratio cognoscendi* - and that these two run in opposite directions'.[16] Each is a partial or limited explanation, correct in its own sphere and needing no correction from the other. Lewis does not object to the order of explanation that proceeds from posited object to observable evidence as cause to effect; he objects to the assumption that the kind of explanation that serves us so well in natural science is the only kind of explanation that satisfies our cognitive interests.[17]

The consequence of this distinction between kinds of explanation is the total methodological independence of the *ratio essendi* (causal explanation) and the *ratio cognoscendi* (reflective analysis):

> Epistemological investigation is, naturally, by way of the *ratio cognoscendi*: that is its peculiar task. Those 'theories of knowledge' which reverse the direction of explanation and give a causal, natural-scientific account, merely substitute a more or less uncritical and psychological methodology, based on dubious assumptions, for their proper business.[18]

That is, even if causal explanations fully satisfies our interests in the *ratio essendi*, the very distinction between the *ratio essendi* and the *ratio cognoscendi* justifies the independence of epistemology from metaphysics. This is why the task of epistemological inquiry can be conducted by 'the reflective method', without even using any of the categories of biology or psychophysics. Once the cognitive semantics and epistemology are taken care of, they will have implications for metaphysics, but epistemology itself does not rest on any metaphysical commitments.

That is not to say that the two have *nothing* to do with one another; Lewis acknowledges the Peircean ideal that

> at the limit, the nature of the real cause coincides with the totality of its conceivably experienceable effects. ... But this does not reverse the disparity between the real nature of the cause and the presently observed and meager revelation of it. Nor does it invalidate the different significance of the two opposed directions which our characteristic modes of understanding may take.[19]

which is to say that *at the Peircean limit*, the *ratio essendi* and the *ratio cognoscendi* converge. Hence naturalism, even if true, simply does not matter for the purposes of epistemology per se; epistemology is methodologically autonomous from metaphysics, even if they converge at the projected 'the end of inquiry'.

This Kantian methodological attitude is markedly distinct from RWS's Spinozistic insistence on *beginning* with metaphysical naturalism, *then* conceiving of perceiving and knowing themselves as natural processes. RWS argues for critical realism in his theory of perception because of his commitment to physical realism in metaphysics; Lewis's critical realism, by contrast, is independent of any metaphysics.[20] Though Lewis is clearly right to argue that his cognitive semantics does not entail a commitment to phenomenalistic epistemology, at this deeper level of the debate – about whether epistemology depends on metaphysics – matters are considerably less clear.

However, RWS's emphasis on grounding epistemology in metaphysics does permit him to raise a serious objection to Lewis – an objection that WSS acknowledges and strengthens considerably. Lewis tells us that the sense of non-terminating judgements depends on the strict implication between non-terminating judgements and terminating judgements. However, by rigorously separating the *ratio cognoscendi* and the *ratio essendi*, Lewis deprives himself of the ability to explain why this strict implication obtains. RWS, by contrast, observes that physical realism 'gives the ground of the predictive hypotheticals' because physical realism can explain why the predictive hypotheticals hold, to the extent that they do. It is precisely this which cognitive semantics cannot do; cognitive semantics is restricted to explicating the *ratio cognoscendi*, without introducing causal-explanatory posits, because cognitive semantics only clarifies the basic structure of our cognitive activity.

This is not quite the end of the issue, because Lewis did insist on a stratum of discourse distinct from the discourse about physical objects, where that stratum functions as a semantic (though not epistemic) foundation for other all kinds of discourses (including that about physical objects). By contrast, RWS did not think that there was any stratum of discourse deeper than, or other than, that of physical objects with properties, the discourse of common sense and science alike. As I understand it, Lewis understood that the first-personal immediate apprehensions of sensuous particulars cannot be combined in a single picture with a third-personal conceptual framework of physical things, no matter how comprehensive the latter. His chief difficulty was that, although he recognized the need for an account of nonconceptual content, his tacit acceptance of the Myth of the semantic Given prevented him from giving a fully satisfactory account of it. The problem faced by Lewis and RWS alike is how to reconcile direct realism about physical objects with nonconceptualism about mental content. Sellars *fils* contributes significantly to solving this problem, partly in virtue of what he accepts from both Sellars *peré* and Lewis.

While much more could be said about the subtle and important differences between Lewis and RWS, I hope to have shown that (1) RWS misunderstands Lewis's cognitive semantics and thereby misinterprets him as a phenomenalist; (2) Lewis ably defends himself against this charge; (3) nevertheless RWS correctly points out that the sharp division of cognitive labor between conceptual explication (the *ratio cognoscendi*) and causal explanation (the *ratio essendi*) allows Lewis to show *that* the predictive hypotheticals hold, but not *why* they hold. It is precisely on this last point that WSS contributes his own criticisms of Lewis, with transcendental naturalism emerging as the *via media* between conceptualistic pragmatism and physical realism. To put in a slogan: if Sellars *peré* is Spinoza, and Lewis is Kant, then Sellars *fils* is (who else?) Hegel.

Sellars Between Physical Realism and Conceptualistic Pragmatism

The complexity of Sellars's own relation to Lewis must not go unnoticed. In his intellectual autobiography, Sellars remarks when he returned to Oxford in 1936 to begin working on his D. Phil, 'the highlight of the year (at least I *think* it was that year) was a seminar in C. I. Lewis's *Mind and the World Order* led by John Austin and Isaiah Berlin',[21] and that he subsequently took Lewis's theory of knowledge course at Harvard in the fall of 1937. In virtually the same breath, however, he also refers to Lewis's increasingly sophisticated articulations and justifications of phenomenalism, which strongly suggests that Sellars shared his father's misinterpretation of Lewis. (Sellars even returns to criticizing Lewis's position – now represented by Firth, who *was* an explicitly committed phenomenalist – in his 1977–8 Carus Lectures.)

The crux of Sellars's *via media* between Lewis and RWS lies in his acceptance of Lewis's pragmatic inferentialism about conceptual content and transcendental positing of nonconceptual content together with RWS's insistence that sensations have only a causal, and not an epistemic, function in perception. Sellars's most targeted contribution to the debate is in 'Physical Realism' (1954), where he critically analyzes Lewis's account of intensional equivalence and the adequacy of Lewis's response to RWS's objections.[22] There Sellars *fils* refers to two other of his recently published papers, 'Is There a Synthetic 'A Priori'?' (1951) and 'Some Reflections on Language Games' (1954). Taking these three papers together, they mark a critical juncture in Sellars's philosophical development, concerned (at least proximally) with reconciling physical realism in metaphysics with conceptualistic pragmatism in cognitive semantics. Though Sellars continues his father's misinterpretation of Lewis's cognitive semantics as a theory of the metaphysics of perception – i.e. conflating sense with reference – he nevertheless identifies a fatal flaw in Lewis's project: its inability to explain how conceptual frameworks are acquired by those who do not already possess them. Once we appreciate the need for an account of concept acquisition that avoids what he calls 'concept empiricism', we will also see that Lewis's 'sense meanings' are entirely dispensable; we will be free of the Myth of the semantic Given. Here I will first lay out Sellars's criticisms of Lewis in 'Physical Realism', then turn to 'Is There a Synthetic 'A Priori'?' as developing the theory of conceptual status that Sellars requires. (Other aspects of the fascinating and subtle differences between Lewis and Sellars, such as their differing attitudes towards the importance of refuting skepticism for epistemology, will not be developed here.)

In the conclusion to 'Physical Realism', Sellars remarks that there 'is no 'sky hook' of *given* meanings to serve as a fulcrum for moving the world of ideas'.[23] All conceptual revision is in the same boat that must be rebuilt while at sea, *a priori* as well as *a posteriori*. Yet this Lewisian insight, shared with Neurath and other pragmatists, itself must be explained by physical realism in order to provide us with a fully satisfactory explanation of the causal ground of the relation between non-terminating and terminating judgements. In order to develop this claim, Sellars stresses that physical realism consists of the complete rejection of the sensory-cognitive continuum – the position that sensations and concepts do not differ in kind. According to WSS, RWS diverged from the realism of Russell and Moore through

> a consistent refusal to equate the fundamental *aboutness* with which thought is about its objects, with the *awareness* with which we are aware of the colors we see. In short, he attacked (and continues to attack) the equation of aboutness (or reference) with acquaintance or givenness.[24]

As WSS frames the issue here, RWS shares with Lewis the rejection of 'the sensory-cognitive continuum', which corresponds in Lewis's terms to the distinction between the given and the conceptual. The intentionality of thought must be sharply distinguished from mere sensory awareness ('nonconceptual content') if we are to understand how the relationship between them constitutes perceptual judgement (and empirical judgement generally).

However, Sellars quickly moves to criticizing Lewis's distinction between the thick experience of objects and the thin experience of the given when he insists that 'while our sensations mediate and control our perceptual knowledge of the physical world, this knowledge is not a second-class knowledge built on a first-class knowledge of colors and sounds'.[25] Clearly, Sellars shares his father's view that, with respect to cognitive semantics, there is nothing deeper or more fundamental than the vocabulary of physical objects – a claim that WSS understands Lewis to deny. As Sellars sets up the terms of the debate, the physical realist objection to conceptualistic pragmatism consists of the following:

> that not all the properties which common sense attributes to physical objects can be analyzed in terms of subjunctive conditionals about perceptions becomes clear once we note that subjunctive discourse of the kind that is relevant to our problem embodies our consciousness of the laws of nature ... this consciousness relates sense perception to bodily and physical occurrences ... [O]nly if one has swallowed some version of the radical empiricist dogma concerning meaning and the given will one know *ab initio* that *red* as a property of physical objects is *analyzable into* hypotheticals.[26]

In other words, the radical empiricist assumes that any statement about 'red' as a property of physical objects can be translated into a set of conditionals. But this translation cannot be carried out; the discourse of physical objects occurs again in the conditionals themselves, because *actions* presuppose the discourse of physical objects, such as one's own body, and the laws of physics. It cannot be the case, Sellars urges, that *all* of physical-object discourse can be completely translated into conditional statements. A further difficulty is that Lewis would need to explain, and yet cannot explain, *why* we would expect that non-terminating judgements strictly imply, and are thus intensionally equivalent to, sets of terminating judgements. At issue here is not Lewis's commitment to the intensional equivalence of non-terminating and terminating judgements, but the ground or basis of that commitment.

At this point, the sophisticated reader of Lewis must point out that Sellars commits a serious error in his use of 'subjunctive conditionals'. As pointed out above, Lewis does indeed hold that the following must be true:

> **There is wine in my glass** if and only if *there is such-and-such transparent shape in my visual field, and the bottom half of the shape is filled with a red liquid* and if I were to take a sip of it, *I would probably be presented with gustatory sensations I have learned to associate with wine on previous occasions.*

On Lewis's cognitive semantics, the biconditional has different characteristics than the subjunctive conditional on the right-hand side. The biconditional, relating the non-terminating judgement to the terminating judgement, is strict implication, since the two are intensionally equivalent. The subjunctive conditional on the right hand side is not strict implication; it is a *probabilistic* statement that holds between the antecedent expressive statement and the consequent expressive statement. In other words, the biconditional is analytic *a priori*, whereas the subjunctive conditional is synthetic *a posteriori* (as probability claims must be, though at this time Lewis was less clear about this point than he should have been).[27]

For this reason, Sellars errs slightly in claiming that Lewis holds that the ascription of properties is analyzable into hypotheticals about the given and meaning. To substantiate that objection to Lewis, we would need an argument to show that strict implication of objective and phenomenal judgements amounts to an analysis of the former in terms of the latter, in the sense of analysis that Russell provided when he showed that definite descriptions could be *replaced* by quantifier expressions. For unless Lewis had a Russellian conception of conceptual analysis (as seems *prima facie* doubtful), it would be far safer to say that Lewis holds that the statements that ascribe properties to physical objects strictly imply, and are therefore intensionally equivalent to, the predictive hypotheticals obtaining between phenomenal states. The phenomenal judgements do not justify or 'ground' objective judgements; rather, phenomenal judgements play a necessary role in making explicit the semantic content of objective judgements. Lewis aims at explicating the sense of objective judgements, not at reducing them to the given and meaning.

However, Sellars is on firmer ground when he points out that the role of action in terminating judgements entails that they are intelligible only against a background of worldly objects, properties, relations, and law-like generalizations (lest we find ourselves confronted with the absurdity of conceiving of bodily movements without any bodily presence in the world, acted upon as much as act-ing). Thus, while any particular non-terminating judgement may be translatable into a set of terminating judgements, this cannot be done for *all* non-terminating judgements *at once*, because each of the terminating judgements itself presup-poses some other non-terminating judgements for its own interpretation.

The substantive objection, then, is that the conceptualistic pragmatist can at best merely *show* that non-terminating judgements strictly imply a set of termi-nating judgements; she cannot *account* for this putative equivalence of intension:

> [In contrast with the radical empiricist, the physical realist] grants, of course, that the process of acquiring concepts of physical objects essentially involves the occur-rence of patterns of sensations arising from our commerce with physical objects, and that the sensations are more intimately related to the go of the organism than are their external causes – but he warns against drawing the conclusion that knowledge and meaning must be more intimately *about* these patterns of sensations than about their external cause.[28]

On the one hand, Sellars's criticism does not quite meet its target. Lewis's view is not that knowledge and meaning are about patterns of sensations, in the sense of *referring* to patterns of sensations. Rather, Lewis holds that non-terminating judgements must be, if they are to have a sense, translatable into terminating judgements, with the logical form of conditionals that take expressive statements as constituents of the antecedent and the consequent. Lewis's stipulation is thus not about reference (or extension) but about sense (or intension), and thus not about the metaphysics of perception (*contra* Sellars *père et fils*) but about the cognitive semantics of objective purport. On the other hand, Sellars points out that only if we depart from cognitive semantics and develop a metaphysical natu-ralism that explains how sensations causally mediate perceptual episodes can we *explain* what the conceptualistic pragmatist at best *shows*, and that such causal mediation plays a necessary role in the acquisition of a conceptual framework.

Yet it must not be thought that Sellars is entirely critical of Lewis. On the contrary, he regards himself as aspiring to reconcile Lewis's conceptualist pragmatism ('phenomenalism') with physical realism, and more precisely, to reconcile Lewis's inferentialism with Sellars *père*'s metaphysical naturalism by showing how physical realism can *accommodate* Lewis's insight that 'the relation between physical object statements and conditional predictions of future experi-ence holds *ex vi terminorum*'.[29] But Sellars makes two significant departures from Lewis. Firstly, the necessity of the relevant biconditionals does not imply that we can simply translate all of the physical-object statements into predictions about future experiences, because Sellars – departing more from Lewis than he indi-cates – does not treat the biconditional here as analytic. Unlike Lewis, Sellars sees that the biconditionals, although necessarily true and hence *a priori*, cannot be analytic. (Post-Kripke, we recognize that necessity does not entail *a priority*.) Secondly, he thinks that physical realism can *explain* why the biconditionals hold by showing how initiation into a conceptual framework requires selective reinforcement of expressions of 'innate' behavioural dispositions as the incipient language-learner causally interacts with her social and physical environments.

For this reason, physical realism accounts for the causal transactions that underlie and generate Lewis's correlations – as Sellars elsewhere puts it, 'espousal of principles must be reflected in uniformities of behaviour' if those principles (and their espousal) is not to seem utterly mysterious and inexplicable.[30] Or, we might say, if the constitutive principles of a conceptual framework are not to be mystified in a version of the Myth of the semantic Given. Lewis locates the right principles that *constitute* the conceptual framework of physical object discourse, but neglects to ground those principles in a causal explanation of how we *acquire* that framework. For this reason, Sellars correctly notes that Lewis does not address how the stipulated correlations between nonterminating judgements and terminating judgements are instituted or generated – how an embodied creature *becomes* a norm-governed user of a conceptual framework. In Lewis's own terms, he cannot explain the origins of sense meanings, or putting the same thought slightly differently, he is committed to the Augustinian picture of language that prevents this problem from being posed.

On this line of reasoning, overcoming the Myth of the semantic Given requires an account of how a conceptual framework is acquired by one who does not already have it, even though the strict implication between objective judgements and phenomenal judgements will hold for anyone who has successfully acquired the conceptual framework of empirical discourse.[31] However, 'Physical Realism' alone does not provide a substantial alternative to Lewis's cognitive semantics; that alternative becomes evident in 'Is There a Synthetic "*A Priori*"?',[32] 'Inference and Meaning',[33] and the important 'Some Reflections on Language Games'.[34]

'Is There a Synthetic "*A Priori*"?' is important for two reasons. Firstly, it appeared shortly after White's 'The Analytic and the Synthetic: An Untenable Dualism' and Quine's 'Two Dogmas of Empiricism', two articles that resulted from the campaign against Lewis that led to Lewis's subsequent eclipse.[35] Sellars's essay was first presented in 1951 and published in 1953. Textual evidence suggests that Sellars was familiar with Quine's 'Two Dogmas of Empiricism', which first appeared in 1950. He certainly would have been familiar with Morton White's 'The Analytic and the Synthetic: An Untenable Dualism', because Sellars published 'Language, Rules, and Behavior' in the same volume as White's essay.[36] Hence Sellars develops a sophisticated criticism at the same time as White and Quine are developing their attacks, though Sellars's is far more nuanced and sympathetic.

Secondly, Sellars advances his alternative by (among other things) further developing Lewis's pragmatic theory of concepts by proposing several distinctions in the course of resolving the question as to whether there a synthetic *a priori* propositions. Importantly, he distinguishes between a narrower and a broader sense of analytic. A proposition is analytic in the narrow sense if the replacement of a defined term with its definition yields a logical truth. A logical truth, in turn, is provisionally defined as any proposition that appears in Russell and Whitehead's *Principia Mathematica* or similar work. By contrast, a proposition is analytic in the broader sense if it is true by meaning alone. (Here it should be noted that the *Principia* is purely extensional language. Lewis himself developed the concept of strict implication precisely because he objected to it on this basis. If 'analytic' means 'expressible in a wholly extensional formal language', then Lewis would be the first to *deny* that propositions 'true by virtue of meaning alone' are analytic!)

Since Sellars proceeds by taking 'analytic' in the narrow sense, the question as to whether there are there synthetic *a priori* propositions quickly becomes the question as to whether there are propositions that are unconditionally assertable ('true *ex vi terminorum*') but not occurring in an extensional logical system. Sellars then aims to show that there are such propositions. However, to accept this, a major obstacle to accepting them must be removed: 'concept empiricism', or the assumption that conceptual content is derived from sense-experience. For if one accepts concept empiricism, then one cannot accept synthetic *a priori* propositions:

(1) concept empiricism entails that every concept of a universal must be satisfied by some particular;

(2) the concept of a real connection is the concept of a relation between universals, not between particulars;

(3) so concept empiricism must deny that we can conceive of real connections;

(4) but there are synthetic *a priori* propositions only if we can conceive of real connections between the properties referred to by the predicates in the proposition; so,

(5) concept empiricism entails the rejection of synthetic a priori propositions, but

(6) concept empiricism is committed to the myth of the given (which one ought to reject);

and hence, by rejecting the myth of the given in all its versions, the door is reopened to synthetic *a priori* propositions.

By 'concept empiricism' he refers to the view that 'the basic concepts in terms of which all genuine concepts are defined are concepts of qualities and relations exemplified by particulars in what is called "the given" or "immediate experience".'[37] The problem with concept empiricism is that it lacks an adequate account of concept acquisition, because the concept empiricist must hold that one's awareness of universals is prior to, and necessary for, learning how to use a symbol. But if learning how to use a symbol just *is* becoming aware of a universal, then the latter cannot explain the former – precisely the difficulty observed earlier in Lewis's account of the relation between sense meanings and linguistic meanings. What is needed instead is 'the abandonment of what has happily been called the metaphor of the mental eye':[38] the view that something can be known to obtain entirely in virtue of one's just seeing it to obtain (however metaphorical the 'seeing').

At this point Sellars notes the affinity between his view and Lewis's:

> If we put this implication in a slightly different way, we immediately establish contact with a characteristic contention of Professor Lewis. All classification of objects, however confident and preemptory, is a venture, a venture which at no point finds its justification in a pre-symbolic vision of generic and specific hearts on the sleeves of objects of experience. Classification resembles the grasping tentacles of an octopus, now tentative, now confident, rather than a salesman's selection of a suit for a customer after a glance at his build. I am afraid, however, that our agreement with Lewis is more shadow than substance. For while he writes in this manner of the interpretation of the given by means of concepts whose implications transcend the given, he also holds that the sensible appearances of things *do* wear their hearts on their sleeves, and that we do have a cognitive vision of these hearts which is direct, unlearned, and incapable of error ... The assumption to which we are committed requires to extend to all classificatory consciousness whatever, the striking language in which Lewis describes our consciousness of objects.[39]

It is tempting to read Sellars as accusing Lewis of accepting a version of the Myth of the epistemic Given. If that were the case, however, then Lewis has a ready reply, because Lewis would not hold that our immediate apprehensions of qualia count as 'the sensible appearances of things'. It is only our conceptual interpretation of qualia that allows those apprehensions to count as appearances *of things*. Moreover, the immediate apprehension of qualia is posited as a necessary condition on empirical content, and not a kind of knowledge in its own right. While Lewis does insist that our 'cognitive vision' of qualia is 'incapable of error', he also insists that their immunity to doubt entails that they have no epistemic status. If we were to interpret Sellars as accusing Lewis of accepting the Myth of the epistemic Given, then we ought to conclude that Sellars is mistaken.

However, if we bear in mind the distinction between the Myth of the epistemic Given and the Myth of the semantic Given, we can see that it actually the Myth of the semantic Given that Sellars is focused upon. Indeed, Sellars has turned Lewis's cognitive semantics against itself: the very same considerations that Lewis applies to classificatory consciousness of objects – that such consciousness is tentative, fallible, and revisable – also applies to all classificatory consciousness as such. The very same considerations that Lewis brings to bear against the epistemic Given, Sellars brings to bear against the semantic Given. It is not just that there is no 'knowledge by acquaintance', but there is no 'meaning by acquaintance', either. In the terms developed in Chapter 2, Sellars recognizes that the Lewisian Dilemma cannot be solved. Once our understanding of the non-discursive dimension of human experience has been *copied from* our understanding of the discursive dimension – which is precisely what Lewis does in accepting the Augustinian picture of language – Lewis begs the very questions he is attempting to answer.

What, then, remains? Sellars tells us that if we are to purge inferential semantics of the Myth of the semantic Given, we will have to accept physical realism:

> A philosopher who rejects the mental eye approach and all its implications is indeed committed to the view that it is by the causal interplay of the individual and his physical and social environment, without benefit of a prehension of eternal objects, whether *in re* or *extra rem*, that concepts, meaningful symbols, arise.[40]

Once the acquisition of a conceptual framework is explained in terms of causal interactions, there is no need for 'sense meanings' to explain how conceptual frameworks are connected to the world of lived experience; instead,

> the conceptual status of descriptive as well as logical – not to mention prescriptive – predicates, is constituted, *completely* constituted, by syntactical rules ... the conceptual meaning of a descriptive term is constituted by what can be inferred from it in accordance with the logical and extra-logical rules of inference of the language (conceptual frame) to which it belongs.[41]

With this move, Sellars takes the decisive step from Lewis's weak inferentialism to the strong inferentialism that becomes systematically elaborated by Brandom. In Brandom's terms, weak inferentialism holds that inferential articulation is necessary for conceptual content, whereas strong inferentialism holds that inferential articulation is sufficient for conceptual content.[42]

The key to Sellars's strong inferentialism is that material ('extra-logical') inference rules, together with language-entry moves (e.g. perceptual reports) and language-exit moves (e.g. declarations of intention) allows Sellars to treat *language itself* as all the discursive intentionality that we need. The meaning of a word lies its norm-governed functional role in inference, together with the language-entry and language-exit transitions, and those norms in turn are explained in terms of the shaping of behaviour in a social and physical context.[43]

If we accept Sellars's construal of 'analytic' as 'true in PM or a similar system', then 'analytic' means 'true in an extensional formal language', hence we should regard Lewis's pragmatic *a priori* not as analytic, but as synthetic. With Sellars, then, one of Lewis's most important ideas – the pragmatic *a priori* – is disentangled from the Myth of the semantic Given and transformed into what Sellars calls material inference rules, both constitutive of a conceptual framework yet also revisable in light of experience.

At work in Sellars's objection to Lewis is, I think, the following line of thought: Sellars accepts (following Carnap) that (i) the analytic is the logical and (ii) intensions are dispensable for logic. Under those Carnapian constraints, Sellars could not have accepted that the extra-logical relations are also analytic. Yet he did accept, following Lewis, the indispensability of intensions for explicating the semantics of ordinary language (including, importantly, both science and philosophy). His solution is to cut the baby in half: the extra-logical rules of inference must be 'synthetic', in the sense that contrast with 'analytic' if we hold that the analytic is the extensionally logical. Yet those rules cannot be *a posteriori* in the sense that our matter-of-factual judgements are *a posteriori*, since the rules are what make judgement possible. Hence the extra-logical rules of inference – i.e. material inference rules – must be synthetic *a priori*, albeit in the pragmatic, Lewisian sense of '*a priori*' according to which the *a priori* is always revisable. Lewis would resist this conclusion because he accepts a broader construal of analyticity, and indeed of logic itself, since he thinks that only an intensional logic can truly capture the structure of human reasoning. Conversely, if there are non-analytic necessary entailments – if there are extra-logical, as well as logical, inference rules – then sense meanings are utterly dispensable.

Despite the significant achievement made in recognizing that Lewis is committed to the Myth of the semantic Given, and in using that criticism to motivate the transition from weak inferentialism to strong inferentialism, Sellars remains – like Lewis and unlike Brandom – committed to 'nonconceptual content'. Indeed, Sellars shares with Lewis the thought that nonconceptual content is not only required by an adequate transcendental reflection on our basic cognitive capacities but also crucial for avoiding the excesses of nineteenth-century idealism represented by Bradley, Bosquanet, and of course Royce. Yet, much like Sellars *père*, Sellars *fils* holds that sensations must ultimately be regarded as playing a causal role. How does WSS hold together the transcendental and the naturalistic sides of his thinking, and in particular, how does he do so with regard to nonconceptual content?

The Concept of 'Non-Conceptual Content'

Through his criticisms of Lewis, Sellars recognizes that we should integrate the conceptualistic pragmatism of Lewis with the physical realism of Sellars *père* in what I call transcendental naturalism: the position that transcendentally specified notions (such as Lewis's biconditionals between non-terminating and terminating judgements) are best conceived of as kinds of conceptual roles that must have naturalistically specified role-players, or as deVries (2010) puts it, 'transcendental structures must be reflected in causal structures'.[44] In O'Shea's terms, this is the norm/nature meta-principle; its importance for Sellars's philosophy in general, and his theory of sense-impressions in particular must not be overlooked.

Firstly, it must be noticed that deVries's claim is *itself* a synthetic *a priori* claim, and more specifically, a transcendental claim. This follows from Rosenberg's analysis of synthetic *a priori* claims as having the structure 'every-must', e.g. 'every event must have a cause'.[45] Here the claim is that every transcendental structure must be reflected in some causal structure; put otherwise, every transcendental structure must be causally realized. The norm/nature meta-principle is thus a synthetic *a priori* proposition about synthetic *a priori* propositions. We must be able to specify not only (at the level of transcendental reflection) *that* specific conceptual roles are satisfied, but we must also specify the constraints on the satisfaction of those roles in ways that are broadly consistent with the ontology of the scientific image.[46] However, the naturalistic transcendental philosopher does not need to specify precisely what the relevant causally realizing items are, let alone tell cognitive scientists where they ought to be looking for them.

The deeper motivation for transcendental naturalism lies in Sellars's commitment to two different lines of thought. Firstly, Sellars accepts a semantic version of 'the naturalistic fallacy': that it is a misbegotten notion to attempt to reduce normative facts to naturalistic facts, if 'reduce' means 'analyze into'.[47] Secondly, Sellars accepts scientific realism in contrast with any sort of phenomenalism or positivism.[48] The former commitment entails that all normative concepts are irreducible to any naturalistic facts, of the sort that figure in a causal-explanatory account grounded in the natural sciences. But at the same time, the causal-explanatory account grounded in the natural sciences is the discourse of ontology; in Sellars's well-known formula, 'in the dimension of describing and explaining the world, science is the measure of all things, of what is that it is and of what is not that it is not'.[49] In light of both commitments, Sellars concludes, on the one hand, transcendental structures, as specifications of kinds of conceptual roles, are irreducible to anything naturalistic, because all conceptual roles are normative statuses. On the other hand, if we were to specify transcendental structures without an eye to causal implementation at all, we run the risk of inflating the results of transcendental philosophy into an ontology – which is to say, venturing forth upon the slippery slope to absolute idealism. Transcendental naturalism is Sellars's *via media* between an idealism that 'ontologizes' the results of transcendental reflection and a materialism that cannot account for normativity, subjectivity, or agency.

Since it is a result of transcendental reflection that we recognize ourselves as perceivers, we must account for the origins of our capacity to recognize ourselves as perceivers without presupposing the very concepts we are trying to explain. How, Sellars asks, could we have acquired the conceptual framework of perception if we did not already have it? To answer this question, Sellars must show both what is mistaken about the empiricist version of the Myth of the Given and provide us with an alternative. As shown above, RWS's neo-empiricist treatment of sensations is a central plank in his critical realism, since it is by treating sensations as causal but not epistemic intermediaries that RWS argues that perceptual episodes are partly constituted by our sensitivity to objects and properties.

What is of interest to me here is not that Sellars allows for sensations *qua* nonconceptual states of consciousness, but the specific role accorded to sensations within the account, and just why the Myth of Jones is supposed to supplant the Myth of the Given.

As already noted above, Sellars argues against the Myth of the Given in many versions. Taking the Myth in the broad, cognitive-semantic sense, the myth consists in the idea that any cognitive item does or can play its cognitive role independent of all other cognitive role-players. When we realize that the Given is a Myth:

> we now recognize that instead of coming to have a concept of something because we have noticed that sort of thing, to have the ability to notice a sort of thing is already to have the concept of that sort of thing, and cannot account for it.[50]

That is, our awareness of things as falling under kind-terms (thus being particular instantiations of kinds) is a *result* of our having acquired concepts, *by way of* (among other things) having been initiated into a linguistic community. Thus, any categorical ontology – any conceptual framework that contains the categories for facts, particulars, and kinds – already presupposes the logical space of reasons. It is central to Sellars's epistemic and semantic holism that no conceptual framework of the sort we use in ordinary experience or scientific reasoning can contain terms for facts without containing terms of particulars and for universals. Facts, particulars, and universals stand and fall together as the categories of any conceptual framework or discursive practice. Hence the advocate of the Given is committed to both epistemic and semantic atomism. In the broadest construal, the Given, in the Mythic sense, is a conflation of the order of knowing and the order of being. One takes some aspect of reality's fundamental structure to simply be identical with one's cognitive grasp of it, such that that cognitive grasping is unmediated by anything else.

At the same time, Sellars regards the concept of sense-impressions as indispensable to correctly explicating any empirical framework. At the conceptual level, this means that in any empirical framework through which the users of that framework conceptualize themselves as perceivers, they must have the concept of sense-impressions. At the causal level, this means that for any beings who understand themselves as perceivers, there must be some set of sense-impressions occurring to them (while leaving open exactly *what* sense-impressions those are). Due to the indispensable role that the concept of sense-impressions plays in our self-understanding as perceivers, the concept of sense-impressions needs to be re-conceptualized as not being Given. Sellars regards the concept of sense-impressions, as the concept of nonconceptual states of consciousness, to be playing an *explanatory* role. It explains why different observation sentences, e.g. 'I see a green apple',; 'the apple looks green to me', and 'it seems to me as though it were a green apple' can be understood as expressing different degrees of endorsing or withholding commitment to the perceptual report, 'I see a green apple.'

Since, on Sellars's account, the function of the concept of nonconceptual contents is fundamentally explanatory, he concludes that sensory states are not originally given to us as sensory states. They are part of an explanatory apparatus that we apply non-inferentially as a result of having been trained to use this particular vocabulary. Sellars argues for this view in what he calls 'the Myth of Jones,'[51] where he suggests that our vocabulary of sense-impressions is an *extension* of our vocabulary in which physical objects are described in Aristotelian vocabulary of the proper and common sensibles. Hence they are not logically independent of one's initiation into the 'space of reasons'[52] and so not, in Sellars's terms, Given in the pernicious sense. Thus, while the 'rawness' of 'raw feels' is indeed nonconceptual, the concept of 'raw feels' does not amount to mere ostensive pointing at brute Givens that can be identified without any drawing on any other conceptual capacities. The concept of a sensations is introduced to explain the nature of perception as distinct from thinking.

To this basic account we must note three qualifications: (i) the distinction between observation terms and theoretical terms is a methodological distinction, not an ontological one; (ii) as a scientific realist, Sellars is a realist about sensations because they successfully explain the difference between perception and thought; (iii) Sellars does not claim that sensations *are* theoretical entities, only that they are *like* theoretical entities. That said, the point of the Myth of Jones is to dislodge the Givenness of thoughts and sensations: 'I have used a myth to kill a myth – the Myth of the Given.'[53]

With this framework in mind, we can turn to Sellars's treatment of sensations in terms of (i) a transcendental specification of the concept of nonconceptual content and (ii) a naturalistic realization of nonconceptual content in terms of the causal role that sensations play in empirical cognition. Sellars begins his magnum opus *Science and Metaphysics* with a nuanced re-interpretation of Kant's distinction between 'intuitions' and 'concepts.'[54] Sellars argues that Kant's use of 'intuition' conceals an ambiguity between intuitive conceptual representations – that is, conceptual representations of *particulars* or of *individuals*, modeled on singular demonstrative phrases, and the receptivity of the senses, which must be *non*conceptual if it is to play the requisite role of 'guiding' thoughts.[55] Sellars thus distinguishes between: (i) minimal objective reports that function as claims about perceptual objects and (ii) sense-impressions proper. The former count as 'intuitions' *qua* the result of the productive imagination; the latter count as 'intuitions' *qua* manifold of sense *prior* to imaginative synthesis. That intuitions *result* from the productive imagination turns on how he interprets Kant's claim that '[t]he *same* function which gives unity to the various representations in a judgement *also* gives unity to the mere synthesis of representations in an intuition.'[56] Sellars takes this to mean that the productive imagination, which generates judgements, also generates sub-judgemental items, modeled after 'this-such' expressions.[57] Thus, the productive imagination, i.e. the understanding insofar as it is playing the role of guiding sensibility, produces 'this white cube' (an intuition) modeled off 'this cube is white' (a judgement). But if intuitions, in one of their roles, are already informed by the deployment of concepts, then we need an account of 'receptivity proper' to explain how our beliefs and judgements are answerable to a world that we do not create, but discover.

Sellars holds that clarifying Kant's notion of intuition is important not only for understanding what Kant was trying to do, but also for understanding why subsequent thinkers did not correctly understand Kant:

> Indeed, it is only if Kant distinguishes the radically non-conceptual character of sense from the conceptual character of the synthesis of apprehension in intuition ... and accordingly, the *receptivity* of sense from the *guidedness* of intuition that he can avoid the dialectic which leads from Hegel's *Phenomenology* to nineteenth-century idealism.[58]

and, much more seriously:

> Kant's failure to distinguish clearly between the 'forms' of receptivity proper and the 'forms' of that which is represented by the intuitive conceptual representations which are 'guided' by receptivity – a distinction which is demanded both by the thrust of his argument, and by sound philosophy – had as its consequence that no sooner had he left the scene than these particular waters were muddied by Hegel and the Mills, and philosophy had to begin the slow climb 'back to Kant' which is still underway.[59]

That is, the distinction between the receptivity of sense and the guidedness of intuitions allow us to recognize that intuitive conceptual representations are 'guided' by something else – what he calls 'receptivity proper' or 'sheer receptivity'.[60] When I perceptually take in how things are, my productive imagination generates perceptual experience by organizing my sensory intake such that I am suitably disposed to make a claim about what I perceive. But this can be the case only if my sensory receptivity to the world has just enough structure for it to guide the productive imagination. It is a transcendental requirement on receptivity proper that it cannot be utterly formless cookie-dough that offers no constraint to the deployment of concepts. Lewis recognized this, which is precisely why he insisted that we must have the ability to recognize relations of similarity and dissimilarity amongst the qualia in order to make some conceptual interpretations appropriate and others not. The dilemma Lewis was unable to resolve is precisely this: that his official conception of the given prevented him from accounting for this recognition. As Sellars recognizes, receptivity proper must have representational purport, and (on pain of collapsing the distinctions between sensibility and understanding) the representations of receptivity proper cannot be conceptual; hence we must distinguish between intuitive conceptual representations and radically nonconceptual representations.

At this point one might worry that invoking nonconceptual representations to play a transcendental role amounts to falling back into the Myth of the semantic Given. After all, Sellars thinks it would a serious error to conflate non-conceptual states of consciousness with merely brute impingements of ambient matter and energy on our sensory receptors:

> But is it genuinely necessary to interpose non-conceptual representation *as states of consciousness* between the 'physical' impact of the sensory stimulus and the conceptual representations (guarded or daring) which finds verbal expression, actually or potentially, in perceptual statements? Can we not interpret the receptivity involved in terms of 'purely' physical states, and attribute to these the role of guiding conceptualization? Why should we suppose that receptivity culminates in a state which is neither 'purely physical' *nor* conceptual? Yet to do just this is, I shall argue, of the greatest importance for the philosophy of mind and, in particular, for an understanding of how the framework of physical science is to be integrated with the framework of common sense.[61]

In short, the ontology of mind requires some third category besides the merely physical and the full-blown conceptual: a category of nonconceptual states of representational consciousness to play the role of non-physical causes. Put otherwise, Sellars has both transcendental and empirical reasons for emphasizing the concept of sensory consciousness.[62] Not only are there nonconceptual representations, then, but they occur as states of consciousness – the content of sensory consciousness – and so are neither, strictly speaking, identifiable with physical items in the causal order described by the natural sciences nor are they identifiable with the full-fledged contents of propositional or discursive thought.

In light of the tight connections Sellars insists upon between conceptuality and apperceptive consciousness (following Kant's achievement in the B-Deduction), Sellars would seem to be calling for an account of non-apperceptive consciousness: a kind of consciousness or awareness the episodes of which are not captured by the 'I think ...' of apperceptive subjectivity. Nonconceptual contents *of consciousness* are states of non-apperceptive consciousness. On his view, such an account requires posing and answering two intimately related questions:

(1) how should we specify what counts as non-apperceptive consciousness?
(2) what is the epistemological status of (some of) the items that count as non-apperceived states of consciousness?

Sellars's response is that the concept of non-apperceptive consciousness has the status of a theoretical posit – we *posit* non-apperceptive consciousness, i.e. sense-impressions, in order to *explain* apperceptive consciousness (the domain of intuitional and judgemental conceptual representations). In other words, the claim that sense-impressions are theoretical posits is his response to *both* (1) *and* (2).

The upshot of both the Myth of the Given and the Myth of Jones is that sense-impressions are non-intentional, and so cognitively semantically neutral, but causally efficacious theoretical posits required by sound transcendental reflection. By denying that sense-impressions have *any* cognitive semantic role, and *only* a causal one, Sellars has demoted sense-impressions from any status as Given; they play no role in constituting empirical conceptual content. Yet Sellars also insists that their causal role occurs as states of non-apperceptive consciousness that constrain the operations of apperceptive consciousness – though entirely causal (and so not part of the rational or normative order), they are part of the mental, not physical, domain. This is why sense-impressions are necessary to flesh out the place of mind in nature: if there were no sense-impressions, then there would nothing to mediate between the mental-cum-rational order and the physical-cum-causal order. Sense-impressions, as both fully (though non-apperceptively) conscious and merely causal, are necessary to bridge the two domains of intelligibility.

But if sense-impressions are nonconceptual states of consciousness, how is the intentionality of perception to be understood? On Sellars's account, the intentionality of perception depends on his account of intentionality generally: perceptions are intentional because they have conceptual content as well as nonconceptual content, since perceptual reports are a kind of 'language-entry transition' (just as declarations of intention are a kind of 'language-exit transition'). The conceptual content of perceptual episodes is understood in terms of how we are supposed to think of perceptual episodes ('seeings' and 'lookings') as modeled on singular demonstrative phrases (plus a 'commentary' which specifies the ways in which the analogy is to be qualified). But in order to distinguish perceptions from thoughts, in keeping with the rejection of the sensory-cognitive continuum, we need to specify the vague formulation that '*something, somehow* a cube of pink in physical space is present in the perception other than as merely *believed in*'.[63]

To understand just how Sellars proposes to account for the intentionality of perception, it will be helpful to examine in more detail Sellars's account of how sensibility and understanding are brought together in what he, following Kant, calls 'the productive imagination'. In his important 'The Role of Imagination in Kant's Theory of Experience', Sellars notes that, as a matter of sheer phenomenology, 'Visual experience presents itself as the direct awareness of a complex physical structure ... opaque objects ... present themselves as three dimensional physical objects which stand in such and such relations to each other and to the perceiver's body'.[64] But while we do see physical objects (or, better put, take

ourselves to be seeing physical objects), what we see *of* them is their facing sides –
that is, the occurring facing side of an opaque physical object is what we *sense* of
it, even though we *perceive* it as a three-dimensional physical object that stands
in relation to other physical objects and to the perceiver's own body. (We do not,
however, perceive the object as having properties or as having causal powers –
that is how the object is conceptualized by the understanding, once the this-such
complexes synthesized by the productive imagination have been made available
for judgement). Considering an apple, of we sense only the red exterior surface,
Sellars asks, 'How can a volume of white volume flesh be present *as actually* in
the visual experience if it is not seen? The answer should be obvious. It is present
by virtue of being *imagined*'.[65] That is, we *imagine* the white flesh of the apple,
and in that sense the white flesh of the apple is actually present in our experience
o f it. Summarizing a complex line of thought, Sellars concludes that 'Roughly
imagining is an intimate blend of imaging and conceptualization, whereas perceiving is an intimate blend of sensing *and* imaging *and* conceptualization'.[66]

What makes this possible – bringing together sensing, imaging, and conceptualization in the right ways – is what Sellars calls the construction of sense-image
models. The construction of sense-image models is guided by two distinct capacities – sensory input on the one hand, and the background cultural and individual
conceptual framework on the other. In this way conceptualization enters into the
products of the synthesis: intuitive conceptual representings expressed as this-
such phrases. When I see a houseplant, my concept of <u>houseplant</u> supplies the
productive imagination with a family of recipes for constructing image-models
that, in conjunction with the construction of an image-model of my own body
and the stimulation of my retinas, guides the construction of 'this-houseplant-
as-seen-from-this-angle-and-at-this-distance-in-this-light', i.e. the synthesis of a
this-such suitable for tokening in a language-entry transition.

Here Sellars carefully distinguishes between what we perceive of the object
and what we perceive the object *as*:

> what we perceive of the object in visual perception consists of those features which
> actually belong to the image-model, i.e. its proper and common sensible qualities and
> relations. Also its perspectival structure. On the other hand, what we perceive the
> object *as* is a matter of the conceptual content of the complex demonstrative thought.[67]

In particular, since the occurrent common and proper sensible qualities and
relations are *all* that we perceive of the object, we do not perceive its causal
powers, nor do we perceive it as a substance with properties. That requires the
employment of the Understanding, which goes beyond what the productive
imagination itself provides. In this way Sellars reaches the important conclusion
that 'the senses do not judge' is correctly understood as the claim that 'the image-
model does not have grammatical structure'.[68]

What, then, are sensations doing in the account of perception? Sellars urges that sensations which must be supplemented with concept-guided images in order to yield perception. Put otherwise, Sellars (following Kant) thinks of perception as an 'amalgamation' of sensation, imagination, and conceptualization. The epistemological status of sense-impressions is that of theoretical posits, as Sellars reaffirms in 'Some Remarks on Perceptual Consciousness':

> the obvious move here is to introduce visual sensations as proto-theoretical states of perceivers to *explain* these results of phenomenological or conceptual analysis ... It is by the introduction of visual sensations that we transcend phenomenology or conceptual analysis. They are not yielded by phenomenological reduction but postulated by a proto-(scientific)-theory.[69]

In the order of being, it will turn out, that it is these sense-impressions which are the *real* object of awareness when we *take* ourselves to be aware of physical objects; we do not, *sub specie Peirceii*, directly perceive physical objects. Rather, we are immediately aware of our own (inner) sensory states which stand in causally well-founded representational relations with the physical (external) objects which are their causes.

To summarize, then: two fundamental commitments structure Sellars's theory of perception: that 'the intentional is that which belongs to the conceptual order',[70] and 'the senses do not judge'. Although sensations are *intensional*, they are not *intentional*, a point easily concealed by the surface-grammar of 'a sensation of red' and 'a thought of red'. (The reports about the sensations, being assertions in various modes of endorsement, *are* of course intentional and not just intensional). In advancing the rejection of the sensory-cognitive continuum, Sellars claims that 'the senses have what I shall call a *pseudo-intentionality* which is easily mistaken for the genuine intentionality of the cognitive order'.[71] Perceiving differs from thinking in having a non-intentional and nonconceptual aspect: the sheer receptivity of sense-impressions. Though sense-impressions are conscious representations, since they are nonconceptual they are also non-intentional.

From this it follows that, in Sellars's strong inferentialism, the intentionality of perceiving is due entirely to its conceptual content. To reject the Augustinian picture of language at work in the Myth of the semantic Given, Sellars maintains that there is only one notion of intentionality: that of conceptuality, as best understood on analogy with language. Thus, linguistic intentionality is at work not only in thought but also in perception itself, in the guise of intuitive conceptual representations, the intuition as a 'this-such'. On the Sellarsian account, the Myth of the Given is 'killed' by the Myth of Jones insofar as Sellars rehabilitates non-apperceptive consciousness *qua* sense-impressions by construing the concept of sense-impressions as a theoretical posit necessary to explain perceptual experience, rather than as a requirement of transcendental reflection *tout court*, as Lewis does. Sellars understands non-apperceptive consciousness in terms of sensations, which are non-apperceptive, non-intentional states of consciousness. The intentionality of perception, on the Sellarsian view, is derived from its conceptual (hence linguistic) content.

It is perhaps due to the unusualness of transcendental naturalism that Sellars's *via media* between transcendental specification (e.g. conceptualistic pragmatism) and causal implementation (e.g. physical realism) has fallen on deaf ears. However, there are also more subtle issues at stake that turn on just how Sellars's acceptance that 'the senses do not judge' leads him to conclude that the senses display at most 'pseudo-intentionality', and that in turn affects how Sellars understands nonconceptual content as a transcendental concept. In the next chapter, I will show how Sellars's account of discursive intentionality, as taken up by Brandom and McDowell, has ironically resulted in a rejection of the concept of 'nonconceptual content'.[72] A close examination of the reasons for the rejection of nonconceptual content by Brandom and McDowell will provide the contrast with the very different treatment of 'nonconceptual content' as a distinct kind of intentionality by Merleau-Ponty (Chapter 5).

4 THE RETREAT FROM NONCONCEPTUALISM: DISCOURSE AND EXPERIENCE IN BRANDOM AND MCDOWELL

Subsequent to the publication of Rorty's *Philosophy and the Mirror of Nature* in 1979, innovative philosophical appropriations of Sellars went into relative eclipse.[1] This eclipse ended in 1994, when Robert Brandom and John McDowell published their respective *magnum opera*, *Making It Explicit: Reasoning, Representing, and Discursive Commitment* and *Mind and World*.[2] Subsequently both Brandom and McDowell have done much to revive a serious interest in Sellars's contributions to epistemology and philosophy of mind (though Sellars's contribution to metaphysics and metaethics have yet to undergo a comparable renaissance). The recognizably Sellarsian strand in their works consists of their commitment to avoiding the Myth of the Given in both the epistemic and semantic versions, to affirming the irreducibility of the normative ('the space of reasons') to the natural within a 'relaxed' or 'liberal' naturalism, and to following Sellars's own lead in moving beyond a Kantian analytic philosophy to a Hegelian one. Yet neither Brandom nor McDowell are Sellarsians in the sense of being mere epigones, nor should their substantial areas of agreement distract us from sober appraisal of their considerable disagreement.

Instead of proposing a comprehensive discussion of each of these fascinating philosophers – let alone a comprehensive comparison – I will keep the subsequent analysis focused on the following questions: (1) does the very idea of experience, as distinct from judgment, require nonconceptual content (in the stipulative sense outlined in Chapter 1)? and (2) does the rejection of the Myth entail the rejection of nonconceptual content? I take Brandom as answering 'yes' and 'yes' respectively, whereas McDowell answers 'no' and 'yes'. These respective answers in turn illuminate their conflicting positions on the concept/intuition distinction. Thus, Brandom takes the critique of the Myth of the Given to entail the rejection of nonconceptual content and *therefore* of the very idea of experience itself, whereas McDowell accepts that the critique entails the rejection of nonconceptual content but nevertheless wants to *salvage* the idea of experience. In what follows I will show why Brandom and McDowell are committed to answering these questions in this way, in contrast to the more 'orthodox' Sellarsian answers I propose here - namely, 'yes' and 'no' - though as I will show in Chapter 5, we will need something like Merleau-Ponty's phenomenology of embodiment to give us better motivation for these Sellarsian answers than Sellars himself provides.

I begin by focusing on Brandom's conception of discursive intentionality as original intentionality, why he treats the intentionality of animals and infants as derived intentionality, and the role of reliable differential responsive dispositions (RDRDs) in perception and action. Here I will argue that the 'two-ply' account of observation that Brandom explicitly endorses (and problematically attributes to Sellars) fails to accommodate properly the difference between the properties of sentient animals and the nature of causal powers generally construed. Brandom's tacit acceptance of a disenchanted conception of nature then motivates the turn to McDowell, who has emerged as a forceful defender of conceptualism about mental content (subject to minor revision in light of his recent work) and who explicitly criticizes Sellars's commitment to 'sheer receptivity'. Though McDowell is implicitly committed to having an account of sentience, his reluctance to elaborate a theory of sentience to complement his account of sapience renders his account of mindedness promising but unsatisfactory. Finally, I will reconstruct and assess the McDowell-Dreyfus debate in order to show just why an adequate account of our mindedness requires taking seriously the phenomenology of embodiment, but without turning phenomenology itself into a new version of the Myth.

Brandom's Rationalistic Pragmatism

Though Brandom is a self-identified pragmatist, he is also, and importantly, a rationalist. Although rationalism and pragmatism are typically regarded as opposing views, it is central to Brandom's project that the best insights of each must be reconciled with the other. This vision is animated by his concern with 'sapience', with the fact of human reasoning. Though he takes as his point of departure that human beings are rational animals, he admits that 'in general I am much more concerned with understanding what it is for us to be *rational* animals than with what it is for us to be rational *animals*' – a matter of emphasis that directly bears on the assessment here of both the Brandom-McDowell and McDowell-Dreyfus debates.[3] Far from accepting that rationalism and pragmatism are incompatible, Brandom appeals to certain insights of the pragmatist tradition (generously construed, à la Rorty, to include the early Heidegger and the late Wittgenstein) in order to *de-intellectualize rationalism*. By this I mean that Brandom both *affirms* with the rationalists the central role played by reasoning in human life and its irreducibility to other forms of intelligibility, but also *denies* that reasoning is best thought of as ultimately grounded in anything like intellectual intuition of essences, as (for example) the awareness of explicit rules would seem to be. By distinguishing between rationalism as a picture of the role of reason in human life and intellectualism as a particular picture of what reason is, and thereby opposing pragmatism to the latter but not the former, Brandom's view can be legitimately called a kind of rationalistic pragmatism.[4]

In order to successfully reconcile rationalism and pragmatism, Brandom accounts for reasoning in terms of social practices rather than in terms of intellectual intuition, albeit social practices of a distinctive kind – namely, linguistic or, to use the Brandomian term, 'discursive' ones. Central to Brandom's account therefore of both normative pragmatics and inferential semantics is a powerful and complicated account of *discursive intentionality*. As discursive intentionality is one of the two kinds of original intentionality I recommend, some attention must be paid to why Brandom argues for discursive intentionality as original intentionality and why he thinks that other salient cases of intentionality – most notably, the non-discursive intentionality attributed to animals and infants – must count as derivative:

> The intentionality, the conceptual content, of noises and marks is borrowed from and dependent on that of the thoughts and beliefs that interpret them, the takings, or practical attitudes that attribute such content. On pain of an infinite regress, it seems necessary to distinguish the *derivative intentionality* such merely interpretable items display from the *original intentionality* their interpreters display ... The theory developed in this work can be thought of as an account of the stance of attributing original intentionality ... Insofar as their intentionality is derivative – because the normative significance of their states is instituted by the attitudes adopted toward them – their intentionality derives from each other, and not from outside the community. On this line, only communities, not individuals, can be interpreted as having original intentionality.[5]

What Brandom gets exactly right, on my view, is that there is a particular kind of original intentionality that necessarily presupposes the linguistic community as a whole. The (social) externalism and (moderate) holism of Brandom's point must be emphasized: there is no discursive intentionality of any kind (not even conceivably) without a linguistic community of some kind. This commitment goes hand in hand with Brandom's emphasis on thinking about intentionality in basically 'lingualistic' rather than 'mentalistic' terms, i.e. that avoiding the Myth of the semantic Given requires holding that the intentionality of language is logically prior to the intentionality of thought. In the 'mentalistic' tradition, it does not make sense to focus on the community as a whole as the locus of intentionality.[6] The logical priority of 'language' over 'mind' is the *right* move, with respect to the kind of contentful states and statuses that Brandom is interested in.

The idea that all and only discursive intentionality is original intentionality plays a central role in Brandom's distinction between *sentience* and *sapience*:

> Sentience is what we share with non-verbal animals such as cats – the capacity to be *aware* in the sense of being *awake*. ... Sapience concerns understanding or intelligence, rather than irritability or arousal. One is treating something as sapient insofar as one explains its behavior by attributing to it intentional states such as belief and desire as constituting reasons for that behavior.[7]

As Brandom makes clear, we sapient animals can treat other animals *as if* they were sapient, which is to say that we interpret their behaviour *as if* they were acting on the bases of beliefs and desires, and this is because, on Brandom's account, any attribution of intentional content must be *ipso facto* attribution of discursive intentional content. The concept of content attributed to the propositionally contentful states of non-sapient animals is derived, rather than original, simply because non-sapient animals are not members of the linguistic community – we can make sense of them, but they can never be among those who can say 'we' to one another. The term 'derived intentionality' in the Brandomian context should be distinguished from the Searlean sense (i.e. the sense that Dennett denies): a traffic light or a computer has derived intentionality because the content of its states is derived from the content of discursive acts, whereas a cat or baby has derived intentionality (in the Brandomian sense) because the *concept* of intentional content attributed to them is derived from the concept of intentional content that is originally at home amongst the community of deontic scorekeepers.

However, this emphasis on language imposes an unnecessary restriction on the kind of account that Brandom is prepared to give:

> The rest of this work presents not only an account of linguistic intentionality (thought of as one sophisticated species in a genus comprising other, more primitive sorts) but a linguistic account of intentionality generally. It is claimed that the propositional contentfulness even of the beliefs and other states intentional interpreters attribute to nonlinguistic animals cannot properly be understood without reference to the specifically linguistic practice of the interpreters, from which it is derived. Original, independent, or nonderivative intentionality is an exclusively linguistic affair.[8]

The unnecessary restriction consists in the transition from 'an account of linguistic intentionality' to 'a linguistic account of intentionality'. On the one hand, he is almost certainly right that only a fully-fledged member of the discursive community can attribute *propositional content* to nonlinguistic animals; only an animal that is able to interpret other animals as playing the game of giving and asking for reasons can attribute to a cat the belief that the toy is under the couch – especially if the content of the attributed state is to function as a premise for reasoning ('the cat believes that the toy is under the couch, so she will meow loudly until I retrieve it for her'). As a member of a discursive community (and a keen observer of domestic feline antics), I am in the right interpretative position to attribute to my cats beliefs that they can neither attribute to each other nor acknowledge themselves as having. This is particularly true if our conception of belief is constrained along Brandomian lines as having the sort of content the tokening of which is normatively constrained by what Brandom calls 'deontic scorekeeping'.[9]

On the other hand, however, it must be emphasized: nothing in Brandom's account of why non-sapient animals have derived intentionality rules out the thought that there is another kind of intentional content, a distinctive kind of *non-propositional* intentional content, which is original with regard to nonlinguistic animals. All that Brandom must be committed to is the thought that *discursive* intentionality is derived with regard to non-sapient animals.[10] In other words, it is entirely optional for him to deny that sentience is marked by its own kind of intentionality. However, since Brandom (following Sellars *contra* Lewis) does not recognize a distinction between intentionality *tout court* and discursive intentionality *per se* – perhaps due to a lingering worry that admitting such a distinction would invite a 'mentalistic' or Cartesian conception of the former – serious difficulties attend his precise articulation of the difference between sentience and sapience. Specifically, as one probes further into the details of his account of perception and action, his conception of sentience threatens to disappear altogether. (By contrast, one important result of distinguishing between discursive and somatic intentionality is that doing so allows us to make sense of the sapient/sentient distinction).

In what follows, I will follow Brandom's own strategy of referring to the account of perception (and, analogously, of action) as a 'two-ply account': the two plies being, most briefly put, reasons and causes.[11] On the side of reasons, Brandom's account depends on his sophisticated and highly technical machinery to show that the game of giving and asking for reasons can only be played by those who can attribute propositionally contentful states to others, who can acknowledge themselves as having such states, and who are able to engage in the 'deontic scorekeeping' that tracks commitments and entitlements to those states. On the side of causes, Brandom's account depends on the concept of a *reliable differential responsive disposition*, or RDRD, in order to explain what makes something count as a perceiver and agent:

> To be a perceiver rather than just an irritable organism is to be disposed to respond reliably and differentially to the perceptible environment by the application of appropriate concepts. To be an agent rather than just a behaver is to be disposed to respond reliably and differentially to applications of appropriate concepts by altering the accessible environment.[12]

That is, what makes something count as a perceiver and agent *rather than* 'just' an irritable behaving organism is that the application of concepts plays an essential role, both in perception (where concepts are applied *in response to* motivationally salient changes in the ambient environment) and action (where concepts are applied *in order to cause* motivationally salient changes in the ambient environment). (It is part of Brandom's pragmatist inheritance, mediated through Sellars as well as Peirce, Dewey, and Rorty that he recognizes that perception and action cannot be understood independently of one another).

Notice, then, that Brandom's question is, 'what else must an irritable and behaving organism be able to do if it is to count as a perceiver and agent?' and *not*, 'what else must something be able to do if it is to count as an irritable and behaving organisms in the first place?' He does *not* ask what distinguishes a sensitive and behaving organism from other kinds of beings. Brandom even goes so far as to admit that an utterly insentient being – a chunk of iron being one of his preferred examples – nevertheless has RDRDs of its own – an RDRD to rust in the presence of oxygen, for example. (I shall return to the importance of this below). What, then, must be added to a set of RDRDs in order for the being in question to count as having empirical content or empirical knowledge?

On Brandom's account, there is an elegant (though not perfect) symmetry between perception and action, a point on which he is indebted to Sellars's account of perception and action as language-entry and language-exit transitions, respectively.[13] What perception and action have in common is that both are explained in terms of the relation between a set of RDRDs and a set of normative commitments and entitlements, thus guaranteeing that we can only understand action in light of perception and perception in light of action:

> the noninferential relations between acknowledgments of practical commitments and states of affairs brought about by intentional *action* can be understood by analogy to the noninferential relations between acknowledgments of doxastic commitments and the states of affairs that bring them about through conceptually contentful *perception*. The causal dimension of acting for reasons – acknowledging practical commitments by acting on them – involves the exercise of reliable differential responsive skills on the *output* side of the game of giving and asking for reasons, just as perception does on the *input* side.[14]

Perception and action count as conceptually contentful for the same reason: because of how the relevant kinds of commitments (doxastic and practical, respectively) are constituted, as those distinctive *kinds* of commitments, by virtue of how generically commitment-instituting discursive practices are brought to bear on the RDRDs of sensory stimulation and purposive behaviour. Hence, perceptions can function as premises in doxastic reasoning, and actions as conclusions of practical reasoning, because of how doxastic and practical attitudes, as commitment-instituting deontic attitudes, are brought to bear on the correlated RDRDs. For example, I am entitled to assert 'it's snowing outside' if I am in the right perceptual circumstances (have a clear view, am not blind, facing the window or outside, etc.), can reliably distinguish between snowing and non-snowing conditions, and have mastered the relevant concepts as the *appropriate* things to say under the conditions.

Notice that I could be a reliable detector of snow, and be able to distinguish perceptually snow from rain, and yet I might have failed to master the right vocabulary, so that I say, 'it's raining' when it is snowing and 'it's snowing' when it is raining. What has gone wrong is not my reliable differential responsive dispositions to the different forms of precipitation, but my training in the discursive practices that commit and entitle me to make assertions about my perceptual discriminations. (Quite possibly Brandom should be committed to a stronger claim that I could not even be counted as a reliable detector of snow unless I were interpreted by co-inhabitants of the space of reasons as being committed and entitled in the right ways). I would, effectively, be a reliable snow-detector in just the same way that a suitably trained parrot can be a reliable red patch-detector.

Importantly, Brandom treats perception and observational knowledge as interchangeable notions. Thus he describes observational knowledge in the same general terms that he describes perception itself:

> The basis of observational knowledge, then, is that it should be possible to train individuals reliably to respond differentially to features of their environments by acknowledging doxastic commitments. These commitments are inferentially related to others that not only play inferential roles but also are themselves appropriately elicited noninferentially by features of the environment ... the possession of noninferential circumstances of appropriate application of some concepts imbues them with empirical content – recognizable as empirical content in virtue of its inferential articulation and as empirical in virtue of its dependence on the noninferential acquisition of commitments to those contents (and of entitlements to those commitments).[15]

That is, so long as the entity in question (i) has RDRDs with regard to its environment; (ii) possesses concepts that are inferentially articulated with other concepts; (iii) is able to non-inferentially apply some of those concepts to its RDRDs (i.e. that not of all its concepts are purely theoretical ones), that would be necessary and sufficient to credit the entity as being a *perceiver* or as *having observational knowledge*. We would be justified in attributing to that putative being the sorts of doxastic commitments whose content counts as empirical facts. Notice that nothing about nonsapient mental states or contents figures in this explanation; there is nothing *essentially sensory* about empirical content. Likewise, the RDRDs of sensitive, behaving organisms make no *essential* contribution to empirical content – for any being that has intentional content at all by virtue of having been trained in the game of giving and asking for reasons, that content counts as empirical solely by virtue of *having* RDRDs *as such*. Whether or not the RDRDs are the particular kind that distinguishes sensitive, behaving organisms from other configurations of causal powers makes no contribution to Brandom's account of empirical content.

There is, in fact, a deep connection between, on the one hand, the fact that sensory consciousness plays no essential role in the RDRDs that, when paired with the right propositionally contentful states and statuses, yield doxastic commitments and entitlements (perception) and practical commitments and entitlements (actions) and, on the other hand, the disappearance of the notion of 'sentience' in Brandom's overall account. Now that we have briefly outlined how norm-governed inferential articulation constitutes the kinds of commitments distinctive of perception and action, consider how Brandom describes exactly what distinguishes us sapient animals from the merely sentient animals:

> We are sentient creatures as well as sapient ones, but our sentience is different from that of those who cannot give and ask for reasons. Described in the language of physiology, our sensing may be virtually indistinguishable from that of nondiscursive creatures. But we not only sense, we also perceive. That is, our differential response to sensory stimulation includes noninferential acknowledgement of propositionally contentful doxastic commitments. Through perception, when properly trained and situated, we find ourselves passively occupying particular responses in the space of reasons ... We are practical creatures, as well as linguistic ones, but our purposive activity is different from that of those who cannot give and ask for reasons. Described in the language of physiology, our motor activity may be virtually indistinguishable from that of nondiscursive creatures. But we not only produce performances, we perform actions. The performances we produce include noninferential responses to acknowledgments of propositionally contentful practical commitments. Through action, when properly trained and situated, we can respond to the particular positions we occupy in the space of reasons by actively altering the nondiscursive environment.[16]

Firstly, it is the distinctive role of 'the space of reasons' to authorize the corresponding demarcation between sensing/perceiving and performing/acting; secondly, the side of our nature that we share with the nonsapient animals is described entirely in terms of 'the language of physiology'. Though Brandom has indeed overcome the *dualism* between reasons and causes in favor of the *distinction* in one important sense – since it is no longer the case that the relation between the two has become utterly inexplicable – I shall nevertheless argue that we need further distinctions at work than that between reasons and causes. In Dennett's terms, Brandom effectively denies that non-sapient animals are semantic engines except in an 'as if' sense. Sensory consciousness plays no *essential* role in observational knowledge; it is neither necessary nor sufficient for the minimal conception of observational knowledge that Brandom aims to explicate.

Brandom's rejection of 'sensory consciousness' is also crucial to his debate with McDowell. In a criticism of *Mind and World,* Brandom argues that the notion of 'sensory consciousness' or 'experience' is simply unnecessary to explain how perception constrains thought, because the RDRDs provide the only constraint – *causal* constraint – that we need in addition to the *normative* constraint that deontic scorekeepers bring to bear against each other.[17] In response,

McDowell worries that eliminating sensory consciousness entails that we cannot make sense of how empirical content is *empirical*.[18] Like McDowell, I aim to show that Brandom's account of RDRDs fails to show how empirical knowledge can count as 'empirical' once the concept of experience is eliminated.

Consider again the RDRDs of the chunk of iron. It reliably responds to different environmental conditions by falling, by rusting, by generating a magnetic field when a live wire is wrapped around it, and so on. Suppose now that a collection of iron bars were inexplicably endowed with reason. It would have to be a collection, and not just one of them, in order for the bars to function as deontic scorekeepers for each other. (There is no private sapience). By Brandom's own lights, these bars would satisfy the necessary and sufficient conditions for observational knowledge: they would have RDRDs to their environment, and they would engage in commitment-instituting discursive practices. Hence they would be able to make observation-reports – that is, to *assert facts* – e.g. about oxygen. On Brandom's account, the fact that iron bars (or, if this example is too outlandish, silicon chips) lack sensory consciousness (on the 'input' side) and purposive activity (on 'output' side) makes no difference whatsoever to their capacity for observational or empirical knowledge, since sensory awareness and purposive activity are merely the specifically animal form of inputs and outputs. The presence of sensory consciousness makes no essential contribution to perception; it is at best a mere empirical fact about how the relevant structures are causally implemented. In other words, consciousness is neither necessary nor sufficient for sentience; sentience requires only that there are causal structures with inputs and outputs.

This, then, is the problem with Brandom's 'two-ply' account of observation, where the causal processes that constitute the RDRDs are one ply and the inferential moves subjected to deontic scorekeeping are the other, and nothing else remains in the account. Brandom must allow for the *logical possibility* of rational chunks or iron, or rocks, or any other finite object; nothing in his account allows him to rule them out (at least not with respect to logical possibility). This is so because the concept of a RDRD is nothing over and above the concept of a causal power, since any finite object that has causal powers to affect its surroundings will therefore have reliable differential responsive dispositions to its surroundings. The differences in causal powers between sentient animals and insentient rocks then fall away, insofar as those differences play no role in specifying the minimal account of observational knowledge and practical reasoning. Put otherwise: Brandom starts off attempting to *explain* sentience in terms of RDRDs, but ends up *explaining it away*, because he sees no essential connection between the concepts of sentience and sensory consciousness. Rational iron bars (or rational silicon chips) must be admitted as possibilities once the conceptual tie between sentience and sensory consciousness is severed. Though this is a consequence of Brandom's account, and not an objection to it, making this consequence explicit will help illuminate why one might feel that Brandom has simply thrown out the baby (animality) with the bathwater (the Myth of the Given).

Indeed, Brandom's insistence on the derived status of discursive intentionality with regard to nonsapient animals, together with his recognition of the intentional content at work in perception and action *and* his refusal to countenance any notion of intentional content apart from discursive intentionality, results in his claim that the sentient but non-discursive creatures do not even perceive and act in a non-derivative sense:

> Our mammalian cousins, primate ancestors, and neonatal offspring – who are sentient and purposive but not discursive creatures – are interpretable as perceiving and acting only in a derivative sense ... Our discursive practices make us semantically autonomous in a sense in which their nondiscursive practices do not.[19]

Though they do, of course, sense and perform in a way that is explainable by the cognitive sciences, their sensory responses do not count as perceptions, nor do their purposive motor performances count as actions, except in a derivative sense – derivative insofar as it is *we* bearers of original intentional (discursive) content who interpret them in terms that they do not interpret themselves. This does not (quite) reduce Brandom's conception of animals to the automata of Descartes, but it comes uncomfortably close. In these terms, Brandom's own criticism of Cartesianism shows only that rationality per se must be conceived in socio-linguistic terms, not that animal embodiment plays any essential role in distinctively human epistemic achievements.[20]

If this is the result of the two-ply account of observation, then one might wonder what generates Brandom's need for that account. Here we must notice how Brandom argues that he has no need for anything like Kant's concept/intuition distinction, hence no need for anything like 'nonconceptual content', and thus no need for any intermediary between RDRDs and propositional states. The main problem with nonconceptual content, Brandom rightly notes, is that if we follow the Kant-Lewis-Sellars line on nonconceptual content – whether Kant's intuitions, Lewis's given, or Sellars's sense-impressions – we shall need some way to account for the normative function of nonconceptual contents, such that sheer receptivity has the right kind of structure to 'guide' the formation of intuitions. We shall need to know how it is possible for something nonconceptual to still have the right kind of form such that some applications of concepts are appropriate or correct and other applications are inappropriate or incorrect. And this runs the risk of inviting us to posit normative constraints *on* normative constraints, which might be (among other things) an open door to a regress-of-constraints that could be slammed shut only by invoking the Myth of the semantic Given.

Needless to say, Brandom is deeply suspicious of the thought that one could cash out anything like nonconceptual yet normative constraint on the attribution of conceptual contents. His alternative is to notice that Kant draws the concept/intuition distinction in such a way as to conflate three different distinctions: form/content, general/particular, and spontaneity (of intellect)/receptivity (of senses). Rather than make one distinction accommodate all three, as he maintains that Kant does, Brandom has three different ways of accommodating each of these thoughts, and so there is no need for anything like 'nonconceptual content' of the sort that Kant, Lewis, and Sellars all insisted upon. Brandom handles these three distinctions as follows: firstly, by adopting Sellarsian strong inferentialism, semantic content is explained entirely in terms of its material inferential role, and so there is no room for any further kind of semantic content to be explained in non-inferential or 'nonconceptual' terms; secondly, anaphoric constructions carry out the work of talking about particulars; thirdly, the RDRDs accommodate the causal impact of the world on our physical apparatus.[21]

Interestingly, however, in response to Macbeth's formulation of Sellars's idea of sense-impressions that

> the noncognitive impressions of sense are to guide minds *dynamically*, as it were, by being, retrospectively, the (ineffable) causes of our finding things out to be thus and so within whatever conceptual scheme we actually employ, and prospectively, through the development of ever more adequate theories of what there is, the (effable) causes of linguistic pictures that in the limit correctly depict those causes.[22]

Brandom replies only that this is a 'fascinating suggestion' regarding 'a dark but important portion of Sellars's system: the maddeningly gnomic and incomplete story about how intuitions guide the application of concepts, where causes meet reasons'.[23] While Brandom does not think that we need such an account, he recognizes that Sellars seems to. Brandom's challenge to the Lewis-Sellars defense of the concept/intuition distinction is precisely to show why anything at all like 'intuitions' are necessary and what precise role they play in the actualization of concepts in experience. As I will show in Chapter 5, however, the phenomenological tradition provides us with a rich set of resources for thinking about 'intuitions' in a way that meets Brandom's challenge and calls into question the adequacy of the distinction between concepts and causes.

Contra Brandom, we would have a firm handle on the sentience/sapience distinction only if we had a robust notion of sensory consciousness as playing a pivotal role in perception(and action), and that in turn requires that our sapient *animality*, and not just our sapient *finitude,* is front and center (as it is for McDowell). That Brandom cannot see why sensory consciousness is essential to perceiving of the sort that a rational animal has – instead, treating it as a contingent fact of our physiological composition – together with his inability to countenance any characterization of RDRDs in terms other than the merely physical, is central to how I want to thematize Brandom's suppression of animality. The disappearance of animality as such, as a kind of intentionality distinct from discursive intentionality, then results in an explication of sentience in terms of RDRDs in which one loses one's grip on the very notion of sentience; hence Brandom's difficult in appreciating that Sellars is explicitly distancing himself from the picture in which there is nothing to mediate between natural causes and normative reasons. For Brandom is, like Davidson and Rorty, Richard and, unlike McDowell, utterly uncritical about the legacy of the Enlightenment:

> The meanings and values that had previously been discerned in things are stripped off along with the supernatural and understood as projections of human interests, concerns, and activities onto an essentially indifferent and insignificant matter. The Enlightenment disenchantment of the world and its assignment to us of responsibility for the norms, values, and significance we nonetheless find in the world are two sides of one coin. Meaningless objects and meaning-generating subjects are two aspects of one picture.[24]

One of the chief difficulties with this account, however, is that once the underlying world-picture consists of strictly bifurcated 'meaningless objects' and 'meaning-generating subjects', we lose our grip on our ability to understand the relationship between them. To drastically compress a complex dialectic of post-Enlightenment thought, the disenchanted conception of nature, in its extreme version, mystifies the emergence of mind in nature and makes it impossible to understand what happens when reasons meet causes. Brandom's rationalistic pragmatism, for all the advances it makes in understanding the fine structure of discursivity, is nevertheless too uncritically accepting of the Enlightenment world-picture for it to not count as a regression from the self-criticisms of the Enlightenment that we find in German Idealism and in American Pragmatism.

McDowell's Transcendental Empiricism

Though McDowell and Brandom have much in common – so much that 'Pittsburgh neo-Hegelianism' is increasingly used to classify them together, sometimes including Sellars – these commonalities should not prevent us from recognizing the profound differences between their views.[25] Though McDowell shares Brandom's view that we must reject the concept of nonconceptual content for the purposes of explicating the very idea of empirical content if we are to avoid the myth of the given (in both its epistemic and semantic guises), McDowell also criticizes certain aspects of the Davidsonian picture that animates Brandom's account of semantic content. On this picture, there are two kinds of constraints on cognitive-semantic content: normative constraint and causal constraint. As Davidson intimates and Brandom explicates, the only source of normative constraint on cognitive-semantic content comes from the deontic attitudes instituted by players of the game of giving and asking for reasons; the only kind of constraint that the world imposes on cognitive-semantic content is causal. McDowell's alternative is that there is a third kind of constraint: the normative constraint of sensible objects, of objects-as-experienced.

More precisely, McDowell holds that objects as present to us in experience exercise normative constraint over judgment by virtue of how experience of those objects passively actualizes the same cognitive-semantic contents that are freely exercised in judgment. Whereas Brandom happily says, 'experience is not one of my words',[26] experience is definitely one of McDowell's words – unlike Brandom (but much like Sellars), the idea of sensory consciousness plays a central role in McDowell's account of how cognitive-semantic content is normatively constrained. But whereas Sellars wants to preserve the idea of sensory consciousness by positing nonconceptual episodes or states of consciousness, i.e. nonconceptual content, McDowell resists. Though McDowell retains the idea of sensory consciousness, all the *content* to that kind of consciousness is conceptual, and so a great deal turns on just what exactly McDowell means by 'conceptual'. Whether McDowell is entitled to an intermediate position between Davidson/ Brandom (all normative constraint is socio-linguistic) and Lewis/Sellars (there are nonconceptual states of consciousness) depends, as we shall see, on the philosophical adequacy of his version of the concept/intuition distinction.

To rehearse the well-known narrative: McDowell aims to dissolve what he calls the 'transcendental anxiety' distinctive of modern philosophy as expressed in the thought, 'How is empirical content [of thought] so much as possible?'[27] This anxiety is 'transcendental' because it results from inquiry into the basic conditions of our cognitive (conceptual and perceptual) capacities. To ask how empirical content is possible is to ask how it is that our cognitive capacities, when exercised properly, make contact with the world. But if we cannot understand how this is possible, we are threatened by the skepticism that perhaps empirical content, objective purport itself, is a chimera – that is an unbridgeable gulf between mind and world. We would be unable to assuage this anxiety if there can even seem to be a gulf between thought (what is thinkable) and world (what is the case). If my thought, 'there is salt on the table' is true, then it is the case that there is salt on the table. But for my (and our) thoughts to be true (or false), they must be about the world as present in my (and our) experience of it. For this reason, we must dislodge the transcendental anxiety – the possibility of an unbridgeable gulf between mind and world – by dissolving the temptations which lure us away from affirming the perfectly innocuous claim that our judgements, when they are true, do not stop anywhere short of the fact that things are thus and so. (Crucially, McDowell regards the anxiety that prevents us from affirming direct perceptual realism as both transcendental in content and historical in context – in particular, occasioned by the advent of the modern natural-scientific conception of nature.)

As long as the modern transcendental anxiety remains in place, we will be caught in an oscillation between the Myth of the Given and coherentism. Since we require reassurance that we are in cognitive contact with the world, and that our judgements are answerable to how things are, we look for something in experience not of our own making. In its most general form, McDowell construes the Myth of the Given as the idea that the space of reasons is wider than the space of concepts.[28] As stressed in Chapters 2 and 3, the Given is any experienceable content that plays a cognitive-semantic role without having any conceptual structure. McDowell's concern with cognitive semantics follows Kant and Hegel – with the intelligibility of thought as such, and in particular, with the intelligibility of empirical content. As a cognitive-semantic fallacy, the Myth of the Given posits nonconceptual content by locating those contents as playing their cognitive-semantic roles and by characterizing the relevant cognitive-semantic roles played, independently of how those contents function within, or with respect to, judgements – which, in turn, have their cognitive-semantic statuses at least partly constituted by their role in reasoning.

The recoil from the Myth occurs because, on the assumption that all thinking is discursively articulated, our access to nonconceptual contents in their cognitive-semantic roles seems mysterious. Unable to guarantee that we have found the lever of Archimedes, we are driven back to coherentism, according to which our judgements do not stand in a cognitive-semantic relation to the world as experienced, but at best a causal one. So coherentism undermines that 'minimal empiricism' necessary for our judgements to even seem to have empirical content'; the 'frictionless spinning in the void' threatens.[29]

On the one hand, then, judgements must stand in an epistemic and semantic – McDowell would say 'rational' – relation to our experience of the world, and not merely a causal one. On the other hand, judgements could have a rational relation with world-involving experience only if there were a transcendentally identifiable point of contact with the world – some cognitive-semantic content apart from the game of giving and asking for reasons. Since that criterion seems impossible to satisfy, we are thrown back onto coherentism, and from thence back into the Given, and so on without respite. Having a grip on the notion of 'judgment' at all requires that we satisfy both conditions at once; the oscillation between the Myth of the Given and coherentism arises because we cannot see how to do so.

With the right distinctions in place, however, McDowell thinks that we can satisfy both conditions: judgements are externally, rationally constrained by the passive actualization of conceptual capacities in sensory consciousness.[30] Perceptual experience is passive as opposed to active, in McDowell's vocabulary, because he follows Kant in thinking of 'activity' in terms of *freedom*. I can freely endorse or withhold assent from judgements, but I cannot freely endorse or withhold assent from perceptual episodes – if what I see is a salt-shaker on the table, then I cannot *not* see that there is a salt-shaker on the table. My concepts of 'salt-shaker' and 'table' are passively actualized in the shaping of sensory consciousness as it relates to the objects experienced.

We should not confuse what is external to judgment with what is external to experience, nor should we posit nonconceptual content ('intuitions', in one of Sellars's senses) merely to vindicate the possibility of empirical content. Rather, perceptual experience necessarily involves the passive actualization of conceptual capacities – as distinct from the active exercise of those same capacities in judgment – and so perceptual experience can be both the external and rational constraint on judgment needed to avoid the oscillation. Since the constraint lies in the passive actualization of conceptual capacities, rather than in their active exercise, it is external to thought (in the sense of 'thought' that matters for McDowell's transcendental project); since the constraint involves our conceptual capacities, it counts as genuinely rational rather than merely causal.

To avoid the oscillation we need only accept that 'receptivity does not make an even notionally separable contribution to the co-operation [of receptivity and spontaneity]'.[31] (Though McDowell has qualified this statement significantly, as we shall see below.) If the contribution of receptivity were even notionally separable to the cooperation of receptivity and spontaneity, then we could specify the cognitive-semantic roles of the contents of receptivity independent of how they function in judgements. So the Myth of the Given assumes that cognitive-semantic roles can be specified independent of their role in judgements, even though cognitive semantics just *is* the articulation of judgements and sub-judgmental contents, *as* sub-judgmental. We have no grip on any cognitive-semantic roles if we abstract entirely from all judgmental function, as the Myth requires.

On McDowell's account, we reject the idea that the space of reasons could be wider than the space of concepts by accepting that the space of concepts/reasons is wider than the space of judgements (in which conceptual capacities are actively exercised); conceptual capacities are always and already at work in the perceptual episodes that permeate the sensory consciousness of a rational animal. McDowell explicitly identifies his affinity with idealism by insisting upon 'the Hegelian image in which the conceptual is unbounded on the outside' there is nothing in our experience that utterly transcends all possible conceptual classification (even if it only by demonstrative phrases).[32]

Importantly, McDowell does not dispense with Kantian intuitions altogether – a feature of his thought that has become much clearer in light of his 'Avoiding the Myth of the Given'.[33] There McDowell both clarifies how conceptual capacities permeate experience and rejects his previous assumption that 'to conceive experiences as actualizations of conceptual capacities, we would need to credit experiences with *propositional* content, the sort of content that judgements have'.[34] Instead, McDowell now distinguishes between discursive conceptual content (what judgements have) and intuitional conceptual content (what experiences have). Non-discursive, intuitional content counts as conceptual because 'every aspect of the content of an intuition is present in a form in which is already suitable to be the content associated with a discursive capacity, if it is not – at least not yet – actually so associated'.[35] In other words, intuitional content is actually conceptual because it is potentially propositional. Along these lines, McDowell also clarifies why sensibility and understanding are both individually necessary and jointly sufficient for both intuitional content and discursive content; it is not that each capacity contributes its own distinct content, but that both kinds of content require both capacities. This clarification also places McDowell significantly closer to Hegel than to Kant.[36]

If the Myth of the Given (à la McDowell) holds that the space of reasons extends further than the space of concepts, and since the unboundedness of the conceptual is needed to avoid the Myth, then either sensed particulars have no intrinsic cognitive authority, or we must expand the domain of conceptual to include sensed particulars. McDowell chooses the latter:

> If an object is present to one through the presence to one of some of its properties, in an intuition in which concepts exemplify a unity that constitutes the content of a formal concept of an object, one is thereby entitled to judge that one is confronted by an object with those properties. The entitlement derives from the presence to one of the object itself, not from a premise for an inference, at one's disposal by being the content of one's experience.[37]

The experienced presence of an object entitles us to judge that the object is as presented because the objectual presentation is itself conceptual, even though non-propositional, and thus accounts for how sensed particulars can have rational authority over judgements (e.g. in giving us reasons for revising those judgements). The mutual adjustment of judgements in light of experiences, and vice-versa, constitutes what McDowell calls 'equipoise'. Yet equipoise is coherent only if the conceptual is at work in both dimensions; that is why the equipoise avoids the oscillation and dissolves the transcendental anxiety.[38]

The result is a *mitigated* concept/intuition distinction, in which the distinction between intuitions and concepts is not a difference between kinds of cognitive semantic content but a difference in the mode of actualization of conceptual capacity.[39] Though this is certainly consistent with *one* of the senses that Sellars assigns to the concept of 'intuition' in *S&M* – intuitions as 'this-such's – McDowell has no room for the *other* sense that Sellars assigns to the concept of intuition – intuitions as sheer receptivity. [40] There is only one kind of cognitive semantic content – conceptual content – but such contents can be *sensibly* present as well as 'intellectually' present (e.g. in thought and judgment). Hence McDowell, unlike Brandom, regards the concept/intuition distinction as philosophically indispensable – but whereas Brandom finds it dispensable because he sees no need for intuitions as a distinct kind of content, McDowell finds the distinction indispensable precisely because he does *not* see intuitions as a distinct kind of content. Importantly, therefore, neither of them accepts Sellars's commitment to finding the intuition/concept indispensable *and* to regarding intuitions as having a kind of content of their own – although this is not, for Sellars, cognitive-semantic content. It is a kind of representational content that plays no normative-functional role, but only a causal-functional one. (Why McDowell finds this notion philosophically dispensable will become clear after we understand better how McDowell understands the division of intellectual labor between philosophy and science.)

The mitigated concept/intuition distinction that McDowell emphasizes is deeply bound up with his commitment to thinking of normal mature human beings as rational animals. Though he shares this commitment with Brandom, McDowell's rehabilitation of intuitions as actualizations of intuitional conceptual capacities, i.e. the passive actualization of conceptual capacities in sensory consciousness, allows him to place more satisfactory emphasis on our animality. As argued above, Brandom's stress on our rationality, rather than on our animality, is connected to his unsatisfactory reduction of sentience to RDRDs. By contrast, we can think of McDowell as striving for equal emphasis on both rationality and animality. He attempts to arrive at this equality of emphasis by locating a self-conception which would allow us to unproblematically accept that

> rational capacities, and hence availability to apperception, permeate our experience itself, including the experience we act on unreflectively in our ordinary coping with our surroundings. Such is the form that animal engagement with the perceptible environment takes in the case of rational animals.[41]

We would now accept that 'the thinking thing is the rational animal', and that 'a *res cogitans* is also a *res dormiens*, a *res ambulans*, and so forth'.[42] The identification of the thinking thing with the rational animal undermines the sheer formality of the Kantian conception of the subject, as the sort of thing that consists entirely in having a disengaged or detached attitude towards its own conditions of sensibility. The moment of truth in the Kantian conception of rational subjectivity lies in what McDowell citing Gadamer, calls 'the free, distanced orientation' towards the world, not in having a deep metaphysical split between sensibility and understanding.[43] But our capacity to have that Gadamerian freedom and distance is itself a fundamentally animal capacity, albeit a capacity of the distinct kind of animal that a rational animal is.

We need to reconcile reason and nature by acknowledging that our rational capacities are themselves natural – but not natural in the natural-scientific way of finding nature intelligible, which consists of constructing testable explanations.

In *Mind and World*, McDowell identifies this kind of intelligibility as 'the realm of law', in which explanations consist of uncovering the laws or law-like regularities that describe some range of physical phenomena. Since then McDowell concedes that biology is not nomological as physics or chemistry are, though the implications of this admission for his general project remain unclear. To acknowledge that rationality is natural, we need to acknowledge the *sui generis* character of our conceptual capacities, vis-à-vis nature qua the realm of law (denying 'bald naturalism'), while on the other hand holding the door shut against any 'transcendence of biology' (denying 'rampant platonism).[44] Whereas bald naturalism dismisses the transcendental anxiety, acknowledging the *sui generis* character of our responsiveness to reasons as such risks conceiving of ourselves as 'metaphysically split, with disastrous consequences for perception and action'.[45]

What is metaphysically special, in one sense – the uniquely human kinds of freedom and obligation – is also metaphysically innocuous, in another sense. This delicate balance turns on Aristotle's notion of 'second nature', reinterpreted through the notion of *Bildung*. Second nature, or *Bildung*, consists of those capacities or abilities acquired through training (not necessarily learning), rather than intrinsic to the kind of thing an entity is. (For example, it is part of the second nature of a domesticated dog to obey certain commands). Likewise, human beings acquire their rational capacities through that particular kind of training called 'enculturation'.[46] By identifying culture with Hegel's 'spirit' (*Geist*), McDowell naturalizes spirit: the dualism between spirit and nature becomes the distinction between naturalized spirit – the acquired conceptual capacities of the rational animal – and utterly disenchanted, spiritless nature.

Importantly, McDowell does not contest the disenchanted conception of nature with respect to the natural sciences – only that this conception of nature is the whole truth about nature, because our rational capacities, *sui generis* though they be vis-à-vis the natural sciences, are nevertheless actualizations of our distinctive (perhaps unique) kind of animality. With the correct picture of our conceptual capacities in a liberated, non-scientistic conception of nature, we can accept that we are fundamentally animals, namely rational animals. McDowell even goes so far as to insist on 'the *traditional* separation of mature human beings, as rational animals, from the rest of the animal kingdom';[47] the rest of the animal kingdom lacks our distinctive 'responsiveness to reasons *as such*'.[48] McDowell thus invokes the Aristotelian idea that normal mature human beings are rational animals in order to reconcile nature, now construed as including but also broader than the modern conception of nature that identifies nature with the realm of natural law, with a Kantian conception of reason as the standing obligation to reflect upon the relation between experience and world-view, and to act under the idea of freedom.

With a broader conception of nature than as a system of laws, we can revive, within an explicitly modern conception both of nature and of reason, the Aristotelian conception of a rational animal. By doing so,

> [w]e can conceive exercises of capacities that belong to spontaneity as elements in the course of a life. An experiencing and acting subject is a living thing, with active and passive bodily powers that are genuinely her own; she is herself embodied, substantially present in the world that she experiences and acts on.[49]

In other words, the concept of a rational animal is that a mature, normal human being is a *part* of the world that also experiences the world *as a world*. In that way, McDowell contends, we can accept Kant's insights into the importance of spontaneity in our self-understanding without any residues of the Cartesian Real Distinction between *res extensa* and *res cogitans*. The adequacy of how, on McDowell's account, experience constrains judgment depends on accepting what he now calls 'intuitional conceptual content', which has Sellars's own disambiguation between Kantian intuitions as 'this-such' representations as a clear antecedent.

We now need to understand why McDowell sees no need for 'sheer receptivity'. Much of the answer to this question turns on McDowell's conception of the proper role of philosophy and how philosophy is distinct from science. In the preface to *Mind and World*, McDowell acknowledges his debt to Strawson as well as Sellars. Apart from the inspiration he draws from specific contributions they made to substantive issues, they also provided McDowell with a model of how to understand his own philosophical project:

> I have been more strongly influenced than footnotes can indicate by P. F. Strawson, especially by his peerless book on Kant's First Critique. I am not sure that Strawson's Kant is really Kant, but I am convinced that Strawson's Kant comes close to achieving what Kant wanted to achieve. In these lectures ... my use of Kant in saying how we should conceive experience – the main thing I try to do here – is Strawsonian in spirit and often in detail.[50]

Whether or not Strawson's Kant is really Kant, we can understand what McDowell takes himself to be doing by noticing how Strawson describes his own project in *The Bounds of Sense* and in *Individuals*.

At the outset of *The Bounds of Sense*, Strawson proposes that '[t]here are limits to what we can conceive of, or make intelligible to ourselves, as a possible general structure of experience' and that Kant's task consists of '[t]he investigation of these limits, the investigation of the set of ideas which forms the limiting framework of all our thought about the world and experience of the world'.[51] It is not an investigation of what is imaginable or possible *per se*, but an investigation into the most general features of the conceptual frameworks which make possible our experience of the world, understood in the broadest sense as any experience of the world which is intelligible as belonging to the experience of beings recognizable as being like us in relevant respects (e.g. being both sensually receptive to the world and possessing conceptual frameworks about the world).

This task is subsequently identified as the 'metaphysics of experience' in *The Bounds of Sense* and in *Individuals* as a 'descriptive metaphysics'.[52] Rather than propose new systems of classifying or interpreting experience, one simply identifies the most general features of possible experience for beings like us. The descriptive metaphysics of experience thus poses the 'How possible?' question with regard to the most general and pervasive aspects of whatever is intelligible to us as a possible experience. For Strawson's Kant, the metaphysics of experience consists of describing how it is possible for us to enjoy experience of unified objects arrayed in spatiotemporal order and interacting with both themselves and with us according to well-defined principles that are both objectively valid and knowable *a priori*.

However, McDowell differs from Strawson by emphasizing the critical function of descriptive metaphysics. Descriptive metaphysics can be critical by liberating us from partial, one-sided, or limited self-conceptions. Such conceptions hold us captive by making certain questions seem compulsory for philosophical reflection. McDowell thus aims at liberating us from the oscillations between coherentism and the Myth of the Given by giving us a dialectically stable descriptive metaphysics. If *Mind and World* is explanatory, it is not explanatory in the way that the sciences provide explanations; it is explanatory only insofar as it aims

> at explaining how it comes about that we *seem* to be confronted with philosophical obligations of a familiar sort, and I want the explanation to enable us to unmask that appearance as an illusion ... [and] reject the appearance that we face a pressing intellectual task.[53]

Thus, rather than present novel theories of knowledge and meaning – perhaps theories which could be empirically tested – *Mind and World* aims to provide a more adequate descriptive metaphysics which will illuminate how it is possible for us to hold a world-view, or stand under the obligation to reflect upon it. Once we have a correct descriptive metaphysics of experience, we will have the tools we need for diagnosing the illusion and seeing through it. In Wittgenstein's familiar phrase, the picture will no longer hold us captive.

Whereas in *Mind and World* McDowell describes his project as an attempt to vindicate 'minimal empiricism', in more recent work McDowell argues that his defense of minimal empiricism requires 'transcendental empiricism', which first emerges in the 1998 Woodbridge lectures as a further development of Sellars's criticism of classical empiricism.[54] In Sellars's view, classical empiricism mistakenly holds that our higher-order theories of the world rest on an independent and presuppositionless foundation of perceptual experience.[55] Crucially, both Sellars and McDowell hold that there is a legitimate sense in which empirical knowledge *does* rest on perceptual experience, by virtue of being our *evidence* for claims about the world. Sellars's point, accepted by McDowell, is that concepts must already be at work in perceptual episodes in order for those episodes to have any epistemic or semantic function at all. Instead Sellars argues that if we are to successfully reject the Myth of the Given (in its empiricist version), we should recognize that semantic holism entails that observation reports are semantically dependent on the conceptual framework as a whole. As with classical empiricism, Sellars maintains that theories are justified in terms of perceptual experiences, and that that dependence is straightforwardly epistemological. But there is another 'logical dimension', which McDowell understands as a transcendental dependence, according to which perceptual experience is made possible by conceptual capacities:

> [w]e can intelligibly credit perceptual experience with objective purport only in virtue of how the conceptual apparatus that constitutes their objective purport fits into the world-view that is, in the other logical dimension, grounded on the deliverances of experience ... The new twist [on the Sellarsian picture] is that, with the conception of Kantian intuitionsthat I am urging, we can put into the picture a downward dependence that is not narrowly epistemological but, like the upward dependence that is already in Sellars's picture, transcendental, a matter of requirements for it to be intelligible that the picture depicts directedness at objective reality at all.[56]

Transcendental empiricism insists on interdependence between perceptual experience and world-view. Without a world-view, perceptual experience as having objective purport would not even be possible; without perceptual experience, world-views as ways in which a view is taken on the world would not even be possible. The conditions of possibility of each lie in the other. On McDowell's reading, both he and Sellars retain the emphasis on *sensory consciousness* shared with traditional empiricism, an emphasis that Brandom rejects.[57] But McDowell criticizes Sellars for insisting that the only way to retain that emphasis, in light of the criticism of the Myth of the Given, is by recasting the contents of sensory consciousness in causal-functional terms.

Early in the Woodbridge Lectures, McDowell admits that he had previously understood transcendental philosophy as a 'sideways-on view', as if it required that we peer around the outside edge of our conceptual capacities in order to see the external constraints to which we are subjected. Beginning with the Woodbridge Lectures, and since, McDowell no longer identifies transcendental philosophy with that particular picture of it; instead, transcendental philosophy is identified only with the investigation of the conditions of possibility of objective purport.

The rejection of the sideways-on view of transcendental reflection dissolves the distinction between the descriptive metaphysics of experience and transcendental philosophy *per se*. McDowell can now happily accept that the descriptive metaphysics of experience, though not a sideways-on articulation of transcendental philosophy, is a version of transcendental philosophy nevertheless. I shall therefore use the term 'transcendental description' to characterize McDowell's position, both in *M&W* and subsequently, in order to motivate the contrast with 'empirical explanation'. By 'transcendental description' I mean a description of the necessary conditions of possible experience. This is a *descriptive* project because it neither revises any of our basic concepts, such as 'experience' or 'world', nor does it depend on the results of empirically well-confirmed theories. (To this extent, McDowell would reject Sellars's insistence that description and explanation necessarily go hand-in-hand). Instead, as a *transcendental* project, it aims only at clarifying and elucidating whatever is necessary for beings like us to have the kinds of experiences that we have. The modality of the claim – what is necessary for any possible experience that belongs to a being recognizably like ourselves – distinguishes transcendental description from empirical explanations and the concepts used in such explanations.

That we are rational animals is not, therefore, an empirical fact about us, as our bipedalism and featherlessness clearly are, let alone any number of distinctive phenotypic or genetic markers. When we think about the distinctiveness of human beings in biological or cognitive terms, we are still operating within the vocabulary of empirical explanations. By contrast, transcendental description aims at illuminating the very possibility of our having any sort of vocabulary, any sort of way of making the world of experience intelligible to us, at all. (Whether this means that transcendental descriptions are a version of the Myth of the semantic Given is a very difficult question). Thus, when we ask, 'what sort of beings must we be in order to have any sort of vocabulary at all?' we are not asking the kind of question that has a straightforwardly empirical answer to be provided by natural or social science. Instead, by thinking of ourselves as rational animals as part of a transcendental description, we understand that the sorts of conceptual capacities distinctive of rationality are actualized in sensory consciousness so as to generate perceptual experiences capable of constraining the operations of free and reflective thought, viz. world-views, vocabularies, and theories.

These two kinds of projects – transcendental description and empirical explanation – must be clearly distinguished: 'But on pain of losing our grip on ourselves as thinking things, we must distinguish inquiring into the mechanics of, say, having one's mind on an object from inquiring into what having one's mind on an object is.'[58] The inquiry into the *mechanics* is classified as an empirical explanation distinct from the transcendental description of *what it is* to have one's mind on an object. Our understanding of knowledge and meaning should not be modeled on the sorts of explanations characteristic of modern science. Rather, that kind of understanding belongs to transcendental description, not to empirical explanation. (It is also true, however, that the distinctive status of transcendental description could not be recognized until the cultural dominance of empirical explanations arose in their modern form; McDowell recognizes this but arguably does not emphasize this fact as much as perhaps he should).

I now return to McDowell's criticism of Sellars (in the Woodbridge Lectures) to show the deep connection between these two themes: his rejection of Sellarsian sheer receptivity, and his commitment to the distinction between transcendental description and empirical explanation. McDowell criticizes Sellars on two points: (1) that intentionality must be world-relational if we are to avoid a picture of thought as 'frictionless spinning in the void'; (2) that one of the constraints on conceptual activity that Sellars provides, namely sense-impressions, is not required. I will agree with McDowell that, as a matter of transcendental philosophy, sense-impressions *qua* causal intermediaries are dispensable. But even if McDowell's interpretation of Sellars were right, that would still not show that we should follow McDowell in abandoning the Sellarsian thesis regarding the non-relational character of intentionality understood as conceptual activity.

In what I take to be a representative passage, McDowell writes:

> Sellars thinks the conceptual representations in perception must be guided by manifolds of 'sheer receptivity', because he thinks that only so can we make it intelligible to ourselves that conceptual occurrences in perceptual experience -- and thereby ultimately thought, conceptual activity, in general – are constrained by something external to conceptual activity.[59]

McDowell understands Sellars as positing something exterior to intentionality as such, i.e. sense-impressions, in order to explain how our conceptual activity is constrained by, or responsive to, something outside of it. Without such constraint, our thought becomes the frictionless spinning in the void that haunts conceptualism, coherentism, and (on some versions) idealism.

'Frictionless spinning' is avoidable, McDowell thinks, only if there is some constraint on conceptual activity which can be brought into view from within the transcendental description of cognitive experience. Notice how McDowell draws the relevant contrast between his view and Sellars's:

> For Sellars, our entitlement to see elements in the conceptual order as intentionally directed towards elements in the real order has to be transcendentally secured from outside the semantical, from outside the conceptual. ... [hence] a transcendental role for sensibility can only be the sort of thing Sellars envisages, a matter of conceptual activity being guided by 'sheer receptivity'. On this view, we *cannot* spell out a transcendental role for sensibility in terms of the immediate presence of objects to intuitionally structured consciousness, as in the reading of Kant that I have recommended. That would be already a case of conceptual directedness towards the real, so it could not figure in a vindication, from outside, of the very idea of conceptual directedness towards the real.[60]

McDowell presents us with two options: either the transcendental role of sensibility is exterior to *all* intentionality, as it is for Sellars, or 'the immediate presence of objects to intuitionally structured consciousness' ensures that the world itself exerts a rational constraint on our thought about it. In other words, perception is an intentional relation with the world.

To see what is at stake in McDowell's criticism of Sellars, I turn now to deVries's criticism of McDowell's position.[61] DeVries worries that McDowell turns to direct realism about perceptual experience because he sees it as the only alternative to construing perception as an epistemic intermediary between thought and reality. If, however, we follow Sellars's insistence that perception involves only *causal* intermediaries between thought and reality, and no epistemic intermediaries, we can retain Sellars's insistence on the non-relationality of intentionality *per se* and explain the intentionality of perception in terms of the intentionality of thought (the concept of which in turn is modeled off the analogy with the concept of the intentionality of language). On the Sellarsian picture, 'perceptions are thinkings, and they possess their logical and cognitive powers because they exhibit the full-blown intentionality of thought', but 'perceptions *also* possess a different *kind* of directedness (or presence), and it is precisely this that the sensible presence inference tries to capture'.[62] The difficulty posed by McDowell's criticism of Sellars is now clear: to distinguish Sellars's view from McDowell's, deVries must invoke *non-intentional directedness*, which is perilously close to a *contradictio in adjecto*. (Arguably this ambiguity is removed if we focus on 'presence' rather than 'directedness'). Sellars and McDowell agree that only the discursive is genuinely intentional; they differ on the nonconceptual component to perception, our epistemic access to the component, and whether that component provides any guidance or constraint on how conceptual capacities are actualized in sensory consciousness.

Why, however, should we prefer the Sellarsian account over McDowell's? As deVries sees it, McDowell denies our ability to tell a sub-personal story about how our knowledge is generated. More accurately, McDowell denies that cognitive science is relevant to epistemology, or to what I have been calling here cognitive semantics. Cognitive semantics is a transcendental project completely separate from what neuroscience can tell us about how cognitive semantical roles are causally realized. Here McDowell's insistence on a broader conception of nature than that of natural science plays a crucial role. Sellars (and deVries) hold that transcendental structures must be realized in causal structures, where those causal structures are described by successful empirical explanation. By contrast, McDowell holds the weaker claim that transcendental structures must be realized in natural structures per se, without restricting the class of those structures to just those causal structures that figure in successful scientific (i.e. law-governed or deductive-nomological explanation). The stronger claim,

McDowell worries, rests on a confusion between what we do in the interests of successful empirical inquiry – posit unobservables in causal explanations of observables – and what we need to do in order to arrive at a dialectically stable transcendental description of our rational animality that will dislodge the anxiety of modern intellectual culture. To this, however, the Sellarsian might object that a fully satisfactory account of our rational animality requires a coherent account of how rational animality is causally realized, both phylogenetically and ontogenetically. McDowell's strict separation between explanation and description prevents him from appreciating this point.

The McDowell–Dreyfus Debate

In 2005, Hubert Dreyfus initiated a debate with McDowell over the legacy of Sellars's criticisms of C. I. Lewis for analytic philosophy of mind. That Lewis (and Sellars's criticism of Lewis) frame the context here is clear from how Dreyfus begins his Pacific APA Presidential Address:

> Back in 1950, while a physics major at Harvard, I wandered into C. I. Lewis's epistemology course. There, Lewis was confidently expounding the need for an indubitable Given to ground knowledge, and he was explaining where that ground was to be found. I was so impressed that I immediately switched majors from ungrounded physics to grounded philosophy ... During that time no one at Harvard seemed to have noticed that Wilfrid Sellars had denounced the Myth of the Given; and that he and his colleagues were hard at work, not on a rock solid foundation for knowledge, but on articulating the conceptual structure of our grasp on reality.[63]

From this intriguing opening salvo, Dreyfus proceeds to accuse McDowell (and, implicitly, Sellars as well) of having replaced the Myth of the Given with 'the Myth of the Mental': the systematic neglect of the role that embodied, absorbed coping plays in making possible the distinctive sorts of conceptual or rational capacities that post-Sellarsian philosophers explore. McDowell for his part, responded by accusing Dreyfus of holding the Myth of the Disembodied Intellect:[64] the myth that the intellect is paradigmatically brought into view in episodes of detached contemplation, which *are* antithetical to absorbed coping. Nor does the Battle of Myths show any particular sign of abating; the accusations of myth-mongering continue in each of their contributions to *Mind, Reason, and Being-in-the-World*.[65]

As the various contributions to Schear's anthology make clear, the issues under examination bear on whether or not there is 'nonconceptual content', the grounds upon which the invocation of nonconceptual content are licensed, the account of concepts in terms of which other kinds of mental content appear as nonconceptual, and how we should describe the similarities and differences between mindedness in normal mature human beings and mindedness in animals and infants. There are also serious interpretive questions at work here as to how to make sense of Aristotle, Kant, Hegel, Husserl, Heidegger, Gadamer, Sellars, and Merleau-Ponty in light of these questions. The contributors also display a plurality of philosophical approaches, including ordinary-language philosophy, philosophy of cognitive science, and phenomenology. There is, however, a further issue at work here that must be explored: whether phenomenology discloses a stratum of experience that is in any sense 'foundational' relative to the assertions examined when we do epistemology, and how exactly we should think about the relation between rationality (sapience) and embodied coping (sentience). (To anticipate, the relation between sapience and sentience requires that we think of sentience as a broader and richer notion than just sensing or having sensations – this point will become central to the discussion of Merleau-Ponty in Chapter 5).

I have already shown (Chapter 2) that Lewis's project of seeking 'an indubitable Given to ground knowledge' must be carefully distinguished from the Cartesian project of seeking indubitable knowledge, since Lewis clearly argues that the immediate apprehensions of sense are indubitable precisely because the very notion of doubt can get no intelligible grip on those apprehensions. But, for that very reason, neither can they count as a distinctive kind of knowledge: Lewis is not an *epistemological* foundationalist. He is, however, a *semantic* foundationalist, in that he does think that there must be immediate and certain content for at least some of our empirical beliefs, otherwise we would not be able to determine the truth-conditions for any of our assertions about the world. Conceptual meanings would be utterly mysterious if it were not the case that each concept is necessarily associated with some range of immediate apprehensions of sense that provide the criteria of applicability for that concept. The real point behind Dreyfus's autobiographical remark is that, despite claiming to share Sellars's criticisms of Lewis – accepting that the Given is a Myth – Dreyfus retains far more of Lewis's general project than he realizes. Though he seems to abandon Lewis's semantic foundationalism, it is more apt to say that Dreyfus transforms Lewis's semantic foundationalism into *phenomenological foundationalism*. (Berendzen uses this term to describe Dreyfus's position in the Dreyfus–McDowell debate, but does not make explicit the connection between Lewis and Dreyfus).[66]

Dreyfus's commitment to phenomenological foundationalism comes through forcefully in his use of the 'ground-floor/upper-story' metaphor he appears to have taken from Todes, who distinguishes between 'the ground floor of perceptually objective experience; and the upper storey of imaginatively objective experience, which presupposes for its objectivity (i.e. for its dependability as living quarters) that the ground floor onto which is built is itself on firm foundations'.[67] In those terms, Dreyfus objects that Sellars and McDowell pay too much attention to the upper stories at the expense of the ground-floor. The problem, of course, is how Dreyfus could possibly be entitled to deploy this metaphor while ostensibly agreeing, with Sellars *contra* Lewis, that 'empirical knowledge, like its sophisticated extension, science, is rational, not because it has a *foundation* but because it is a self-correcting enterprise which can put *any* claim in jeopardy, though not *all* at once'.[68] This is not to say that one *cannot* be both a phenomenological foundationalist and an epistemological anti-foundationalist; it is to say that Dreyfus has not shown us that he is entitled to assert that he is.

One might object that Dreyfus's autobiographical remark is a mere rhetorical flourish that does not bear on the central issues. But I think that, far from being a mere anecdote, Dreyfus's mention of Lewis points to the very heart of the issue. Insofar as both Dreyfus and McDowell would agree that, as McDowell puts it in his preliminary response, '[t]here is more to our embodied coping than there is to embodied coping of non-rational animals',[69] the question is, how is this 'more' to be understood? And more specifically, what is the background picture of intellect/rationality/mindedness which motivates the sense that there is 'more' to our embodied coping than there is to the embodied coping of the (putatively) non-rational animals? On Dreyfus's account, the 'more' that we rational animals enjoy is just built on top of whatever it is we share with animals and infants- which is not, of course, a *bare* Given for Dreyfus, but rather a *richly structured* Given that is available for phenomenological disclosure and description. In contrast, McDowell thinks that this 'more', however articulated, permeates all the way down to our embodied coping skills. On this view, the acquisition of rational conceptual capacities 'trickles down' and thoroughly transforms the sorts of embodied coping skills that we have, such that there is no possibility of factoring out the embodied coping skills of a rational animal and aligning them with the embodied coping skills of a non-rational or pre-rational animal.

Among the various issues at stake here between Dreyfus and McDowell is whether one has a neo-Kantian conception of the intellect or a neo-Hegelian conception. For if one has a neo-Kantian conception, as Dreyfus apparently does, then one will look for something non-intellectual or non-rational to account for the embodied coping skills that give the neo-Kantian view such difficulty, and then it will seem almost irresistible to thematize something like 'non-conceptual intentional content' as Dreyfus does, following in the wake of Heidegger and Sartre. On the other hand, if one has a neo-Hegelian conception, as McDowell does – partly mediated by Sellars and Gadamer and developed in conversation with Brandom, Pippin, and others – then one will turn towards a less intellectualistic, more practice-oriented conception of rationality, the understanding, and mindedness. (In the Schear anthology, several contributors – Braver, Noë, Siewart, and Rouse – propose somewhat different versions of what Noë calls 'de-intellectualizing the understanding', i.e. conceiving of conceptual activity as grounded in perceptual-practical skills rather than as standing in contrast to them. On my reading, McDowell's conception of the understanding is not as 'intellectualistic' as Dreyfus took it to be).

To focus this wide-ranging debate about how we are to think of rationality, the intellect, understanding, conceptuality, and mindedness, we should distinguish between two quite different questions at work here:

(1) is there *nonconceptual intentional* content, or is all intentional content *ipso facto* conceptual as well?

(2) are the most paradigmatic exercises of rationality best thought of as instances of deliberation that *stand back* from its object, or as specific ways of being *engaged with* the objects?

As I see it, McDowell and Dreyfus largely end up talking past one another because of differences in what they take for granted: McDowell reasons *from* the engaged picture of rationality *to* the rejection of nonconceptual intentional content, whereas Dreyfus reasons *from* the acceptance of nonconceptual intentional content *to* the disengaged picture of rationality.

By this I mean that McDowell's philosophical starting-point is an Aristotelian account of normal mature human beings as rational animals that are distinct from non-rational animals because the acquisition of rational capacities permeates our animality, and from this he concludes that 'our embodied coping is more than the embodied coping of non-rational animals';[70] this, conjoined with the worry that 'non-conceptual content' entails the Myth of the Given, yields McDowell's thesis that there is no nonconceptual content specifiable as such by transcendental description, and so even our embodied coping is conceptually structured. Dreyfus, on the other hand, begins with the existential-phenomenological descriptions of absorption – being 'in the flow' as one runs after a bus or plays expert-level chess, to use his favorite examples – in contrast with theoretical reflection. On that basis, and conjoined with a neo-Kantian picture of what theoretical reflection consists of (a crucial part of the background for Heidegger, Sartre, and Merleau-Ponty), Dreyfus concludes that the former does not display the conceptual capacities of the latter.

Though admittedly a crude sketch, this way of putting the salient differences between Dreyfus and McDowell shows how conceptuality, rationality, and subjectivity are entangled. Genuine resolution of the debate may well involve prying them apart in some way or other, and in particular, distinguishing the insights of the phenomenology of embodiment from Dreyfus's problematic use of Todes, wherein Todes treats our bodily comportments as a 'foundation' for objective judgment. If we call this kind of bodily comportment a 'perceptuo-practical Given', then the real difficulty is to completely extricate the perceptuo-practical Given from both the epistemic Given and the semantic Given. This in turn requires drawing a line between somatic intentionality (the home of the perceptuo-practical Given) and discursive intentionality (which, when properly elucidated along Sellarsian/Brandomian lines, would explain why both the epistemic and semantic Givens are Myths). In short, we need a way of conceiving of the practical Givenness of embodied coping skills as *not* playing any sort of foundationalistic role with respect to the discursive practices that are paradigmatic of the sorts of cognitive-semantic contents distinctive of fully actualized rational animals. To construct that account, I now turn to Merleau-Ponty's description of the perceptual and practical habits that comprise our embodied coping.

5 SOMATIC INTENTIONALITY AND HABITUAL NORMATIVITY IN MERLEAU-PONTY'S ACCOUNT OF LIVED EMBODIMENT

Both Sellars and Merleau-Ponty insist that rejecting the sensory-cognitive continuum – that there is a difference in kind and not just of degree between perceiving and thinking – requires that perception involves a concept of non-conceptual content, but that insisting on the role of such a concept in no way licenses the empiricist version of the Myth of the Given. In that regard Merleau-Ponty would seem to agree with Sellars in a way that neither Brandom nor McDowell do, but this agreement is unfortunately superficial. The salient difference is that Sellars argues that we cannot completely explain what it is to perceive until we introduce into our account something that is posited for theoretical reasons, in the interests of explanatory adequacy – i.e. sense-impressions. By contrast, Merleau-Ponty holds that the nonconceptual aspect of perception is brought into view through phenomenological descriptions alone, i.e. phenomenological description is both necessary and sufficient for securing our cognitive grip on the notion of nonconceptual content. We do not need to posit anything in order to secure a fully adequate understanding of perception. The difficult point to appreciate is that Merleau-Ponty is able to do so *without* committing himself to the Myth of the semantic Given. (On the question whether phenomenology commits the Myth of the Given, see Appendix).

The aim of this chapter is to show, in other words, how Merleau-Ponty succeeded where C.I. Lewis failed. In doing so, Merleau-Ponty is also able to satisfy the demand for transcendental friction. To anticipate: what gives friction to our judgements, embedded as they are in our discursive practices, is that as essentially embodied beings, we are creatures not just of rules (norms) but *also* of habits. The upshot of this discussion will be to show that the distinction between norms (à la Brandom) and habits (à la Merleau-Ponty) gives us a different and better understanding of what Kant was trying to capture in his distinction between concepts and intuitions. (One crucial difference is that the concept/intuition distinction is primarily introduced for the criticism of theoretical reason, whereas the norms/habits distinction is distinctively pragmatic. In that regard my project contributes to the nineteenth- and twentieth-century trend of giving Kantian themes a more pronounced and explicit orientation towards pragmatism).

To establish these (perhaps, seemingly) audacious claims, I will proceed as follows. First, I will examine how Merleau-Ponty describes the perceptuo-practical structure of lived embodiment. *Phenomenology of Perception* (henceforth *PP*) traces the route from perception to movement and from movement to perception.[1] In explaining how this functions, I will make explicit and defend Merleau-Ponty's implicit views about the role of habits and skills in both ordinary and pathological perceptuo-practical context-specific, object-oriented comportments, in order to show this kind of activity counts as both a specific kind of intentionality – *motor* intentionality – and a specific kind of normativity – namely, *habitual* normativity. By 'habitual normativity' I mean that our habitual ways of engaging with objects are subject to implicit norms of correctness, insofar as our engagement with objects comes with varying degrees of success and failure, and that this engagement is bodily and habitual in that it is not instituted by the social practices of deontic scorekeepers. (As a terminological matter, I use 'motor intentionality' when explicating Merleau-Ponty's specific views in *PP* and 'somatic intentionality' when presenting my own, because 'motor intentionality' does not connote perceptual sensitivity).

Crucial to Merleau-Ponty's diagnosis of the need for sound phenomenology is his dialectical criticism of what he calls 'intellectualism' and 'empiricism'. Intellectualism assumes that all intentionality is the intentionality of judgement, whereas empiricism assumes that all intentional content can be explained in terms of causal relations between sensations. Merleau-Ponty argues that these are historically opposed positions, each living off the criticism of the other, and that we need a dialectical critique of this very opposition in order to understand why phenomenological descriptions are correct. In these terms, I will argue that Sellars's theory of perception is deeply problematic because it attempts to be *both* intellectualist *and* empiricist by using empiricism to compensate for intellectualism, and conversely. Since he attempts to be both an empiricist and an intellectualist, in Merleau-Ponty's terms, he retains the assumptions shared by both views and against which Merleau-Ponty advances a dialectical criticism. The result of that criticism, applied to Sellars, is that while Sellars correctly recognizes the need for both conceptual and nonconceptual elements in perception, his neglect of the precise role of embodiment prevents him from getting the phenomenology quite right and indeed, from doing justice to his own best insights. Finally, I will show how the perceptual-practical field can count as a kind of givenness – what Robert Hanna calls 'the Grip of the Given' – without falling into the Myth of the semantic Given. This part of the argument will be developed through close criticisms of both Jay Rosenberg and Robert Hanna.

The central claim to establish here is that, because the habitual normativity of somatic intentionality lacks the requisite sort of *rational* authority that the Given would have to have in order to be genuinely Mythic, the 'practical Given' is not vulnerable to the criticism of the Myth of the Given. We should accept that there are two different kinds of intentional semantic content and avoid the Myth of the semantic Given with regard to both kinds. If we can follow Sellars and Brandom with regard to discursive intentional semantic content and Merleau-Ponty with regard to somatic intentional semantic content, then the bifurcated account of intentionality will be largely vindicated.

Motor Intentionality and Habitual Normativity

As has been pointed out by numerous Merleau-Ponty scholars, Merleau-Ponty aims at depicting and dislodging the unstable oscillation between (neo-Kantian) 'intellectualism' and (neo-Humean) 'empiricism'.[2] A comparison between Merleau-Ponty and the Sellarsian tradition is promising precisely because Merleau-Ponty also aims, in his own distinct way, at rejecting the sensory-cognitive continuum by insisting on a difference in kind between perceptual awareness and discursive thought. The problem with both intellectualism and empiricism is that neither view draws the distinction in the right place, because both fail to notice and elucidate correctly the fundamental structures of our situated, bodily grip on the world. 'Empiricism' assimilates perception to merely causal impingements (e.g. Hume, Quine, and Davidson); 'intellectualism' assimilates perception to discursively structured cognition (e.g. Kant of the *Critique of Pure Reason*, the early Husserl, and Dreyfus's McDowell). Neither is able to do justice to what it is to see, to grasp, and to touch. Despite their opposition, both empiricism and intellectualism are versions of what Merleau-Ponty calls 'objective thought', by which he means the assumption that the world as we experience it consists of fully determined objects and properties.[3] An indictment of each reveals the inadequacy of objective thought as such and the necessity of turning to phenomenology. Yet Merleau-Ponty is also aware of the tendency towards transcendental idealism in Husserl's phenomenology.[4] Consequently Merleau-Ponty attempts to liberate transcendental phenomenology from idealism while at the same time arguing that physicalism, i.e. any view that purports to explain perception exclusively in mechanistic terms, cannot account for the intentional content of perception.

To make this account work, Merleau-Ponty must show us how to think of our situated cognitive grip *on* the world as having, as its necessary condition of possibility, our bodily presence *in* the world. That is, we would avoid physicalism (what Merleau-Ponty also calls empiricism) by acknowledging the intentional and normative character of purposive bodily action, but we would also avoid idealism (what Merleau-Ponty also calls intellectualism) by acknowledging the difference in kind (with regard to cognitive semantics) between motor intentionality and discursive intentionality. Though Merleau-Ponty might be accused of conflating epistemological and metaphysical views here, there are at least strong historical associations between idealism and intellectualism and between empiricism and physicalism. (This is not to endorse Merleau-Ponty's implicit assumption that empiricism and physicalism are ultimately compatible, though that issue is too complicated to address here.)

To distinguish between discursive intentionality and motor intentionality, we must introduce a distinct kind of intentional 'mental' content which is distinct from the kind of content that is paradigmatically exemplified in thought, judgement, belief, and inference. (I have put 'mental' in scare-quotes here because one of Merleau-Ponty's philosophical goals is to reject the conceptual distinction between 'the mental' and 'the physical'.) In light of this, we should recognize that the perceptual field of human experience has a basic structure irreducible to propositional thought and that 'The world is not what I think, but what I live: I am open to the world, I unquestionably communicate with it, it is inexhaustible'.[5] I want to focus on two of Merleau-Ponty's themes: the necessary interdependence of perception and movement and the necessary distinction between perception-movement and thought (though this distinction receives one crucial qualification). On this basis I will show how Merleau-Ponty both avoids conceptualism about perceptual experience – and may even invite re-consideration of the very concepts of 'perceptual judgement' and 'observational knowledge' – and shows that bodily perception itself is a distinct kind of intentionality.

Early on, Merleau-Ponty asserts that the later Husserl correctly distinguished between different kinds of intentionality:

> Husserl distinguishes between act intentionality – which is the intentionality of our judgement and of our voluntary decisions (and is the only intentionality discussed in the *Critique of Pure Reason*) – and operative intentionality (*fungierende Intentionalität*), the intentionality that establishes the natural and pre-predicative unity of the world and of our life.[6]

As a preliminary consideration for why operative intentionality, pre-predicative as it is, deserves to be called any kind of intentionality at all, consider two features of the classical conception of intentionality: aboutness and directedness.

These are distinct in the following way. When I am thinking about what I might have for lunch, the possible state of affairs represented in that thought – the various lunch-options – directs my perception and action. (If I am in a café, a menu becomes motivationally salient, etc.) The content, or intentional object, plays a directive role; that is essential to what makes it intentional content. But that content is also specifiable in a fine-grained way as what I am thinking about, what I have thought about in different contexts, and what I can say that I am thinking about if asked. Operative intentionality is 'pre-reflective', in Reutner's sense, because it lacks aboutness: there is no distinct intentional *object* even notionally separable from the intentional *act* directed towards that object.[7]

The Husserlian concept of operative intentionality, which Merleau-Ponty transforms into the concept of motor intentionality, lacks the act-object structure of the intentionality of our judgement, and so it does not individuate contents in the fine-grained way that discursive intentionality does. But it does have directedness; it is the intentionality of purposive behaviour, and it is this kind of intentionality that Merleau-Ponty defends as 'a new conception of intentionality'[8] relative to those of Kant or the more well-known (and earlier) Husserl.

The central organizing concept for Merleau-Ponty's new conception of intentionality is what he calls variously 'the body schema'[9] and 'the intentional arc'.[10] This concept is developed in three stages: firstly, by drawing upon Gestalt theory on the figure/ground structure of perception ('The perceptual "something" is always in the middle of some other thing, it always belongs to a "field")';[11] secondly, by drawing on the psychology (especially the psychopathology) of movement; thirdly, by showing that perception and bodily movement are interdependent. In the course of developing the first and second stages, Merleau-Ponty also shows that the two dominant foils for his view – intellectualism and empiricism – cannot adequately account for the phenomena of perception and action. Since it is crucial to the present argument that Sellars's theory of perception is at once overly intellectualistic and overly empiricist, I shall postpone till the next section a detailed examination of Merleau-Ponty's criticisms of both intellectualism and empiricism, since those criticisms are crucial for appreciating what is problematic about Sellars's theory of perception. Instead I shall devote the remainder of this section to explicating Merleau-Ponty's positive theory of perception as a necessarily embodied form of non-discursive intentionality.

Central to Merleau-Ponty's understanding of perception is his acceptance of the thesis of Gestalt psychology that all perception has a figure/ground structure: to perceive is always to perceive some determinate X (the 'figure') that is determinate by virtue of how it stands apart from the perceptual background (the 'ground'). One perceives a cup on the table *as* a cup on the table by virtue of (among other things) the perceptual ground against which the cup-on-the-table contrasts, such as: the underside of the table, the table-legs, the rest of the room, and the other objects on the table (if there are any). Crucially, Merleau-Ponty insists that what we directly perceive (in the epistemological sense, not the causal sense) are *objects* and not (for example) 'sense-data' or 'sense-impressions'. In keeping with the general tenor of the phenomenological *epochē* or reduction – the 'bracketing' of posits and assumptions – Merleau-Ponty does not offer a

causal explanation of perception at all. Much as we saw with McDowell's attitude towards scientific explanations of mindedness, Merleau-Ponty's concern
lies with describing what is to perceive rather than with explaining the mechanisms whereby perception is causally realized.[12]

As an explication of what it is to perceive, Merleau-Ponty affirms direct realism; to perceive is to perceive what is objective-for-us. Part of what distinguishes
Merleau-Ponty's direct realism from McDowell's, however, is his careful exploration of the fact that our perceptual sensitivity is never towards a single object in
isolation. Rather, to be perceptually aware of an object is always to be perceptually aware of *objects*; 'To see the object is to plunge into it … because objects
form a system in which one object cannot appear without concealing others'[13]
and 'each of them arranges the others around itself like spectators of its hidden
aspects and as the guarantee of their permanence'.[14] There must be a plurality of
perceptible objects in order for any specific object to be presented as the figure,
and the rest as the ground, of that specific perceptual encounter.[15]

Yet we still want to know, what produces and accounts for the figure/ground
structure of perception? On Merleau-Ponty's account, the figure stands out from
the ground only insofar as one adopts the right bodily posture towards it; otherwise the figure is indeterminate. It is our bodily posture that *produces* the object
as determinate, or (put otherwise) that resolves its perceptual indeterminacy. To
see the cup on the table *as* a cup on the table requires adopting the right distance
from it: neither so far away that it is just 'stuff in the room', nor so close that
one perceives only the sheen of the porcelain. But if all perception has a figure/
ground structure, and the figure/ground structure is only intelligible because of
the role of bodily behaviour, then perception is only intelligible in light of bodily
behaviour, which is why Merleau-Ponty is entitled to claim that 'one's own body
is the always implied third term of the figure-background structure, and each
figure appears perspectivally against the double structure of objective space and
bodily space'.[16] So it is not just that all perceptual content conforms to a figure/
ground structure, but also that one's own body is necessarily implicated in that
structure and makes it possible.

The perceptual and the practical are therefore interdependent, partly because
'The movements of one's own body are naturally invested with a certain perceptual signification, they form a system with external phenomena so tightly woven
that external perception 'takes account' of the movements of the perceptual
organs'.[17] As a result it must be the case that 'I throw my perceptual intentions
and practical intentions against objects that appear to me, in the end, as anterior
and exterior to those intentions, and which nevertheless exist for me only insofar
as they arouse thoughts or desires in me'.[18]. Consequently, 'the perception and
the movement form a system that is modified as a whole'.[19] Put otherwise, there
is a direct connection between object-perception and purposive behaviour, not

mediated by discursively articulated thought, that plays a transcendental role in constituting our basic structure of bodily agency and, indeed, of basic bodily consciousness, or what Merleau-Ponty calls the body-schema.

Here a brief contrast with Lewis's account of terminating sentences is illuminating. Recall that for Lewis a terminating sentence has the form, 'S being given, if A then E' where 'S' and 'E' are expressive statements that convey an immediate apprehension of sense and 'A' is an action. For example, it being given that I am seeing a book in the left-hand side of my visual field, if I turn my head to the left, I will see the same book in the center of my visual field. Terminating judgements of this sort form the semantic basis for the sense ascribed to non-terminating or objective beliefs. Merleau-Ponty shares this general insight into the relation between perception and action, but conceives of the relation as being far more intimate. Instead of thinking of perception as consisting of discrete sense-experiences that are connected by actions, Merleau-Ponty thinks of perceiving and acting as different aspects or poles of experience. The entanglement of perceiving and moving explains *why* Lewis's terminating judgements are correct. Put otherwise Lewis's account of terminating judgements merely reconstitutes the original unity of perceiving and moving in terms of the role that actions – conceived of independently of perception -- mediate between immediate apprehensions of sense. By contrast, Merleau-Ponty keeps the original unity of perception and movement in central focus.

In keeping with phenomenology generally, Merleau-Ponty refuses to tease apart intentionality and consciousness.[20] Just as perceptuo-practical comportments characterizes a distinctive kind of intentionality, they also characterize a distinctive kind of consciousness. (Merleau-Ponty's refusal to separate out intentionality and consciousness will bear on a criticism of Rosenberg in Chapter 5, subsection 3: 'Before Jones: The Myth of Julia'). Instead, Merleau-Ponty develops an account of bodily consciousness as *non-apperceptive consciousness*: 'Consciousness is originally not an 'I think that', but rather an 'I can'[21] and reflex and perception are 'modalities of a *pre-objective perspective* that we call "being-in-the-world"'.[22] This kind of consciousness is non-apperceptive because it is pre-personal; 'every act of reflection, every voluntary taking up of a position is established against the background and upon the proposition of a pre-personal life of consciousness'[23] or put otherwise, one's lived body is not only directed *towards* but also *aware* of the motivationally salient objects in its perceptual milieu. This is not to say that it is the body which is perceptually aware *rather than* oneself, but to say that bodily awareness is one's own awareness without the thematization of itself as awareness that characterizes self-consciousness, or apperceptive consciousness.

Unfortunately, Merleau-Ponty confuses this concept of a pre-personal or pre-subjective consciousness with the concept of the lived body as *another* subject,[24] and to that extent he invites McDowell's reasonable objection that there are too many person-like things in the picture.[25] To forestall this objection, I will restrict my attention to Merleau-Ponty's description of a *pre*-personal or *pre*-subjective consciousness. For example, consider my bodily awareness of the contents of the room in which I am sitting while I, the 'thing that thinks' or apperceptive consciousness, struggles to convey my understanding of Merleau-Ponty. While I am aware of my bodily situatedness in the room, that awareness is on the fringes of my thought; it is my articulation of Merleau-Ponty that occupies my attention, not the feeling of the keys beneath my fingers. What justifies Merleau-Ponty's use of 'I' to describe the life of pre-personal consciousness is that Merleau-Ponty is *describing*, in the rich discursive idiom of philosophy, what is going on at the pre-personal level. Phenomenology here is not a linguistic or symbolic expression of immediate experience but a specific kind of conceptual articulation, namely the kind that acknowledges the life of non-apperceptive consciousness on which it depends.

Since this kind of consciousness is not, first and foremost, the apperceptive consciousness of the 'I think', it is best characterized as not only pre-subjective but also as pre-objective. When Merleau-Ponty says that 'the pre-objective unity of the thing is the correlate of the pre-objective unity of the body',[26] I take him to be saying the following:

(1) awareness of oneself *as* a subject and awareness of the object *as* an object are strictly correlated;

(2) there is a different kind of mutuality at the level of the lived body which is a correlation of pre-subjective consciousness and pre-objective perceptual 'objects'.

More precisely, the perceived thing of non-apperceptive consciousness is not *quite* an object – though it has its own kind of unity – for two reasons: first, because it lacks the requisite determinacy for the attribution of properties (e.g. qualities, sortals, causal dispositions); second, because it lacks the requisite determinacy for the assigning of completely precise spatial-temporal location. (These are distinct because the former specifies what the object is, and the latter specifies where and when the object is.) Instead we should think of the pre-objective unity of the thing and the pre-objective unity of the body as 'poles' of the perceptuo-practical 'field'. But this field *does* have a distinct polarity – the 'to' of purposive movement and the 'fro' of perceptual sensitivity – and therefore has its own kind of pre-reflective intentionality, i.e. directedness without aboutness. (A cat's activities can be directed towards toys, food, or birds without the cat's being able to classify these objects *as* objects or have thoughts *about* them in the full-fledged sense.) This is why Merleau-Ponty would not think (*contra* Rosenberg; see Chapter 5, subsection 3: 'Before Jones: The Myth of Julia') that non-apperceptive consciousness is 'pure positional awareness' but instead is a kind of intentionality: because the pre-objective unity of the thing is identified with the figure/ground structure that oscillates around a perceptual norm, though it is not an object with well-defined properties and powers.

It must be noted that Sellars would also happily accept that properties, just like causal relations, are *conceived*, not *perceived*; where Merleau-Ponty would take issue with Sellars is the claim that the vocabulary of the proper and common sensibles is the 'ground floor' of inquiry, in the sense that this vocabulary is the vocabulary of last resort when questions or challenges to more theoretically rich perceptual reports become salient in the course of inquiry. Rather, Merleau-Ponty would say that the vocabulary of common and proper sensibles is still too deeply intertwined with the rest of 'objective thought'; what we need is a description of perceptual phenomena which is not dependent on the implicit ontology of objective thought, and that the vocabulary of the common and proper sensibles cannot satisfy.

Much as there is a distinctive kind of bodily consciousness paired with the distinctive kind of bodily intentionality, there is also a distinctive kind of bodily normativity that can be called 'habitual normativity'. The crux of habitual normativity is that there are perceptual norms, e.g. that one must be the right distance from an object, a distance which co-varies with the kind of object one is perceiving, in order to perceive it correctly as the kind of object that it is, and that is accomplished when the perceived object meshes with the capacities inherent in one's bodily movements. The lived body completes the figure/ground structure precisely by virtue of effectively 'gearing' into the world, which is to say that 'If the body provides the ground or the background of the perception of movement … it does so as a perceiving power, insofar as it is established in a certain domain and geared into a world'.[27] This gearing provides the body's own norms for successful perception, because 'I perceive correctly when my body has a precise hold on the spectacle'[28] – though it is never a 'complete' hold, and so I never perceive everything that is perceivable in any specific perceptual encounter.

This kind of normativity consists of perceptual norms that in turn reside in bodily habits adopted towards perceptual objects. Though it is distinct from the kind of normativity whereby deontic scorekeepers hold each other accountable for their assertions and other linguistic acts, it counts nevertheless as a kind of normativity just because there are success-conditions; one can always misperceive by failing to adhere to the relevant perceptual norm.

Hence, when Merleau-Ponty says that 'The distance between me and the object is not a size that increases or decreases, but a tension that oscillates around a norm';[29] we should understand this norm-laden tension in terms of perceptual habits make possible smooth and effective bodily activity *and*, conversely, that smooth and effective bodily activity is necessary for successful perception. The norms of correct perception are intrinsic to the organism-environment relation, not grounded in the norms of a linguistic community. (This is where

Merleau-Ponty picks up on the neo-behaviourist or 'second-base' view of intentionality Haugeland discusses; see Chapter 1). In other words, while there are social-linguistic norms that play an essential role in the intentionality of *sapient* or rational animals, there are also the habitual, bodily norms of perception and action that characterize non- and pre-rational animals. Haugeland also points out, correctly, that biological normativity (as he calls it) cannot do all the work that a socio-linguistic account can do, which is precisely why I hold that we need *both* accounts to carry out slightly different (but interrelated) aspects of transcendental cognitive semantics.

These bodily norms are the habits of perception and movement, which is why I call this kind of normativity habitual normativity. By habit I do not mean specific habits which one can have – good habits or bad habits – but rather the general fact of having habits at all, or that there is a general style of habit-having that structures all of one's specific habits through which one inhabits one's habitats (i.e. environments). Habits for Merleau-Ponty are always, simultaneously, both perceptual and motor; 'every habit is simultaneously both motor and perceptual because it resides, as we have said, between explicit perception and actual movement, in that fundamental function that simultaneously delimits our field of vision and our field of action'.[30] The ground of all habit is the body: 'my body is the primordial habit, the one that conditions all others and by which they can be understood'.[31] That is, having a habit is a specific mode of embodiment, both in terms of how one's body is related to the environment (e.g., is one an early riser or a night owl?) and in terms of the organizations repeatedly taken by the parts of the body towards each other (e.g., does one tend to play with one's hair or stroke one's beard?). Characteristically, Merleau-Ponty affirms, since we are concerned here with a kind of *normativity*, it cannot be rendered fully intelligible in terms of the natural sciences (given Merleau-Ponty's conception of natural-scientific intelligibility).[32] Yet since we are concerned with *bodily* habits, we are concerned with a kind of meaning or significance distinct from that of discursive judgement; 'The acquisition of a habit is surely the grasping of a signification, but it is the motor grasping of a motor signification'.[33]

To further elucidate the concept of a motor signification, Merleau-Ponty distinguishes 'motives' from both 'reasons' and 'causes', as motives are a kind of purposiveness in behaviour that structure the coupling of perceiving and acting and that cannot be explained in terms of either mechanistic, efficient causation or discursively articulated thought. As part of his general project of breaking free of the conceptual distinction between 'the mental' and 'the physical', Merleau-Ponty gives us a phenomenology according to which 'the phenomenological notion of *motivation* is one of those 'fluid' concepts that must be formulated if we want to return to the phenomena'.[34] Likewise Merleau-Ponty also contrasts 'intellectual signification' with 'motor signification', which he describes as 'an anticipation or grasp of the result assured by the body itself as a motor power, a 'motor project' (*Bewegungsentwurf*), or a "motor intentionality".[35] As Wrathall nicely puts it, Merleau-Ponty insists on a 'space of motives' distinct from and irreducible to both the logical space of causes and the logical space of reasons, if the latter is construed narrowly as the domain of inferentially articulated and normatively evaluable judgements.[36]

Having described Merleau-Ponty's description of lived embodiment thus far, the skeptic might still wonder why we should grant the claim that this counts as (i) a kind of intentionality *per se* and (ii) a different kind of intentionality from what I have been calling discursive intentionality. Both lines of response are required here because the Sellarsian tradition can be deployed to criticize Merleau-Ponty from two different directions: either that what makes perception and action different from discursive thought is not just non-discursive but also non-intentional representational content (Sellars on sheer receptivity, and Brandom on RDRDs) or that perception and action are intentional precisely by virtue of sharing the same kind of intentionality that discursive thought has (Sellars on language-entry and language-exit transitions, and McDowell on intuitional conceptual content).

In response to (i), notice that neither sense-impressions (the Sellarsian approach) nor RDRDs (the Brandomian approach) can do justice to the embodied features of human existence. Sense-impressions are explanatorily inadequate because they are, as a matter of 'sheer receptivity', entirely passive. Against this, Merleau-Ponty acknowledges that there is a moment of passivity in sensory consciousness but denies that the kind of passivity of mechanistic causation is descriptively adequate: 'what we call passivity is not our reception of an external reality or of causal action of the outside upon us; it is being encompassed, a situated being ... that we perceptually start over and that is constitutive of us'.[37] That is, our situated and embodied being-in-the-world involves being attuned to motivational saliences that belong to a different logical space than those of mechanistic causation, even if the mechanistically causally related items are non-physical (as Sellars's sense-impressions *qua* states of consciousness are). Hence sense-impressions are normatively inert, unlike the habitual normativity displayed with regard to perceptual things.

Likewise, assimilating motor intentionality to RDRDs would require what Levine calls a 'deflationary conception of habits'.[38] As argued in Chapter 4, the concept of a RDRD is nothing over and above the concept of a causal power. But if we deflate motor intentionality to fit Brandom's model of RDRDs, we lose sight of the purposive, directed character of bodily habits. The concept of a RDRD is fleshed out entirely in term of brute, mechanistic causation; it neither allows for the flexibility and teleological character of bodily habits nor for the fact that bodily habits display a perceptuo-practical kind of normativity. So we should insist on at least a *conceptual* distinction between the fundamentally tele-ological character of motor intentionality and the fundamentally mechanistic character of physico-chemical regularities generally, even if we were to accept (*contra* Merleau-Ponty) that the former can, in some to-be-defined sense, be explained in the terms of the latter.

But just as we should insist on a conceptual distinction between intentional content and efficient causation (whether mechanistic or 'paramechanical'), so too we should insist on a conceptual distinction between motor intentionality and discursive intentionality. Discursive intentionality conforms to what Evans calls the Generality Constraint: for someone to understand the thought that *a* is G, she must be able to think it possible that *b* is G or that *a* is H – the same predicate is applicable to different individual constants.[39] (For present purposes we can think of inferentialist semantics as specifying why the Generality Con-straint holds). The point is that even though inferential semantics is holistic, concepts could not even function as nodes in an inferential nexus if it were not the case that propositional content is compositional. Brandom's priority of infer-ential role over representational content does not deny that propositions are decomposable; it explains *why* they are, by showing the specific contributions that sub-propositional components play in inferential licensing and pragmatic commitment. Hence inferential semantics is committed to the decomposability of judgement, which follows in turn from the Generality Constraint.

By contrast, bodily habits do not conform to the Generality Constraint at all. On Merleau-Ponty's view, the figure/ground structure of the perceptual field is non-decomposable and bodily habits are context-specific and situation-spe-cific. If I develop the habit of always driving the same way to work, such that I can stop paying explicit attention to the route and pay more attention to NPR, then if my habit is disrupted due to construction, I find that the old habit of dif-fuse attentiveness to the road no longer works when I need to find an alternative route. Conversely, having developed that habit, I may find myself driving to work without having arrived at that destination through deliberate reflection, if I am sufficiently distracted.[40] But if this shows that bodily habits are too context- and situation-specific to conform to the Generality Constraint, then they cannot be actualizations of discursive intentionality. Though habits are generalizable – they are context- and situation-specific type-wise, not token-wise – they are not generalizable in the way that thoughts must be in order to satisfy the Constraint. Satisfying the Constraint requires decontextualization and abstraction that in turn requires compositional semantic contents. Hence, bodily habits must be both intentional *and* distinct from discursive intentionality: that is, they must be motor intentionality.[41]

What, however, is the relation between motor intentionality and discur-sive intentionality? On one widespread reading – that of Dreyfus and Todes

– the former acts as a 'foundation' for the latter. Presumably it would take some theoretical finesse to reconcile phenomenological foundationalism with the epistemic and semantic anti-foundationalism so prominent in the Sellarsian tradition. But we are spared from having to do so, because Merleau-Ponty's position on the relation between motor intentionality and discursive intentionality does not neatly fit into the foundationalistic picture.[42] In summarizing his discussion of the pathological case of Schneider – among whose deficiencies was an inability to imitate precise gestures on command, although he could effortlessly perform ordinary habits acquired before his injury – Merleau-Ponty writes that:

> the life of consciousness – epistemic life, the life of desire, or perceptual life – is underpinned by an 'intentional arc' that projects around us our past, our future, our human milieu, our physical situation, our ideological situation, and our moral situation, or rather, that ensures that we are situated within all of these relationships. This intentional arc creates the unity of the senses, the unity of the senses with intelligence, and the unity of sensitivity and motricity. And this is what goes limp in the disorder.[43]

This is the key move that prevents Merleau-Ponty from being a phenomenological foundationalist (as Dreyfus arguably is and Todes certainly is): though Merleau-Ponty does clearly distinguish between 'the life of consciousness' (i.e. the life of *apperceptive* consciousness) and 'the intentional arc', the intentional arc *includes* the symbolic functions of culture, ideology, and morality *as well as* perception ('sensitivity') and behaviour ('motricity'). It does not therefore exclude the symbolic functions that are clearly mediated by, among other things, moves in the game of giving and asking for reasons.

Here it is helpful to contrast Merleau-Ponty's descriptions with Kant's principle that the same function that gives unity to the manifold of sense also gives unity to the judgement – a Kantian doctrine that Sellars and McDowell accept.[44] Against Kant, Merleau-Ponty insists that the intentional arc is a distinct kind of intentionality, different from that of judgement *per se,* which underpins and unifies perceptual sensitivity and with motricity. Since the intentional arc *also* unifies conceptual capacities with perceptual sensitivity and motricity, the intentional arc is not a substrate for the intellect that has a completely free-standing functioning of its own. The difference between Kant and Merleau-Ponty is that, for Kant, intuitions have the same kind of unity as judgements, whereas for Merleau-Ponty perceptuo-practical intentionality has its own kind of unity – the pre-objective unity of the thing, the pre-objective unity of the body – which is *in turn* unified with the unity of conceptually mediated judgement in order to produce normal human intentional experience. Though there is a difference between the intentionality of perceptual synthesis and of intellectual synthesis, normal (non-pathological) human experience shows that they are intertwined. (Merleau-Ponty also establishes his distance from Dreyfus in talking about how 'the world' is perceived. Merleau-Ponty endorses the *Welt/Umwelt* distinction; he does not think that what is perceived is just the environment and that the world is merely a conceptualized structure on top of a base of environment-perception.[45])

Importantly, one advantage of distinguishing between sensible and intellectual intentionality is that this distinction does not align with the passive/active distinction. It will not do, as McDowell repeatedly suggests, to identify perception with the passive actualization of conceptual capacities that are also actively exercised in judgement. Rather, we should notice that *both* somatic intentionality and discursive intentionality have what might be seen as an 'active moment' and a 'passive moment'. In somatic intentionality, the passive moment is feeling and the active moment is acting. The case in discursive intentionality is more complicated, but I would suggest that the passive moment is *believing*, since in the normal cases we find ourselves *saddled* with beliefs as a result of how we are informed about our physical and social milieus. The active moment in discursive intentionality is, however, inferring. Trying to force the discursive/somatic distinction into the active/passive distinction does not fit the phenomenological facts.

Sellars's Bifurcation of Somatic Intentionality

Thus far I have presented only a rough sketch of Merleau-Ponty's account of perceptuo-practical intentionality and habitual normativity. We now need to see what theoretical virtues this account has over those of Lewis and Sellars. I shall argue that Sellars, anticipated by Lewis, effectively bifurcates somatic intentionality into an intellectualistic component and an empiricist component: language-entry transitions and sheer receptivity, respectively.[46] The price paid for this bifurcation is that Sellars is unable to do full justice to his own insight, borrowed from Wittgenstein, that what he calls sheer receptivity plays a role in guiding language-entry transitions.

The crux of the problem is that Sellars, much like Lewis, holds what should be called 'empiricist intellectualism'. Though Merleau-Ponty situates these schools in opposition to each other, we can understand Lewis and Sellars as trying to overcome this opposition by reconciling them within a single view. Sellars's empiricist intellectualism lies in the priority he accords to judgement in his theory of intentional content, on the basis of which observations and volitions, though not judgements *per se*, have intentional content by virtue of having *propositionally structured* content. To compensate for this 'intellectualization' of perception, Sellars then introduces sensations in order to explain what makes experience different from thought. From this theoretical starting-point it is impossible to appreciate that 'to perceive in the full sense of the word (as the antithesis of imagining) is not to judge, but rather to grasp, prior to all judgement, a sense immanent in the sensible',[47] because the assimilation of the intentionality of perception *per se* to the intentionality of thought loses sight of what is specific to perception before judgement comes on the scene. The classical intellectualist is one who begins with the correct acknowledgment that sensations lack intentional content – a point on which Sellars and Merleau-Ponty are sufficiently Kantian to agree – but then makes the fateful mistake of thinking that '[j]udgment is often introduced as *what sensation is missing in order to make a perception possible*'.[48] This is, I will argue, is quite close to Sellars's view.

As Sellars understands perception (see Chapter 3), the perceptual object is presented to us in two different modes: as sensed and as imagined. Thus, we *sense* an object's colored facing surface and *imagine* its non-facing colored surface, as well as its colored interior or volume. ('Sense' here is understood in terms of Sellars's 'seeing of' – what we see *of* the object is different from the object that we see.) The unity of common and proper sensibles that characterizes a perceptual object results from the activity of 'the productive imagination', which Sellars (here following Kant very closely) understands as using the concept of the object, *together with the concept of the subject's body*, as a recipe for constructing sense image models of perceived objects. The difference between merely imagined objects and genuinely perceived objects then turns on whether or not the construction of the sense-image model is constrained by the sheer receptivity of sense-impressions. (It follows from this, interestingly enough, that Sellars must ultimately *deny* that we directly perceive physical objects; rather, we directly perceive sense-impressions that we *mistakenly categorize* as properties of physical objects).[49] Thus, while Sellars is hardly a strict intellectualist, he shares a deep commonality with the intellectualist tradition. The cardinal difference is that Sellars does not introduce judgement as what sensation lacks to make a perception, but rather *posits sensation as what judgement is missing in order to make a perception possible*. Though this is indeed a substantive difference from traditional intellectualism, it is not sufficient to rescue Sellars's view from Merleau-Pontyian criticisms.

To see how Merleau-Ponty would object to this theory, notice that he points out that 'intellectualism lives on the refutation of empiricism, and in this refutation it is judgement that serves the function of overcoming the possible scattering of sensations'.[50] In much the same way, Sellars holds that the construction of the image-model, guided by the conceptual recipe, unifies the manifold of sense-impressions and synthesizes the *tode ti*, the this-such, which in turn is the content of the perceptual act (or, in Sellars's 'Mentalese', the complex demonstrative phrase that takes the place of subject-term in perceptual judgement or report). The image-model, guided by the concepts that in turn are characterized by their role in the space of reasons, is the unification of the manifold of sense. However, the unity is imposed on the manifold of sense-impressions. The sense-impressions taken by themselves are a *mere* manifold that is suffused with unity only by the productive imagination as the image-model is constructed.

We can see here that Sellars would count as an intellectualist, in Merleau-Ponty's sense, even though Sellars is not a *classical* intellectualist. The classical intellectualist completely assimilates perception to judgement such that

> rather than being the act of perceiving itself grasped from the inside by an authentic reflection, judgement – which was introduced in order to explain the excess of perception over the retinal impressions – itself becomes a mere 'factor' of perception charged with the task of providing what is not provided by the body; rather than being a transcendental activity, it becomes a mere logical activity of reaching a conclusion.[51]

Unlike the classical intellectualist – and this is precisely where Sellars draws upon empiricism to correct the excesses of intellectualism – Sellars does not treat the productive imagination as merely a logical or epistemic capacity. Instead the productive imagination draws upon our logical and epistemic capacities in constructing image models that are in turn constrained by sense-impressions in the case of veridical or genuine perception. Sellars's intellectualism consists rather in his commitment that there is no unity in the perception that is not transcendentally first in the intellect (even though Sellars is not an innatist about the intellect itself, as his criticisms of both Kant and Lewis make clear).

Since our concept of the intentionality of thought is analogically modeled off our concept of the intentionality of language, Sellars suggests that we locate the intentionality of perception and action in terms of 'language-entry transitions' and 'language-exit transitions'. In language-entry transitions, we transition from perceptual experience to linguistic expressions by reporting what one perceives (e.g. 'I see a ...'); in language-exit transitions, we transition from linguistic expressions to action by declaring what one intends to do (e.g. 'I shall ...'). (Of course observation reports are not the only kind of language-entry transition nor are declarations of action the only kind of language-exit transition). On the Sellarsian account, both perception and action are fundamentally norm-governed by virtue of their relation to language; the norms that make issuing a perceptual report correct or incorrect are those constitutive of the conceptual framework (subject to social mores about the appropriateness of making the particular perceptual report under the particular conditions). However, we must notice that the language-entry and language-exit transitions are not *themselves* applications of the material inference rules, although they are *governed* by such rules. Strictly speaking, the only applications of the material inference rules are to inferences themselves, and Sellars is sensitive to the distinction between inference *per se* and perception and action. The contention here is that he is not *sufficiently* sensitive to this distinction, not that he lacks it entirely. By contrast, Merleau-Ponty insists on a different kind of consciousness and intentionality, governed by its own kind of habitual normativity, in which perception and action are necessarily unified and upon which our capacity to make perceptual reports and declarations of intention depends.

Merleau-Ponty considers what the intellectualist would say about one's perceptual encounter with a cube, even one made of glass. (The Sellarsian reader is invited to replace the glass with pink ice if she wishes). What the intellectualist would say, Merleau-Ponty asserts, is that

> it is rather by conceiving of my body as a moving object that I can decode the perceptual appearance and construct the true cube … The object and my body would thus
> , certainly form a system, but it would be a cluster of objective correlations and not, as we said above, a collection of lived correspondences. The unity of the object would be conceived of – but not experienced as – the correlate of the unity of our body.[52]

In other words, Merleau-Ponty's intellectualist thinks of perception as the solution of puzzle with clues provided by the senses. Against this, Merleau-Ponty notes that one's awareness of the discursively articulable explication of the concept cube does not suffice to bring us into cognitive contact with the singular, perceptual thing. We must be able to imagine that the six equal faces encloses a space, and 'if the words "enclose" and "between" have a sense for us, they must borrow from our experience as embodied subjects'.[53] Only essentially and necessarily embodied intelligences could imagine or perceive what a cube is, regardless of one's cognitive grasp of the definition: 'the cube with six equal faces is the limit-idea through which I express the carnal presence of the cube that is there before my eyes and beneath my hands in its perceptual evidentness'.[54] It is hard to see how, precisely, Sellars would object to this. However, consider how Merleau-Ponty then proceeds to elaborate on this point:

> I have no need of taking an objective view of my own movement and of bringing it into the account in order to reconstitute the true form of the object behind its appearance. The account is already settled, the new appearance has already entered into composition with the lived movement and is offered as the appearance of a cube. The thing and the world are given with the parts of my body, not through a 'natural geometry', but in a living connection comparable, or rather identical, to the living connection that exists among the parts of my body itself.[55]

Whereas Sellars invites us to think of the construction of the image-model as involving a recipe that draws upon the concept of the object and the concept of the subject's body, Merleau-Ponty points out that this is unfaithful to the transcendental description of embodied perception. We do not start off with antecedent grasp of the object, on the one hand, and of our body, on the other hand, and then bring them together in constructing the image-model. Instead our perceptual awareness of the thing and our own purposive bodily movements are much more deeply intertwined at a level of pre-conceptual – or at any rate, pre-discursive –

intentionality and consciousness. 'External perception and the perception of one's own body vary together because they are two sides of a single act',[56] not because we have an antecedent grasp of the thing, on the one hand, and the body, on the other, and then combine them in perception, but rather because perceptual experience is this original unity of lived bodies and perceived things.

As noted earlier, Sellars emphasizes the role of imagination in perception. Non-facing colored surfaces are not merely believed in, which would be compatible with their absence ('intentional inexistence'), but are present to us, albeit present *as imagined*. By contrast, Merleau-Ponty emphasizes that the figure-ground structure of perception renders the non-facing sides of things present to us not only as not believed in, but also not as imagined. We do not *imagine* the non-facing sides of things, because their non-facing sides are present to us as possible seeings: what would be actually seen if we were to pick up an object, manipulate it, walk around to its other side, or what we can ask others to describe what they see of it, to pass it to us or catch it as we toss it to them, and so forth. In contrast, we cannot physically manipulate objects that are only imagined, and our intersubjective discourse with regard to imagined objects (e.g. dystopias and utopias) is constrained in qualitatively different ways than our discourse with regard to perceived objects. We cannot explain perception in terms of sensing and imagining, because both sensing and imagining are fully determinate, whereas perception is essentially indeterminate and ambiguous. (Though I do not know how many stripes an imagined tiger has, it is fully determined for me in my imagination *as* a tiger with stripes. I do not have to get myself into the right bodily comportment with regard to it in order to render it for consciousness as a perceptual figure against a perceptual ground, as I do when I see a tiger in a zoo or in the wild). Moreover, we would not know even what imagining is if we did not understand the difference between perceiving and imagining. In fact, it is crucial to stress that, unlike Sellars (but much like McDowell) Merleau-Ponty endorses a relational account of perception and a disjunctivist account of the difference between perception and hallucination.[57]

Though Merleau-Ponty joins with Sellars in resisting both epistemic and semantic empiricism, in the empiricist tradition that runs from Locke through Mach to Carnap, Merleau-Ponty would distance himself from Sellars by insisting on the distinction between motor intentionality and discursive intentionality, which is to say, by rejecting intellectualism. Though Sellars, following Wittgenstein and Ryle and anticipating Brandom, would happily insist that rules are a matter of knowing-how, this pragmatist re-conception of discursive intentional content is nevertheless a pragmatism of the intellect that does not give the body its due. To that extent, Sellars would not appreciate Merleau-Ponty's insistence that

By saying that this intentionality is not a thought, we mean that is not accomplished in the transparency of a consciousness, and that it takes up as acquired all of the latent knowledge that my body has of itself. Resting upon the pre-logical unity of the body schema, the perceptual synthesis no more possesses the secret of its object than it does the secret of one's own body.[58]

The difference between perceptual synthesis and intellectual synthesis is that in the former, one feels pulled toward towards the object as the appearances coalesce into the appearances *of* this single, particular object, whereas in the latter, the reflecting subject gathers together the appearances into a reflectively produced model or conception.

Both the figure-ground structure of perception and the interdependence of perception and movement are obscured by the conjunction of empiricism and intellectualism. Rather, it is the living body, the body as subject, that must be disclosed in order to understand what it is to perceive and why it is the case that 'the body is a natural myself and, as it were, the body is the subject of perception'.[59] Taking seriously the structure of the perceptual field and the embodied subject of perception and action enables a full appreciation of how the perceptual-practical field has its own kind of intentionality, an intentionality of embodied perception. Perception is not a 'mental' act but fundamentally a *bodily* one. It is *the lived body* that perceives, neither a disembodied mind nor a corpse or other merely physical object. But this conception – that perceiving is a power of the lived body – is not fully available to Sellars because he conceives of the body in terms of the scientific image, i.e. as ultimately just a system of particles. Thus, one of the deepest strain of the Cartesian legacy – the 'splitting' of the lived body into a purely mechanistic component and a purely rational component – is not overcome in Sellars's work, although he does do a great deal to overcome the Cartesian conception of rationality per se, by following in Kant's footsteps.

What makes Sellars's intellectualism an *empiricist* intellectualism is that the productive imagination must be constrained by a moment of passivity – which the empiricist tradition has always correctly recognized – and that it cannot be the case that everything in perception results from the productive imagination. In this regard Sellars's empiricist intellectualism is a descendent and heir of Lewis's own empiricist intellectualism, in which the pure given is posited through transcendental reflection in order to avoid idealism. Only an empiricist intellectualism can rescue intellectualism from its complicity with idealism; on that point Lewis and Sellars are exactly right. But Merleau-Ponty argues that the oscillation between intellectualism and empiricism in the history of modern epistemology belies their deep commonality:

The kinship of intellectualism and empiricism is in this way much less visible and much more profound than is believed. It does not merely stem from their common use of the anthropological definition of sensation, but rather from the fact that both maintain the natural or dogmatic attitude, and the survival of the notion of sensation in intellectualism is but a sign of this dogmatism.[60]

Though Sellars is certainly a good enough pragmatist to understand the ontology of science as a *product* of inquiry, his empiricist intellectualism indicates that he does not entirely shake off the ontology of science into how he conceives of the methodological and epistemological starting-point of inquiry.

The flaw of both intellectualism and empiricism is that they seek to explain the conditions of possibility of judgement by using concepts that only make sense in light of judgement. The phenomenological reduction, in which one tries to pry apart our awareness of our experience from the customary explanations, shows what is mistaken in both empiricism and intellectualism. This is not to say that what is purely described is Given in the Mythic sense, though that would be the case if it were possible to complete the reduction and arrive at a purely described stratum of experience (see Appendix). But that is not Merleau-Ponty's view; on the contrary, we must go through the antinomies of objective thought in order to see that the phenomenological descriptions are true.[61] If empiricism and intellectualism both err by taking for granted that objects are fully determined, neither can properly pose the question of how perceptual determinability comes about. Doing so requires explicating the role of the plurality of pre-objective perceptible and motivating things and the plurality of pre-subjective embodied consciousnesses in explicating the figure/ground structure. The figure/ground structure is precisely what makes it the case that the figure stands out from the ground only if one adopts the right bodily posture towards it; otherwise the figure is indeterminate. It is our bodily postures that *produce* the object *as* determinate, that resolve its perceptual indeterminacy.

The figure/ground structure of perception is missing from Sellars, and I would argue that he is in fact incapable to noticing it because he never notices that perceptual objects are indeterminate to begin with; on the contrary, for him sensory states are always fully determined.[62] Sellars therefore evades the importance of indeterminacy and ambiguity for an adequate phenomenology of perception, as distinct from the more-or-less determinate nature of thinking, sensing, and imagining (which is not to say that these are all the same kind of determinacy). He correctly avoids the one-sidedness of both empiricism and intellectualism, but only by combining the two. In doing so, Sellars has committed one of the cardinal sins of philosophy; to use Wittgenstein's well-known phrase, he permits a picture to hold him captive.[63] His picture of the perceptual situation is that a solitary subject confronting a solitary object; omitted from this picture is both the *plurality* of objects that necessitate the figure/ground structure of perception and the *plurality* of subjects that are also, for Merleau-Ponty, partially co-constitutive of perceptual experience (since the object-hood of the perceived object is partly constituted by its perceivability by another embodied subject who can see a side that is not facing me or with whom I can share a perceptual episode). Though Sellars insists on a plurality of subjects in the space of reasons, there is no intersubjectivity in the explication of perception itself.

With this in place, we can finally show exactly why it is that Sellars's empiricist intellectualism prevents him from doing justice to his some of his own best insights. Recall that Sellars, much like Lewis, insists on nonconceptual content in order to avoid the slippery slope to idealism:

> My objection ... is not to the idea that some such trichotomy is involved, nor to the contrast between the 'receptivity' of sense impressions and the *guidedness*, to use a relevant concept from the *Investigations*, of the flow of conceptual representations proper involved in normal perceptual activity ... If it [the manifold of sense] is, as I take it to be, non-conceptual, it can only guide 'from without' the unique conceptual activity which is representing of *this-suches* as subjects of perceptual judgement ... it is only if Kant distinguishes the radically non-conceptual character of sense from the conceptual character of the synthesis of apprehension in intuition ... and accordingly, the *receptivity* of sense from the *guidedness* of intuition that he can avoid the dialectic which leads from Hegel's *Phenomenology* to nineteenth-century idealism.[64]

It is not enough, that is, to just distinguish between *this-suches* and the more complex perceptual reports in which this-suches take the subject-term; we must also distinguish between this-suches and something else, 'sheer receptivity'. If this-suches have guidedness, then sheer receptivity must be what is doing the guiding. But how exactly does it do so?

If we turn to the passages from the *Philosophical Investigations* to which Sellars directs our attention, what we find is considerably more ambiguous than *Science and Metaphysics* would have us believe:

> But when we read, don't we feel the look of the words somehow causing our utterance? – Read a sentence. – And now look at the following sequence [here Wittgenstein inserts a line of squiggles] and utter a sentence as you do so. Can't you feel that in the first case the utterance was *connected* with seeing the signs and in the second went on side by side with the seeing without any connection? ... One might rather say, I feel that the letters are the *reason* why I read such-and-such. For if someone asks me, "Why do you read it *this* way?" – I justify it by the letters which are there. But what is supposed to mean: to *feel* the justification that I uttered or thought? I'd like to say: when I read, I feel a certain *influence* of the letters on me – but I feel no influence on what I say that from series of arbitrary squiggles.[65]

What interests Wittgenstein here and in the passages that follow is what it is to feel influenced or guided by the letters one reads.[66] Though Sellars is interested in explaining the actuality of what it is that doing the guiding, he misunderstands the phenomenology of reading to which Wittgenstein directs our attention, and likewise cannot fully accommodate Wittgenstein's suggestion that it is a serious mistake to try to *explain* this feeling of influence or guidance in terms of *either* a mechanical (or paramechanical) causation *or* the result of deliberate reflection. This influence is nothing other than what Merleau-Ponty calls habit, which he describes in the following term:

> But if habit is neither a form of knowledge nor an automatic reflex, what is it? It is a question of knowledge in our hands, which is only given through a bodily effort and cannot be translated by an objective designation ... The question is often presented as if the perception of the letter written on the paper came to awaken representation of the same letter, which in turn evoked the representation of the movement necessary to reach it on the keyboard. But this language is mythological. When I glance over the text offered to me, there are no perceptions awakening representations, but rather wholes that arrange themselves at the present moment, endowed with a typical or familiar physiognomy. When I place my hands before my machine, a motor space stretches beneath my hands where I will play out what I have read. The word that is read is a modulation of visual space, the motor execution is a modulation of motor space, and the whole question is how a certain physiognomy of 'visual' wholes can call forth a certain style of motor responses ... But this power of habit is not distinguished from the one we have over our body in general ... To understand is to experience the accord between what we aim at and what is given, between the intention and the realization – and the body is our anchorage in a world.[67]

It is not much of stretch, I submit, to say that the 'mythological' language to which Merleau-Ponty objects is the 'paramechanical' style of explanation that Wittgenstein exposes. The relevant difference between Sellars and Merleau-Ponty here is that, while Sellars acknowledges the importance of the concept of guidedness, his empiricist intellectualism prevents him from fleshing out the idea of habit as a distinct kind of non-intellectual intentionality. Conversely, whereas Sellars (unlike Merleau-Ponty) is interested in explaining how perceptual episodes are causally instantiated, he would have been better served if he had gotten the phenomenology correct with regard to the phenomena he is trying to explain. If he had, perhaps he would not have found it necessary to invoke sensations at all, or perhaps they would have played some other kind of explanatory role.

Merleau-Ponty, by contrast, provides a description of motor intentionality that shows us just what habitual normativity consists in and why it is that the visual appearance of the letters is coordinated with endowing them with sense – because of how motor intentionality and discursive intentionality are intertwined through the intentional arc that unifies intellect with sensitivity and with motricity. Since Sellars lacks the conceptual resources to go beyond the exceedingly simple picture of the perceptual encounter – one in which a solitary subject is perceptually encountering a solitary object – he does not begin with enough complexity to do justice to embodied perception, and so he cannot discover the idea of motor intentionality and the idea of habit. But this in turn prevents him from exploiting correctly Wittgenstein's point about influence or guidedness, because that which is doing the guiding or influencing must be, in some fundamental way, *active* in the process. Sheer receptivity, since it is construed as purely passive, can only passively constrain the formation of this-suches, but this does not fit the phenomenological facts.

Importantly, Merleau-Ponty does not insist that ordinary perceptual experience can occur entirely without tacit conceptual application, as we saw in the explanation of the intentional arc; rather, he holds that ordinary perceptual experience necessarily involves intentional content different in kind from those paradigmatically employed in acts of judgement. What we call 'perceptual judgements' would then involve *both* kinds of intentional content, both perceptual and propositional, bearing a complex relation to each other. Merleau-Ponty can accept that awareness of spatio-temporally locatable, repeatable particulars bearing specifiable properties requires the application of concepts. The particulars are repeatable in the sense that one can with identify some particular – a person, an animal, or object – as being the same particular, in a perceptual encounter, that one has previously encountered. He also holds there is a lived ground of embodiment in which bodies 'gear into' circumambient motivationally salient stimuli. As this lived ground is both pre-objective *and* pre-subjective, it is non-apperceptive intentional consciousness. The necessary distinction between the pre-objective dimension of bodily intentionality and the fully objective dimension of apperceptive consciousness is also at work in Merleau-Ponty's criticism of other philosophers:

> every perception is a communication or a communion, the taking up or the achievement by us of an alien intention or inversely the accomplishment beyond our perceptual powers and as a coupling of our body with the things. If this was not noticed earlier, it is because the becoming aware of the perceived world was made difficult by the prejudices of objective thought. The consistent function of objective thought is to reduce all the phenomena that attest to the union of the subject and the world, and to substitute for them the clear idea of the object as an *in-itself* and of the subject as pure consciousness. Thus, objective thought cuts the ties that unite the thing and the embodied subject and leaves behind only sensible qualities for composing our world (to the exclusion of the modes of appearing we have described), and preferably visual qualities, because they have an autonomous appearance, because they are less directly tied to our body, and because they present us with an object rather than introducing us into a milieu.[68]

Neither empiricist nor intellectualist theories of perception can understand the thing perceived *as distinct from* whatever is conceptualized, imagined, or sensed. Thus, whereas Sellars urges that 'perceiving is an intimate blend of sensing *and* imaging *and* conceptualization',[69] Merleau-Ponty would contend that Sellars misunderstands perceiving because Sellars is too deeply committed to what

Merleau-Ponty calls 'objective thought', or the picture we have of the world as we experience it before the phenomenological reduction has begun. More precisely stated, since Sellars does in fact understand and practice phenomenology, he has not carried the reduction far enough, and so he does not understand perception as having its own structure that is unanalyzable into sensing, imaging, and conceptualization. This does not show that somatic intentionality is both necessary and sufficient for ordinary perceptual experience; rather, it shows only that somatic intentionality *as distinct from discursive intentionality* is necessary for ordinary perceptual experience and thus for empirical content.

Though I have given some reasons for why I think Merleau-Ponty's understanding of perception is to be preferred over Sellars's own, I have not yet touched on one very important part of the problem: the debate over whether somatic intentionality is a candidate for 'non-conceptual content'. Sellars, as noted, *is* committed to nonconceptual content – a fact that has been at the source of much interpretative controversy. With Merleau-Ponty the situation is considerably more complicated, owing in large part to an ambiguity in the concept of 'non-conceptual content' itself.

Before Jones: The Myth of Julia

Let us imagine a pre-Jonesean Rylean called Julia. With the aid of time-travel, Julia reads both *Making It Explicit* and *Phenomenology of Perception*. She would not understand Brandom on the appearance/reality distinction, and she would not understand Merleau-Ponty's criticisms of what he calls 'sensations'. But she would understand perfectly well how deontic scorekeeping institutes propositionally contentful states (beliefs, desires, etc). and statuses (commitments, entitlements, etc.), as long as she could understand herself to be correlating those states and statuses with overt linguistic behaviour (e.g. utterances). Brandom's inferential semantics and normative pragmatics apply just as well to the (pre-Jones) Ryleans as it does to us, though they lack any conception of an internal process or content. Along the same lines, however, Julia would also be able to appreciate how the body-schema is co-constituted along with the perceptual field, and she would be able to understand that there is a logic of purposive activity distinct from the logic of propositionally articulable thought. In other words, she would be able to grasp the gist of both books, though the dialectical setting and specific targets would make no sense to her.

What Julia would not understand, pre-Jonesean as she is, is that there is something analogous to deontic scorekeeping that transpires inside the person when she (and others) is not engaged in intersubjective discourse (or that the same is true of others). Likewise, she would not understand that she (and others) have sensory states that are (roughly) the same when perception and action are properly tied together ('the intentional arc') and when they are decoupled (illusions, hallucinations, mental images, etc.). Lacking that grasp on those concepts, she cannot master looks-talk. Though she will be able to discriminate between bodily postures that allow for optimal perceptual grip on the perceptual object and postures that do not, she would lack the right conceptual repertoire for reporting on these differences that are, *to us*, introspectively available on account of our having mastered noninferential use of the relevant concepts.

What, though, of the specific concepts introduced by Jones: the concept of thought and the concept of sensations? Specifically, what about the ostensibly nonconceptual character of sense-impressions? These are absent from the Myth of Julia; they enter the scene only when Jones teaches the Ryleans how to introduce theoretical posits to explain what is otherwise inexplicable to them. These are, however, occurrent internal states of the perceivers – something going on 'inside' them – rather than modes of the perceiver's way of being in the world. A psychological theory such as those of Jerry Fodor or David Rosenthal would be unintelligible to her, because she lacks the right conceptual repertoire for understanding what those are supposed to be theories *about*. Yet she would be able to understand what Brandom and Merleau-Ponty are talking about, because no theoretical positing is involved in their account. On the account urged here, however, she would therefore be able to combine those two accounts and grasp the distinction between discursive intentional content and somatic intentional content.

What we ought to learn from the Myth of Julia is that there is a substantive difference between 'non-conceptual content' at the *pre*-personal level and the *sub*-personal level. The former is the role of lived embodiment in perception and action as conceptualized by Merleau-Ponty's 'radical reflection',[70] whereas the latter is the states of the organism as conceptualized by theoretical postulation in psychology and/or neuroscience. Is somatic intentionality therefore any kind of nonconceptual content?

Here we face a terminological decision. Given the distinction between discursive intentionality and somatic intentionality, should we pair conceptuality with discursivity or with intentionality? (Perhaps this is a false dichotomy, if there are different kinds of concepts that are associated with the two kinds of intentionality). If, however, we endorse the Sellarsian/Brandomian view of concepts, in which a concept is a node in an inferential nexus, then somatic intentionality, as non-discursive, would indeed be nonconceptual intentional content. But it would not be nonconceptual content in the sense that has figured prominently in analytic philosophy of mind since the term was introduced by Evans, because nonconceptual content in that sense is sub-personal – it is not even phenomenologically available. If that is right, then anti-nonconceptualist arguments such as those put forth by McDowell might not pertain to somatic intentionality.

This point deserves further exploration, because the conflation between pre-personal nonconceptual intentional content and sub-personal nonconceptual content, which is not intentional in *any* sense, can be discerned in two of the most philosophically interesting uses of the philosophy of embodiment for the debates over conceptual and nonconceptual content: those of Rosenberg[71] and Hanna.[72] Both Rosenberg and Hanna put forth versions of what I would consider the right view: that at the level of transcendental description, we can identify a kind of content that (a) has something like a cognitive-semantic role (b) is distinct from propositionally-articulated content, and (c) does not commit the Myth of the Given even given the conjunction of (a) and (b). However, neither Rosenberg nor Hanna is sufficiently attuned to the pre-personal concept of nonconceptual content and the sub-personal concept of nonconceptual content; accordingly it is not entirely clear just how far they would accept (a)–(c).

The perceptuo-practical Given is not Mythical because it lacks the right kind of logical or epistemic structure and normative force to play the kind of semantic or epistemic role that Sellars recognized as Mythic – that is, the kind of epistemic role that Russell gives to sense-data or the kind of semantic role that Lewis gives to immediate apprehensions of sense. More precisely: habitual normativity lacks the kind of *authority* that deontic scorekeepers exercise with regard to each other. The key difference is that habitual normativity is located at the level of the organism-environment relationship (what Haugeland called the 'second-base' or neo-behaviourist position), whereas deontic normativity is located at the level of the social practices *between* organisms (what Haugeland called the 'third-base' or neo-pragmatist position). The kinds of normativity at work constrain perception, thought, and action in different dimensions, and are orthogonal to one another, although in normal human life they interpenetrate so smoothly as to be, strictly speaking, inseparable (except perhaps in pathological cases). As long as we maintain this distinction between the different kinds of normativity, we can accept the normativity of somatic intentionality without committing the Myth of the sematic or epistemic Given. We would be committing the Myth of the Given if and only if a linguistic expression of a perceptuo-motor habit was necessary and sufficient to count as having the same normative authority as the commitments and entitlements that constitute the pragmatic dimension of the space of reasons.

Much of the present project has been anticipated by Jay Rosenberg, who also bridges the distance between Kant, Sellars and existential phenomenology in *The Thinking Self*. What Rosenberg does not do, however, is avail himself as fully as he might have of Merleau-Ponty's distinctive contribution to phenomenology; as a result he conflates the Sellarsian and Merleau-Pontyian strategies. Instead, Rosenberg begins his exploration of what might be meant by 'non-apperceptive consciousness' through a reading of Sartre's requirement that pre-reflective consciousness, since it must be self-consciousness in order to be consciousness at all, must be pre-reflective self-consciousness.[73] If we reject this assumption – that all consciousness must be self-consciousness – the way is open to thinking of pre-reflective consciousness as "'pure' positional awareness"[74] and consequently, '*[a] pperceptive* consciousness comes to be thought of as resting on a foundation of pure positional awareness, a "directed" consciousness which is *of* objects but which is not at the same time in any sense even "implicitly" a consciousness-*of-conscious-ness*'[75] and that, in light of the tight (Kantian) connection between apperceptive consciousness and conceptual representation, '*conceptual* representation must rest on a *fundamentum* of *non-conceptual* representation'.[76] The problem with Rosenberg's view is how he characterizes such nonconceptual representations.

On the one hand, Rosenberg correctly notes that nonconceptual representation must characterize *some* kind of awareness. To bring this into view, he considers the case of a cat stalking a quail. Insofar as the cat lacks apperceptive consciousness – she is not aware of herself *as a cat*, or even aware *of her own awareness* – she also lacks *conceptual* representations of the contents of her awareness. (To reject this assumption – that is, to hold that the cat can have conceptual representations without self-awareness – is to reject the Kantian view of the interdependence of conceptual representations, object-consciousness, and self-consciousness to which Rosenberg is explicitly committed). So the cat is not even 'aware of the quail *as an object* (independently existing, spatio-temporally continuous, and categorically determinate'[77] Yet, at the same time, the cat is aware of *something*. But what, if not aware of an object? As Rosenberg sees it, the quail 'surely has *some* internal counterpart, in the cat's perceptual state, and it remains true that this internal counterpart 'stands *in* for' the quail itself in that complex organic state'[78] – an attribution that is justified on the basis of its explanatory power.

Rosenberg correctly notes that the cat's pure positional awareness has 'the structure of a perceptual field partitioned into *figure and ground*'[79] which he then describes in an analogical extension of the Aristotelian distinction of form and matter. Hence the cat's nonconceptual representation of the quail has the general form of 'it is *so much* (form) of *such-and-such kind of stuff* (matter)'[80] and the specific form of '*an aviform quantum of mottled brown*'[81] (bearing in mind that the analogical language is here, in Sellarsian fashion, strictly qualified by a commentary). Importantly, Rosenberg treats the inner states of the cat as performing roles that are functionally analogous to the conceptual roles of judgment, such as serving as premises and conclusions in inference.

What has gone wrong here is that, in the absence of sustained attention to Merleau-Ponty's identification of non-apperceptive consciousness *with the lived body*, Rosenberg has conflated two very different (but equally valuable) projects: the phenomenological description of non-apperceptive consciousness as a specific mode of *experience*, and the Sellarsian positing of non-apperceptive consciousness as a specific kind of *explanation*. The phenomenologist of embodiment would happily agree that the cat's stalking of the quail is a kind of non-apperceptive consciousness, and would, if she were to accept Kant's Mutuality Thesis, agree that this is not conceptual consciousness. But, she would insist, the nonconceptual consciousness is not a fact about the cat's 'inner states', whether cognitive or neurophysiological; it is a fact about the cat's way of being in the world, and the criterion of accepting this claim is one of descriptive adequacy, not explanatory power (to the extent that these are separable, which neither Sellars nor Merleau-Ponty would insist upon). Though she would undoubtedly appreciate Rosenberg's remark that 'the most fundamental (pre-conceptual, pre-apperceptive) forms of consciousness have the teleological character of proto-intentions',[82] and that Merleau-Ponty is especially useful for understanding this thought, she would nevertheless contend that there is a substantive difference between treating non-apperceptive consciousness as *pre*-conceptual and *pre*-apperceptive (as Merleau-Ponty treats motor intentionality) and treating non-apperceptive consciousness (as Sellars treats sense-impressions) as a theoretical posit at the level of *sub*-personal explanation.

A similar conflation between the pre-personal and sub-personal senses of 'non-conceptual content' can be found in lurking in Hanna's otherwise helpful distinction between 'the Myth of the Given' and 'the Grip of the Given'. In two recent papers, Robert Hanna argues that the critique of the Myth of the Given, as an argument for conceptualism about representational content, is far more problematic than it is taken to be.[83] That critique can fuel an attack on a 'sensationalist' conception of nonconceptual content, but this, Hanna maintains, is 'not really a thesis about *representational* content at all, but rather only a generally discredited thesis about how *phenomenal* content relates to conceptual content'.[84] Here Hanna offers an illuminating, high-altitude narrative of the reception of Kant and Hegel in early twentieth-century epistemology by which he concludes that 'what is being rejected by McDowell under the rubric of "non-conceptual content" is nothing more and nothing less than *Hegel's misinterpretation of Kant's philosophy of cognition*'.[85] The lesson we ought to draw from this account, Hanna argues, is that we should distinguish between the Myth of the Given and what he calls the Grip of the Given as two different ways of thinking about nonconceptual content. According to Hanna's version of the Myth, the Myth is the idea that non-representational, purely phenomenal content plays some sematic or epistemic role. The Myth, Hanna argues, is itself a Myth – it is a view that does not even deserve to be taken seriously enough to be refuted. By contrast, the Grip of the Given is a way of thinking about nonconceptual content that Hanna endorses. According to Hanna, the Grip of the Given suggests that we think about nonconceptual content along quite different lines than what is suggested by the Myth:

> Non-Conceptualism is a thesis about *representational content*, and *not* about sen-
> sory or phenomenal content – even if Non-Conceptualism does indeed have some
> non-trivial implications for the nature of sensory or phenomenal content. So it is
> nothing but a philosophical illusion to think that the Myth of the Given actually
> applies to Non-Conceptualism. This illusion can thereby be aptly dubbed *The Myth
> of the Myth of the Given* ... Non-Conceptualism says that our pre-discursive and essen-
> tially embodied encounters with the world, insofar as they are directly referential, and
> insofar as they are guided and mediated by non-conceptual content, are inherently
> *proto*-rational *cognitive* and *practical* encounters, not *non*-rational, *non*-cognitive, and
> *non*-practical encounters with it.[86]

I agree with Hanna that the Grip of the Given is necessary for singular cognitive reference and competent judgment and inference; somatic intentionality is
precisely an account of how the given gets its grip on our cognitive semantics.
But on Hanna's construal, 'the Myth of the Given' holds that 'non-conceptual
content is nothing but the unstructured causal-sensory "given" input to the
cognitive faculties, passively waiting to be carved up by concepts and propositions'.[87] By contrast, as he puts it, the Grip of the Given states that 'essentially
non-conceptual content can provide rational human minded animals with an
inherently spatio-temporally situated, egocentrically-centered, biologically/
neurobiologically embodied, pre-reflectively conscious, skillful perceptual and
practical grip on things in our world'.[88] Though Hanna does not put the point
quite this way, the Grip of the Given is missing from Sellars's approach because
he assumes that non-apperceptive consciousness must also be non-intentional,
i.e. sensations. By contrast, the 'grippiness' in the Grip of the Given is precisely
that of non-apperceptive (because essentially nonconceptual) and yet intentional (because directed at spatio-temporal objects and events) consciousness,
which is – for Merleau-Ponty, if not for Kant – essentially bodily consciousness
and bodily intentionality.

Yet unlike Kant, Merleau-Ponty undertakes a detailed description of motor
intentionality as logically distinct from discursive or intellectual intentionality
and shows why intellectualism cannot account for the Grip of the Given. Indeed,
Merleau-Ponty would go so far as to say that the slippery slope to idealism can
be avoided only by insisting on the distinction between discursive and somatic
intentionality, rather than in subjecting discursive intentionality to an empiricist
correction. Though Hanna may be right in contending that Kant had a concept
of nonconceptual content as a species of representational (and not merely phenomenal) content,[89] Kantian nonconceptual content is probably not *intentional*
content, and it certainly is not motor intentionality. As such, Kantian nonconceptual content cannot take us all the way to elucidating the Grip of the Given,
or what Merleau-Ponty eloquently describes as how our perceptual and practical
intentions are how the body 'gears into' the perceptual objects it encounters.

On the Sellarsian account, the Myth of the Given is 'killed' by the Myth of Jones. Sellars rehabilitates non-apperceptive consciousness *qua* sense-impressions by construing the concept of sense-impressions as a theoretical posit necessary to explain perceptual experience. By contrast, Merleau-Ponty specifies non-apperceptive consciousness by claiming that 'these clarifications allow us clearly to understand motricity unequivocally as original intentionality. Consciousness is originally not an "I think that" but rather an "I can".[90] We should follow Merleau-Ponty, as well as Rosenberg and Hanna, in distinguishing between the 'I think' of *apperceptive* consciousness and the 'I can' of non-apperceptive or bodily consciousness – that is, between the consciousness of judging and the consciousness of doing, respectively. Doing that adequately requires distinguishing the Myth of Julia from the Myth of Jones. Non-apperceptive consciousness is not an explanatory posit at the sub-personal level, but rather a descriptively necessary feature of embodied consciousness-in-the-world at the pre-personal level, and of what makes rational animals like us a kind of *animal*.

6 THE POSSIBILITIES AND PROBLEMS OF BIFURCATED INTENTIONALITY

In setting up the present project, I proposed the need for a new account of intentionality – what I call bifurcated intentionality. Two philosophically salient reasons motivated this account: the need to respond to Rosenberg's eliminativism about intentionality and the need to satisfy the demand for transcendental friction. In order to construct the account, I turned to resources drawn from C. I. Lewis, Sellars, Brandom, McDowell, and Merleau-Ponty. Throughout the goal was to show why we should think about intentionality in terms of both sociolinguistic norms and bodily habits. We need the first move – the Sellarsian move that explains our grasp on the concept of the intentionality of thought in terms of our grasp on the concept of the intentionality of language – in order to avoid the Myth of the semantic Given. But we need the second move – the Merleau-Pontyian move that introduces the new conception of intentionality located in bodily habits and 'the Grip of the Given' – in order to satisfy the need for transcendental friction more successfully than Lewis, Sellars or McDowell are able to. Moreover, this distinction allows us to preserve, in a modified form, a deep insight shared (thought in different ways) by both Sellars and Merleau-Ponty: that we should reject the sensory-cognitive continuum

I now aim to pull together the disparate threads at work here to show in more detail how the account of bifurcated intentionality works and how it resolves two of the major debates considered here: McDowell's criticism of Sellars, and Dreyfus's criticism of McDowell. I then turn to two recent accounts offered by philosophers similarly positioned between analytic pragmatism and phenomenology- by Rebecca Kukla and Mark Lance and by Mark Okrent- to show how bifurcated intentionality supplements, in different ways, their respective projects. Finally, I return to Alex Rosenberg's eliminativist challenge and take up the question, 'can intentionality be naturalized?' in light of bifurcated intentionality. The answer to that question, I will show, depends on whether one adopts scientific naturalism or a more liberal or relaxed naturalism.

Myths of the Given and Transcendental Friction

We are now in a position to distinguish the Merleau-Ponty thesis and the Sellars thesis to shed new light on the Myth of the semantic Given, using the insights developed by Hanna and Rosenberg respectively. The Merleau-Ponty/Hanna thesis holds that

> (1) non-apperceptive consciousness and somatic intentionality are neces-
> sary for having a cognitive grip on sensuous particulars as the pre-reflec-
> tive, pre-discursive intentional correlates of embodied perception and
> action.

At first glance, this would seem to conflict directly with Sellars's 'psychological nominalism' that

> *all* awareness of *sorts, resemblances, facts*, etc., in short, all awareness of abstract enti-
> ties – indeed, all awareness even of particulars – is a linguistic affair ... not even the
> awareness of such sorts, resemblances, and facts as pertain to so-called immediate
> experience is presupposed by the process of acquiring the use of a language.[1]

Taking psychological nominalism seriously, as clarified and developed by Rosenberg, yields the Sellars/Rosenberg thesis:

> (2) apperceptive consciousness and discursive intentionality is necessary for
> having a cognitive grip on sensuous particular *as particulars*. We acquire
> a grip on particulars *qua* first-order sortals (e.g. 'cat' and 'mouse') and
> get a grip on first-order sortals via metalinguistic sortals (e.g. 'particu-
> lar', 'kind'). Both metalinguistic sortals and first-order sortals, qua both
> of which enter into complex semantic and epistemic relations with
> other metalinguistic sortals, are necessary to have a full-fledged grip on
> particulars.

The important difference between (1) and (2) is that in (2), but not in (1), the metalinguistic concept of 'particular' is explicitly playing a cognitive-semantic role. The cognitive semantic issues at work in Sellars's 'psychological nominal-ism' concern the application of universals to particulars, with its coordinated metalinguistic issues of recognizing universals as universals and recognizing particulars as particulars. For it is the concept of 'particular' as a kind of meta-linguistic sortal that plays a cognitive semantic role, not particulars as objects of perceptuo-practical encounters. One would not be committing oneself to the Myth of the semantic Given to point out the role of lived embodiment in how particulars, as the figures in a figure/ground structure, become available to (non-apperceptive) consciousness. What, then, of the relation between (1) and (2)?

Earlier I argued that one problem with the Myth of the Given is that it is far more protean than typically realized. To clarify matters, I distinguished the Myth of the semantic Given from the Myth of the epistemic Given. The Myth of the semantic Given is the thought that one could be aware of, and so conceptually grasp, a concept – including the concept of 'particular' – as playing its cognitive-semantic role independently of its relations with other cognitive semantic items in the context of perception, thought, and action. For this reason I distinguish between 'grasping a particular' and 'grasping a particular as a particular'. The latter involves awareness of one's grasping that particular, and that in turn requires a grasp of the metalinguistic sortals for classifying the concepts under which the particular falls. The contrast between the Merleau-Ponty/Hanna thesis and the Sellars/Rosenberg thesis now allows us a more refined characterization of the Myth of the semantic Given: the Myth of the semantic Given is the thesis that (1) is *necessary and sufficient* for (2).

In other words, the Myth of the semantic Given holds that having a cognitive grip on sensuous particulars, correctly understood (à la Merleau-Ponty/Hanna) as the pre-reflective intentional correlates of embodied perception and action, is necessary and sufficient to have a cognitive grip on sensuous particulars *as particulars*, correctly understood (à la Sellars/Rosenberg) as grasped by means of bringing them under concepts, where the use of the concept involves mastery of the relevant metalinguistic sortal under which the concept falls. (Moreover, it would be a further episode in the Myth to think that this latter kind of cognitive grasp or awareness – of particulars as particulars – could be achieved independently of having a cognitive grip on any other metalinguistic sortals). Someone who held this position would say that grasping (via perceiving) the particular wooly blue of a carpet is necessary and sufficient for grasping the fact that the carpet is wooly blue (together with the awareness that one has grasped a fact), even if she grasped neither any other facts nor any other metalinguistic sortals. But one would *not* commit oneself to the Myth of the semantic Given if one held that (1) is necessary but *not* sufficient for (2), or that awareness of particulars is necessary but not sufficient for awareness of particulars *as* particulars. It is this last claim – that awareness of particulars is distinct from, necessary for, and also insufficient for awareness of particulars as particulars – that contains the key to resolving the various problems and debates that I have thus far been concerned with.

For one thing, this characterization of the Myth of the semantic Given gives new perspective to what went wrong with C. I. Lewis's cognitive semantics and why Sellars was correct to criticize him. Lewis commits himself to the Myth of the semantic Given because he does think that perceiving the similarities and differences amongst the qualia is necessary and sufficient for grasping the universal-particular relations amongst the qualia prior to any and all conceptual interpretation. As shown above (Chapter 2), Lewis recognizes the need to explain what constrains conceptual activity, and recognizes further that the undifferentiated flux of sense-experience cannot constrain anything. But, recognizing that, he imports back into the description of qualia metalinguistic sortals that only make sense once conceptual interpretation has taken place. This is precisely why the right way of understanding Sellars's criticisms of Lewis is to see that Lewis committed the Myth of the semantic Given. By contrast, Merleau-Ponty does not commit the Myth of the semantic Given because he does not insist that (1) is necessary and sufficient for (2), only that (1) is necessary for (2). However, Merleau-Ponty does allow us to rescue a deep insight of Lewis: that we do need something other than discursive intentionality in order to avoid the slippery slope to idealism, or to use the language introduced in section 1.2, to satisfy the demand for transcendental friction. (For this reason, I think that Rosenthal and Bourgeois are correct to recognize an generic affinity between Lewis and Merleau-Ponty – which I explain in terms of recognizing the demand for transcendental friction – but they are mistaken as to its specific character, because they do not see that Lewis commits himself to the Myth of the semantic Given and Merleau-Ponty does not.[2]) How, then, is the demand satisfied?

This proposal tells us what the general relation is between discursive intentional content and somatic intentional content – that the latter constrains the former – but it does not yet tell us *how* this constraint is implemented. Here we might be tempted by two extremes that ultimately should be avoided. At first, McDowell's view of the relation between discursive conceptual content and intuitional conceptual content suggests a way of proceeding: the latter constrains the former because the former *explicates* the latter. Intuitional conceptual content is, implicitly, what the unfolding of discursive intentional content must be true to. Attractive as this solution is, however, it is not available here because bifurcated intentionality pushes the two kinds of content further apart than they are on McDowell's account. The two kinds of intentional content are not, *pace* McDowell, the same kind of intentional content present to consciousness in two different modes. At the other extreme, to say that somatic intentionality merely furnishes the occasion for issuing something with propositional content is clearly unsatisfying, since one might as well say the same about the triggering of sensory receptors. The relation has to be both less close than on McDowell's view and closer than on the mere occasion view. Where does this leave us?

As I see it, the most plausible suggestion is this: the propositional content of a linguistic act (whether declarative, optative, indicative, imperative, etc.), if it has any empirical dimension at all, is 'answerable' to the perceptual content of the experience of the worldly feature (the figure/ground structure) singled out by the propositional content insofar as there must be some range (perhaps not fully determinate range) of perceptual experiences, the phenomenological description of which would correspond to the explication of the propositional content in question, though the figure/ground structure of somatic intentionality precludes assigning privileged descriptive status to the common and proper sensibles. The astute reader will note that this proposal is in effect, though in a different idiom, Lewis's account of non-terminating judgements and terminating judgements, though shorn of the Myth of the semantic Given that distorted Lewis's account. Unlike Lewis, however, I do not insist that the relation between the explicated propositional content and the phenomenological description of the perceptual content take the form of a strict (biconditional) implication, nor do I insist that the phenomenological description of the perceptual content be exhaustive or complete. Nor is there a privileged vocabulary for phenomenological description, since even phenomenological descriptions are in principle revisable. Indeed, as Merleau-Ponty stresses, the impossibility of a complete description is entailed by the new conception of intentionality, because the embodied agent lacks the requisite 'distance' from its own content implicit in the thought of being able to survey it all at once or completely. Hence there is an ineliminable distance between the two kinds of content.

It must also be stressed that, in keeping in line with Lewis and Sellars, this proposal is about minimally necessary features of empirical content, which is to say that it is a thesis concerning the empirical dimension of *senses*, not about *reference*, a point that must be raised in order to forestall the kinds of objections that Roy Wood Sellars raised against Lewis. In keeping with the general pragmatist spirit of Lewis and Wilfrid Sellars, the 'correspondence' between propositional content and perceptual content should be thought of as part of an intersubjective discourse and as fallible and so subject to revision. The constraint that perceptual content provides to propositional content is no foundation or ground, and certainly no touchstone of certainty.

I now want to show how the account of bifurcated intentionality can be used to resolve two debates examined earlier: the McDowell–Sellars debate and the McDowell–Dreyfus debate. Briefly restated: the McDowell–Sellars debate, as based on McDowell's criticisms of Sellars in the Woodbridge Lectures and responses to McDowell by deVries and Jay Rosenberg, concerns (a) the substantive relations between intentionality, relationality, and perception and (b) the methodological relation between science and philosophy. Sellars both treats intentionality as non-relational – as not involving a relation between the mind and the world – and perception as intentional. Hence he concludes that perception is non-relational. Given those commitments, he concludes that the moment of 'friction' in perception must come from its non-intentional component, i.e. he holds that a theory of perception requires the postulation of sense-impressions in the interest of explanatory adequacy. Against this, McDowell holds that we have very good reasons to think that perception is world-relational, if disjunctivism is correct,[3] and further that it is a conflation of transcendental description and empirical explanation to make postulated entities do any transcendental work. A salient advantage of bifurcated intentionality is that we can accept Sellars's thought in a modified form: that *discursive* intentionality is not world-relational. This is fully consistent with a modified version of McDowell's thesis about perception as the claim that *somatic* intentionality (the kind of intentionality distinctive of perception) is world-relational.

Somatic intentionality is world-relational because a perceptually and structurally unified world unfolds for us as experienced through the (relative) unity and stability of our bodily orientations and engagements with our environments. By contrast, Sellars insists that intentionality is not world-relational. Specifically, he denies that there is a single relation between thought and world denoted by the concept of 'intentionality'. Since (as he argues) the grammar of intentional ascription is at home in explicating the structure of semantical relations, 'intentionality as a relation between thought and world' is a kind of category mistake. He arrives at this view through his epistemic and semantic holism: the meaning of a term depends on both its norm-governed inferential relations with other terms and its associated norm-governed language-entry and language-exit transitions, although Sellars also holds that once a piece of language has been mastered, it can be non-inferentially applied, as with reports of sense-impression. As we have already seen, the intentionality of language is all the intentionality that Sellars thinks there is, and so there are no intentional relations that are also at the same time and in the same sense relations with the world. However, I suggest here that if we restrict the Sellarsian account of intentionality to discursive intentionality, we can preserve the merits of Sellars's account while still conceding something important to McDowell.

While there are good Merleau-Pontyian reasons for affirming a relational theory of perception,[4] there are also compelling reasons to retain Sellars's non-relational treatment of what I call here discursive intentionality – an insight that, as Sellars himself puts it, is 'a thesis I have long felt to be the key to a correct understanding of the place of mind in nature'.[5]

In particular, the non-relationality of discursive intentionality is central to Sellars's nominalistic treatment of the problem of universals, according to which universals are the shadow cast by language, or as Kraut puts it, 'metaphysical claims that initially appear to state language-world connections -claims about the relation between predicates and properties, for example – are, on Sellars's theory, construed as normative claims about appropriate linguistic usage'.[6] This is not to say that Sellars's nominalistic treatment of universals should be accepted without question or criticism, but rather to point out its philosophical significance. It is not too much exaggeration to say, as Ken Westphal put it, that

> There are five truly great theories of particulars and universals, their relations and our knowledge of them. Four are those of Plato, Aristotle, Kant, and (do not be incredulous) Hegel. As accounts of those issues, these theories converge very significantly, thus throwing their subtle and profound differences into illuminating relief. Historically, the fifth such theory would be Ockham's, although because Sellars is a

modern philosopher deeply concerned with the relations of mind and world, rendered so problematic by the rise of modern science, Sellars's nominalism is the fifth such theory.[7]

Such a theory should only be abandoned for much stronger reasons than McDowell's theory of direct intentional perception will license.

Bifurcated intentionality can be seen now as the thought that discursive activity is constrained by something *both* external to it *and* a kind of intentionality, namely somatic intentionality. Acknowledging somatic intentionality preserves the strength of McDowell's insight that intentionality must somehow bear on the world, if it is not to somehow be frictionless spinning in the void, without committing ourselves to the further thought that our conceptual capacities, when not defective, themselves reach all the way out to the lay-out of reality. So it is entirely optional for us to worry, as McDowell does, about the pitfalls of allowing an external constraint on intentionality *per se*. Rather, conceptual activity is constrained by something *both* exterior to it *and* intentional: the unity of the lived body, in tracing out and unifying various perceptual adumbrations, transcendentally guarantees the presence to consciousness of things as perceived.

Taking Merleau-Ponty seriously also allows us to concede two significant points to McDowell's critique of Sellars: firstly, that some kind of world-relational intentionality is required, and secondly, the external constraint on thought is not an explanatory posit for the purposes of transcendental philosophy. But in doing so, we need not abandon, as McDowell does, the non-relationality of discursive intentionality. Consider what might be lost if we affirm McDowell's view of intentionality in light of broader Sellarsian considerations. McDowell rightly affirms both the relationality and the intentionality of perception, but his reticence to distinguish between the intentionality of perception and the intentionality of language entails that all the old problems of 'intentional inexistence' will resurface.[8] If my seeing a coffee-cup is an intentional relation between my visual awareness and the coffee-cup, and there is no salient distinction between the intentionality of perception and the intentionality of thought, then is my thinking of unicorn an intentional relation between my conceptual capacities and the (absent) unicorn? Is the unicorn an 'unactualized possibility'? (What is that, if not an entity in some possible world, to which my conceptual powers grant me a quasi-magical access?)

In short, whereas Sellars holds the following:

(1) intentional content is non-world-tracking (the signifying/picturing distinction);

(2) perceptual episodes have intentional content (as language-entry transitions, including but not limited to observation reports);

(3) perceptual episodes have world-tracking representational content (the

representational purport of sense-impressions);
I urge instead that
(a) discursive intentional content is non-world-tracking;
(b) perceptual episodes have somatic intentional content (phenomenologi-
    cally considered);
(c) perceptual episodes have world-tracking representational content (natu-
    ralistically considered).

The difference between my view and Sellars's is that I treat the intentionality
of perceptual episodes as itself world-relational, just because it is distinct from
the non-relational intentionality of thought and talk. The world-relationality
of somatic intentionality follows from the relational theory of perception held
by McDowell and by Merleau-Ponty. The difference between my view and
McDowell's is that I treat the intentionality of perception as distinct from the
intentionality of thought and talk, just because the former is world-relational and
the latter is not. (Though I do not discuss (c) here, I see no reason to deny (3) as
long as the distinction is drawn between phenomenological concepts and explanatory concepts). As suggested above, the problem with rejecting (a) is that doing
so leads one right back to all the problems of 'intentional inexistence', realism
about universals, and so on. If one is tempted both by Sellars's nominalistic treatment of universals and by McDowell's disjunctivism about perception (or any
argument that holds that perception is both direct and intentional), then what
one needs is something like the bifurcated account of intentionality offered here.

The account of bifurcated intentionality also resolves the McDowell–Dreyfus debate. Above I examined McDowell's reasons (in his Woodbridge Lectures)
for rejecting sheer receptivity, I also noted that McDowell (in his exchange with
Dreyfus) accepts Dreyfus's insistence on embodied coping skills – provided that
the logical space of embodied coping skills is not construed as a 'foundation' for
the logical space of reasons. So if embodied coping skills are not 'foundational'
(*contra* Todes and Dreyfus), then how should we think of their relation to conceptual capacities? The answer is: we should think of embodied coping *as* sheer
receptivity. More specifically (and provocatively), embodied coping is what
sheer receptivity should have been if Sellars had not identified, under pressure
from his commitment to identifying intentionality with conceptuality and conceptuality with discursivity, sheer receptivity with sense-impressions – a series of
moves that Sellars shares with Lewis. That is, we should agree with Sellars (and
Lewis) that some form of sheer receptivity is a transcendental requirement on
an adequate conception of mindedness, and agree with McDowell that theoretical posits should play no role in transcendental description of mindedness.
The thought that we cannot satisfy both requirements without relapsing into
the Myth of the Given is precisely the thought that must be dislodged, and the
way to do so is to see how the phenomenology of embodied perception discloses
how embodied coping skills play the role that Sellars assigns to sheer receptivity.

The appeal to the phenomenology of embodied perception is intended to dislodge the grip of the assumption that rational conceptuality is the paradigm of intentional activity, transcendentally viewed – consider how the tradition has been receptive to the notion of 'spontaneity' – and then it will seem that only that which is passive can provide friction. Rather we ought to accept that there is a kind of proto- or quasi-normativity, a kind of nonconceptual (at least non-discursive) intentionality, that can indeed satisfy the demand for transcendental friction. It is only the assumption that the conceptual is the intentional – an assumption shared by Lewis, Sellars, and McDowell – that has prevented us from noticing that we needed to find it. One might object that embodied coping, or bodily habits, are simply far too 'active' to play a role analogous to sheer receptivity. On the contrary, however – the assumption that receptivity must be passive is an assumption I aim to reject. The 'sheerness' means only that receptivity is construed without any concepts added to it, where concepts in turn are construed in inferentialist terms. Hence all that the notion of sheer receptivity requires is a contrast with spontaneity *qua* the inferential and noninferential use of discursive commitments, and that requirement is satisfied by noticing that receptivity has a different kind of structure than that of moves in the space of reasons. That notion does not require that receptivity be purely passive; receptivity can be active, in the very ways that Merleau-Ponty and other phenomenologists of embodiment describe.

The thesis that somatic intentionality constrains discursive intentionality does not require a commitment to picturing this constraint as a 'foundation'. Instead, we can think of the metaphor as more 'horizontal' than 'vertical'. This much has already been anticipated by Dreyfus himself when he remarks at the very end of his *Inquiry* debate with McDowell, 'To avoid any suggestion of an indubitable ground-floor from which other phenomena are derived, we could, following Heidegger and Merleau-Ponty, call this a *horizonal* rather than a ground-floor/upper-story dependency relation'.[9] We do not have to think of somatic intentionality as involving any violation of the avoidance of the Myth of the Given, because the normativity of bodily habits constrains (but does not determine) the normativity of social norms, and so does not have the same kind of authority as those norms have over deontic scorekeepers.

Whereas McDowell would insist that conceptual norms are constrained by the objects themselves, he is correct only insofar as it is our bodily habitual engagements with objects that provide us with one kind of normativity distinct from that of deontic scorekeeping itself. Since the kinds of conceptual capacities distinctive of socio-linguistic norms are not the only kind of intentional content involved in perception, and bearing in mind the non-relationality of discursive intentionality, we have the thesis that perception (and, indeed, action) involve both a non-relational component – social or instituted normativity, the kind of normativity in which we are answerable to other sapient animals – *and* a relational component – habitual normativity, the kind of normativity in which bodily habits gear us into our environments. However, it must be immediately conceded that a great deal of human life involves neither 'pure' norms nor 'pure' habits, but the very interesting hybrid of norms and habits that are *skills*. Fridland conceives of skills as an intermediate category between actions and concepts, but I take it as a minor adjustment to that view to think of skills as an intermediate or hybrid between habits and norms.[10] For this reason, however, I want to keep the transcendental focus on habits *rather than* on skills, which is why I do not talk of 'embodied coping skills' as Dreyfus does.

In response to McDowell's concern that 'there are too many person-like things in this picture', it must be pointed out that non-apperceptive conscious-ness means that we do *not* have too many person-like things in the picture, but that subjective consciousness is constrained by pre-subjective consciousness (which is, however, only cognitively available to apperceptive consciousness through conceptually mediated descriptions, i.e. phenomenology). On these grounds, the major contributor to the Schear anthology whose views are closest to mine is Zahavi, who observes that

> Even if it could be argued that there is no commonality between the protosubjectiv-ity of animals and infants and the full-fledged subjectivity of those humans who have been initiated into a language ... I don't see how one could deny that the former con-stitutes a necessary condition of possibility for the latter ... [but] one would have to concede that an exploration of this basic but fundamental fact of our experiential life doesn't capture that which is distinctive about human consciousness.[11]

As argued above, bifurcated intentionality specifies how awareness of particulars, as made possible by non-apperceptive consciousness, is a necessary condition of possibility for awareness of particulars as subsumed under concepts by an apper-ceptive consciousness.

In order to flesh out this picture more adequately, I want now to turn to one important challenge faced by the nonconceptualist account of non-apper-ceptive consciousness. In his excellent article on Merleau-Ponty's account of motor intentionality, Jensen argues that we should not interpret Merleau-Ponty as holding that absorbed coping is a fully autonomous capacity that is revealed under pathological conditions, but itself a symptom of the pathology, and that the normal condition involves a much closer unity of conceptually mediated judgement, perceptual sensitivity, and bodily movement ('motricity'). From this he concludes

> the challenge faced by the non-conceptualist ... is to show why we should not regard the disintegration of motility and intellectual capacities found in pathological cases as a disintegration of an explanatory primary co-operation of motility and spontaneity, rather than as a disturbance of an autonomous level of non-conceptual intentionality distinct from the level of conceptual capacities.[12]

On the reading offered here, I do not want to claim that motility is 'autonomous' with respect to spontaneity, a thesis which threatens us with the Myth of the Given. Am I then committed to holding that it is spontaneity *together with motility* that is explanatorily primary? Yes, but only with the further caveat that the explanatory co-primacy of motility with spontaneity requires seeing both *as kinds of* intentionality, rather than thinking that the intentionality of motility is somehow inherited from, or derived from, that of spontaneity.

In holding that there is a distinct kind of intentionality, motility or somatic intentionality, which is not derived from the intentionality of discursive spontaneity, the view defended here might seem to imply that motor intentionality is foundational to spontaneity. A 'foundationalistic' construal of the role of motor intentionality does not sit easily with Sellars's commitment to epistemic and semantic anti-foundationalism nor with the 'horizonal' metaphor adopted (then abandoned) by Dreyfus. The problem here can be sharpened by considering the debates about 'original' and 'derived' intentionality. Brandom, a faithful Sellarsian on this point, puts the issue as follows:

> The theory developed in this work can be thought of as an account of the stance of attributing original intentionality. It offers an answer to the question, What features must one's interpretation of a community exhibit in order properly to be said to be an interpretation of them as engaging in practices sufficient to confer genuinely propositional content on the performances, statuses, attitudes, and expressions caught up in those practices? ... If the practices attributed to the community by the theorist have the right structure, then according to that interpretation, the intentional contentfulness of their states and performances is the product of their own activity, not that of the theorist interpreting that activity. Insofar as their intentionality is derivative – because the normative significance of their states is instituted by the attitudes adopted toward them – their intentionality derives from each other, not from outside the community. On this line, only communities, not individuals, can be interpreted as having original intentionality.[13]

Does the attribution of original intentionality to communities structured by the right kinds of normative statuses imply that the motor intentionality is merely derived, or a sort of 'as if' intentionality somehow falling short of the genuine article? Conversely, if motor intentionality has some priority over discursive intentionality, does the Myth of the Given threaten in a new guise?

I think that it does not, but only by virtue of keeping a sharp eye on the distinction between transcendental descriptions and empirical explanations, and specifically, on the distinctive status of cognitive semantics. In developing bifurcated intentionality, I have intended only to answer the question of transcendental cognitive semantics with respect to empirical content, i.e. how is empirical content possible? Social norms and bodily habits are individually necessary and jointly sufficient for empirical content, because the latter provides with a situated, bodily grip on particulars, and the former provides us with a conceptual framework for inferentially and noninferentially applying universal to particulars and for explicating the relevant metalinguistic sortals. Thus, for the purposes of transcendental cognitive semantics, social norms and bodily habits are *equally* original or 'co-original'. [14]

The bifurcated account of intentionality also thereby enables a deeper appreciation of Sellars's early remark

> To say that man is a rational animal, is to say that man is a creature not of *habits*, but of *rules*. When God created Adam, he whispered in his ear, 'In all contexts of action you will recognize rules, if only the rule to grope for rules to recognize. When you cease to recognize rules, you will walk on four feet'.[15]

I would add only that, as rational *animals*, humans are both creatures of rules (or: norms) *and of habits*. Thus, bifurcated intentionality does better justice than do the language-centered accounts of Brandom and McDowell at capturing our rational animality: the rationality of norms and the animality of habits.

Words Made Flesh (Compare and Contrast)

The appeal of both the Sellarsian emphasis on language and the phenomenological emphasis on experience, esp. embodied experience, has not been lost on many philosophers who have attempted to do justice to insights drawn from both traditions (as well as several others).[16] I now turn to three philosophers who have advanced similar views – specifically, I will examine Lance and Kukla[17] and Mark Okrent. Whereas Kukla and Lance emphasize the normative pragmatics of discursive practices and aim for a more concrete and embodied conception of those practices than Brandom achieved, Okrent emphasizes the importance of an intentionality of purposive animal behaviour upon which the intentionality of rationality depends. (For reasons of space I will not examine in detail the work of Joseph Rouse, though his account is closely aligned both with both Lance and Kukla's and with Okrent's). Throughout I shall highlight the few areas of contention that stand out against a background of overwhelming agreement.

In their *'Yo' and 'Lo'* and other co-authored works, Kukla and Lance carefully develop a normative pragmatics highly sympathetic to the cognitive semantics developed here. Central to their account is their criticism of what they call 'the declarative fallacy' which afflicts 'any philosophy of language, including a pragmatic account, which takes the declarative as the privileged and paradigmatic speech act'.[18] On their view, the declarative fallacy has afflicted much analytic philosophy of language. The problem with the focus on declaratives is that declaratives have a distinctive place within the space of reasons, and ignoring other kinds of linguistic acts will lead to a highly distorted conception of normative pragmatics that structure the space of reasons. Taking declaratives as paradigmatic involves treating a particular as a false universal – what is necessary is to take stock of the whole structure of the space of reasons, not just one part of it.

Specifically, they claim that all normative statuses apply to speech acts in two different ways: in terms of having inputs and outputs (the normative status governing the production of the speech act and the normative changes resulting from an entitled act), and in terms of whether the inputs and outputs are agent-neutral (to all) or agent-relative (to one person or a restricted set of persons). Declaratives have agent-neutral inputs and outputs: the entitlement needed for justified assertion of a declarative is not indexed to particular person or particular social position.

But there are also three other kinds of speech acts: those with agent-relative inputs and agent-neutral outputs (baptisms), those with agent-neutral inputs and agent-relative outputs (prescriptives), and those with agent-relative inputs and outputs (imperatives, promises, etc). Though Lance and Kukla share a great deal with Sellars, Brandom, and McDowell, they also hold the declarative fallacy distorts the characterization of discursive practices insofar as 'McDowell and Sellars ... take as an unshakeable starting point that insofar as a state has a *discursive* or *conceptual* structure, it has, or is directly derivative upon something that has, a *declarative, propositional* structure'.[19] Dislodging the accumulated weight of the declarative fallacy requires understanding how the space of reasons is concretely inhabited first-personally and second-personally, not just third-personally, as the focus on declaratives implicitly assumes.

Along with pragmatists and phenomenologists, Lance and Kukla insist that 'meaning and normativity are phenomena that are ineliminably grounded in socially located human bodies, that reductionism and classical representationalism are bankrupt practices in philosophy of mind and epistemology'[20] but they worry that classical pragmatism and phenomenology of embodiment have 'tended to privilege embodied practice over discourse and thought, seeing the former as more fundamental and more interesting than the latter'.[21] Though this is certainly worrisome as a claim about Merleau-Ponty, as I hope to have shown, it is certainly fair to the phenomenological foundationalism of Dreyfus and Todes. On this specific point, Lance and Kukla follow Rouse on emphasizing that normative transactions between competent language-users only make sense in the context of concrete, embodied behaviour. As Rouse puts the cardinal point in the context of the debate between McDowell and Dreyfus, 'the material-inferential proprieties that govern our use of words in turn presupposes a rich practical-perceptual grasp of the ongoing discursive practice that constitute a natural language'[22] such that '[c]onceptually articulated discursive practice is a distinctive way in which practical-perceptual bodily skills can develop through an extended process of niche construction and coevolution of language and language users.'[23] However, Rouse admits that there remains the difficult issue of how to understand 'the difference between nonhuman animals' vague and inarticulate disclosure of their environment, and our discursively articulated world ... no degree of complexity and flexibility in responsiveness to environmental cues is sufficient by itself to constitute a conceptually articulated grasp'.[24] It is for precisely this reason that I have stressed that somatic intentionality is *necessary but insufficient* for the kind of empirical content that manifests itself in our cognitive experience.

Indeed, Kukla, and Lance press a line of criticism against Sellars and Brandom much the same as that pressed here: that they do not possess a sufficiently robust picture of lived embodiment, as when they note that

> when authors such as Sellars and Brandom discuss *practices*, the lived, acting body planted in a concrete environment does not remain in view ... we aim to plant discursive practices firmly within the embodied material terrain. For us, concrete action, centrally including the act of perceiving, will form the *substance* of language and not just a means of entering or exiting it.[25]

The question is whether there is any normative status that attaches to perceptual and practical intentions distinct from how they are taken up in the space of reasons.

To answer that question, however, we first need to see how Lance and Kukla explain the normative status of perception. Much like Brandom and McDowell they contend that 'nonconceptual content' raises more questions than it answers. For one thing, it is 'difficult to understand how such conceptual content can be accountable to the nonconceptual contents of perception'[26] and such accounts 'leave open large questions about what kind of content they are pointing to.'[27] These objections are valid with regard to nonconceptual content as an explanation of sub-personal cognitive processing, but they do not pertain to somatic intentionality as a description of pre-personal experience. The first objection is not relevant because bifurcated intentionality holds that discursive practices are a non-world relational instituted normativity constrained by a world-relational habitual normativity; the second is not relevant because the phenomenology of embodiment precisely specifies both the kind of content and our mode of access to it.

Though they reject 'nonconceptual content', Kukla and Lance also raise serious objections to McDowell's conceptualist account of perception:

> The problem is that McDowell doesn't distinguish between propositional content and the different kind of discursive content distinctive of perception. The upshot is that everyone, *including McDowell* himself, has presumed that if what is absorbed in perception is not a full declarative judgement, but still engages our concepts, then it must somehow be a proto-*declarative* ... like Sellars, McDowell often simply equates the propositional and the conceptual, presuming that insofar as our concepts are exercised in perception, the form that perception takes must be propositional form.[28]

Hence Lance and Kukla do not wish to reject the Sellarsian point that observations are a distinct kind of skill that presupposes being situated in the space of reasons; 'observation is a matter of events in the world licensing the actions of epistemic agents'.[29] Perceptions are not judgements, not because they are outside the space of reasons, but because they occupy a different role in the topography of that space than judgements do; 'they take up, acknowledge, or recognize the normative significance of worldly events and objects. They put us into singular, first-personal receptive contact with the world and thereby make us answerable to it'.[30] In this way Lance and Kukla aim to incorporate perception fully into the space of reasons – thereby avoiding the Myth of the Given, in light of the epistemic and semantic status of observations – without conflating the distinction between perceptual content and propositional content, as they (and I) argue that McDowell has done.

More recently, Kukla and Lance have elaborated significantly on their conception of how objects are invested with normative significance for us. As an aside, they note,

> by the time the sensible manifold can show up to me as synthesized into objects, we are already taking things as having a conceptually articulate structure and hence as already planted within the space of reasons. McDowell for one, is often concerned with the earlier problem of how sensibility can be received as organized in this way in the first place. For the most part, we are just not attempting to solve this ground-level problem here.[31]

By contrast, bifurcated intentionality *is* an attempt to solve this ground-level problem by specifying how bodily comportments and habits introduce a kind of normativity and intentionality into our dealings with particulars that is then taken up by, and transformed by, our discursive practices

In further contrast with Brandom, Kukla and Lance stress the transcendental significance of the first- and second-person perspectives; on their view, it is 'not only that language *as we find it* [that] involves agent-relative, essentially first-personal discursive practices, but that any functioning language with the capacity to make empirical claims *must* involve such practices'.[32] To compress the argument here, this is because the very concept of empirical content requires observations (what they call 'recognitive episodes'), which involves being able to issue a recognitive (as well as to take oneself to be doing so and to be recognized by others as doing that), and that requires acknowledging the first-person perspective of the person whose observation it is. So without the first-person dimension of recognitives built into the discursive practices of the language-as-used, it would be impossible to understand that language as containing any claims with empirical content.

While I cannot but applaud their general project of making the theory of discursive practices more concrete and embodied, I have one reservation about the resulting account of perception. Specifically, it elides the subtle but important distinction between *perceiving* and *observing* or *conducting an observation*.

I agree that observations are a distinctive achievement of rational agents, which put us in the position of being held accountable by the world. But this is different from the kind of embodied perceiving that gears us into the world in the first place and which Merleau-Ponty describes. Perceiving is an organismal habit before it is a norm-governed skill. The observatives on which the totality of our empirical knowledge rests are themselves the result of the *transformation* of perceptual habits through initiation into the discursive community. On the one hand, Kukla and Lance are correct to point out that Sellars, McDowell, and Brandom commit the declarative fallacy, and that we should not conflate discursive structure with declarative form. On the other hand, this important critique not only does not affect the conception of discursivity at work here, but also the conception of bifurcated intentionality can be used to show precisely how there are basic structures of our embodiment that are taken up into first-personal and second-personal placings in the space of reasons. (There is a parallel point to be made here about actions).

This does not mean that I want to privilege embodied habits *as opposed to* discursive practices, as Dreyfus and Todes do. Such prioritization (and opposition) entails a version of phenomenological foundationalism that does not capture Merleau-Ponty's position, as many have shown. Rather, Merleau-Ponty aims to show that our imaginative, symbol-generating and linguistic capacities are necessarily our ways of being embodied in the world. However much we should bring concepts down to earth as features of our discursive practices, we should not reject the distinction between discursive practices *as such*, in all the rich poly-dimensionality to which Kukla and Lance draw our attention, and embodied habits *as such*. The difficulty here is to avoid conflating the causal priority of habits over norms, both phylogenetically and ontogenetically, with transcendental priority. Transcendentally considered – that is, with respect to cognitive semantics – discursive practices and bodily habits are co-original, individually necessary and jointly sufficient.

The cardinal distinction between bifurcated intentionality and the normative pragmatics Kukla and Lance develop concerns the exact relation between language and embodiment. Kukla and Lance insist that no theory of discursive practices can account for empirical discursive content if it lacks the pragmatics of first and second person perspectives. But somatic intentionality explains how it is even possible for objects to be invested with normative significance in the first place, in the ways that they describe: it is possible for us to invest instituted or discursive normative significance in objects because they are already geared into our bodily habits, especially insofar as those habits are transformed into skills:as distinct from skills. Lance and Kukla also recognize that it would be a version of the Myth of the Given to insist that the act of merely perceiving something is *sufficient* to license the kinds of normative commitments that are taken up in the space of reasons. The reason why my cats cannot license observation reports is because they lack standing in the space of reasons, despite the exceptional attunement of their perceptual sensitivity. My point, however, is that there is a kind of normativity and intentionality distinct from that of discursive practices, and which serves as a necessary condition of possibility for the latter. While Brandom's reliance on RDRDs, on the one hand, and declaratives, on the other, may explain why he puts too much emphasis on our rationality, rather than put equal emphasis on both our rationality and our animality, Kukla and Lance are well-positioned to take bifurcated intentionality seriously.

Whereas Lance and Kukla take their point of departure from the normative pragmatics of natural languages, Okrent argues that our theory of intentionality must be grounded in a robust account of animal behaviour. He shares with pragmatists (broadly construed) the methodological starting-point that 'the intentional content of thoughts should be understood as deriving from their relation with actions, rather than the other way round.'[33] This broadens out the Sellarsian approach that puts the explanatory priority on *language* rather than on *action*, as Okrent does. But to dissolve the circularity that would threaten if we were to explain both the intentionality of actions in terms of thought and also that of thoughts in terms of actions, we need a separate way of understanding the intentionality of actions that depends on 'making teleological language intelligible in a way that neither reduces it to physical terms nor depends on any causal relation between the items displaying the teleological features and the intentional states of agents'.[34] The key to Okrent's approach lies in his emphasis on *goals* rather than on *functions*. That is, we first have to construct an account of goal-oriented behaviour, and only then supplement it with an account of rationality which will, in turn, illuminate the intentionality of beliefs and desires in terms of their explanatory role in rational action. Okrent's term for this explanatory strategy is 'pragmatic', as distinct from representationalist and causal-functionalist strategies, both of which accord explanatory priority to the intentionality of mental states.

The chief difficulty that Okrent faces is how to characterize teleological explanations. On the one hand, we intuitively recognize the appropriateness of teleological explanations even when dealing with obviously non-rational animals. (Okrent's favorite example is the *Sphenx* wasp.) Yet Okrent, following Davidson (though also Brandom), denies that non-rational animals have beliefs and desires, so cannot explain the wasp's behaviour in terms of her beliefs and desires. At the same time, 'goal-directed explanations differ from causal explanations in that they are intensional and from deductive nomological explanations in that they don't seem to appeal to any laws'.[35] How, then, do we distinguish teleological explanations from causal explanations, on the one hand, and from rational explanations, on the other?

We do so through a multi-part strategy that explains the goal-orientedness of an act in terms of (i) classifying it as a specific kind of act; (ii) explaining the role that acts of that kind play in the overall pattern of behaviour, and then (iii) explaining the overall pattern of behaviour in terms of the kind of agent, qua living organism, whose behaviour it is. But what is the goal of the living organism? Okrent's surprisingly Aristotelian answer is: itself. The goal of a living thing is the perpetuation of its own living activity, which in turn allows Okrent to say:

> [w]e can now see why all goal-directed behavior is the behavior of an agent that has itself as a goal. An event has a goal only if it stands under a nonarbitrary norm, a norm that establishes the goal of the act. Such nonarbitrary norms for the evaluation of acts depend on relations among the act, other acts of the same agent, and, crucially, the goals of the agent itself. *Agents* have goals only if what they are, their being, specifies a norm against which the agent is to be evaluated. And only living things stand under such nonarbitrary norms and so have goals of their own. It thus follows that only the acts of living things can have a goal.[36]

However, it must be stressed, Okrent's quasi-Aristotelianism about the goal-directedness of living things does not signal any reticence towards 'Darwinism', broadly construed. (The resurgence of creationism and 'intelligent design' makes it necessary to say so). Rather, he thinks that teleological explanations are not adversely affected by the shift from typological to populationist thinking inaugurated by Darwin, and he also argues, *contra* Millikan, that explanations in terms of biological functions depend on teleological explanations.[37]

Teleological explanation is only part of the puzzle, however, because it applies equally to nonrational and rational animals, and so cannot tell us anything about what makes rational animals distinct – and only rational animals have intentional contents, beliefs and desires, of the sort that have made intentionality such a philosophical conundrum. The next part of the puzzle is Okrent's account of what he calls 'instrumental rationality', in which the agent is able to *acquire* new goals by *learning*, and specifically, 'the ability to learn to respond effectively to a range of situations by engaging in novel, but goal- and situation-appropriate, activity',[38] which means that the organism's biologically determined goals do not determine all the means that it can employ in satisfying those goals. The organism can have behave in ways that are goal-oriented but not goal-determined.

Instrumental rationality, however, is insufficient to account for what is distinctive of human agency; for example, human beings can act in ways contrary to their biological purposes (e.g. martyrs and ascetics) on the basis of principles. To account for this dimension of human life, which Okrent (following both Aristotle and Kant) calls 'practical rationality', Okrent introduces a distinctively Kantian emphasis on the role of *reflection* as making possible an ontologically distinct kind of agency: 'Natural agents are caused to act as they do by their natures. Reflective agents act as they do because they accept reasons from which they can infer actions that are appropriate given those reasons.[39] Crucially this involves recognizing that the reasons are the right ones upon which to act, and not merely reasons that are acted upon. To this Kantian point Okrent adds an evolutionary account as to how practical rationality might have evolved from the kinds of instrumental rationality that we share with other primates. But this by no means that we entirely transcend our animality; on the contrary,

> just as instrumental rationality is a system of behavior that depends on and survives in a pool of teleological necessity and success, practical rationality is a system of behavior that depends on and survives in a pool of mostly instrumentally rational action.[40]

In other words, Okrent's picture of normal mature human beings as rational animals involves a delicate balance between an Aristotelian-Kantian-Davidsonian conception of rationality and an Aristotelian-Darwinian conception of animality.[41]

It should be stressed that Okrent's account is also taken up by Rouse, who points out that it is necessary to 'understand how perceptual-practical engagement itself becomes conceptually articulated and thereby contentful'.[42] First, we need to start off in the right place by understanding that 'organisms teleologically, as directed toward the goal of maintaining and reproducing their characteristic life-cyclical pattern under changing circumstances', where neither organism nor environment can be understood separately, and which exhibits 'reflective rather than determinative teleology'.[43] That is, while all organisms exhibit an indefinite but purposive exploration of its environment, the acquisition of discursive practices transforms the determinative teleology of animal habituality into the reflective and open-ended teleology of distinctively human practico-perceptual engagements.

Much like Okrent, I hold that nonhuman animals are not merely interesting automata that could, even in principle, be explained entirely in terms of physical laws, and we both want to say that the emergence of language makes possible forms of explanation – *rational* explanation – that are inappropriate to the lives of non-human animals. Despite these considerable similarities, there is one crucial difference between Okrent's strategy and mine: as I have developed the view here, somatic intentionality is not the intentionality of purposive behaviour ('teleology', in his sense) because teleology functions for him as an explanatory concept, whereas for me somatic intentionality is a transcendental concept that we invoke in order to carry out the cognitive semantics of empirical content. (It would be a further question to examine the similarities and differences between teleology and somatic intentionality.)

As I see it, bifurcated intentionality sits at the cross-roads of Kukla and Lance, on the one hand, and Okrent, on the other. Lance and Kukla pursue a 'top-down' approach; they begin with the normative pragmatics and inferential semantics of Sellars and Brandom and ask what must be the case in order to make the space of reasons concrete and embodied. Okrent, on the other hand, pursues a 'bottom-up' approach; he begins with the teleology of living organisms – with what makes the reliable differential responsive dispositions of organisms different from those of iron bars – and asks what must be added to it in order to generate practically rational animals. Bifurcated intentionality firmly occupies the philosophical space at which those projects converge, by showing why discursive practices and bodily habits are equally required in order to explain the possibility of empirical content.

Can 'Intentionality' Be 'Naturalized'?

We can finally return to Alex Rosenberg's eliminativist challenge to the very concept of intentionality with which we began. Recall that, according to Rosenberg, a fully consistent philosophical naturalism cannot accommodate the very concept of intentionality. As Rosenberg sees it, the only plausible bearer of intentional states and contents is the individual brain. But our best empirically confirmed theories to date of how brains represent their environments show that brains do not represent their environments in terms of anything sentential. Instead brains represent their environments by mapping them.[44] But since, according to Rosenberg, the very concept of intentionality entails that intentional contents are propositional or sentential, and since there is nothing else *in rerum natura* that can be the bearer of intentionality besides the brain, we must conclude that intentionality cannot be naturalized. It cannot be accommodated by metaphysical naturalism. (One might construe the same basic argument as a *reduction ad absurdum* of naturalism, or more precisely, an argument for why naturalism cannot be true. One philosopher's *modus ponens* is another philosopher's *modus tollens*.)

In light of the account of bifurcated intentionality developed here, and especially in light of both the Sellars/Brandom shift from the intentionality of thought to the intentionality of the discursive community and the Merleau-Ponty shift from the intentionality of thought to the intentionality of the lived body, we can see one fatal flaw in Rosenberg's argument: the specific conception of intentionality that it presupposes. Rosenberg's argument takes as its target the 'first-base' position (in Haugeland's term), the neo-Cartesians – or perhaps better, the 'neuro-Cartesians'. For it is only if one first assumes that intentional propositional contents are individual and mental does it then makes any sense to suppose that the individual brain is the right place to look for the causal processes that instantiate those contents. If, however, one begins by rejecting this Cartesian assumption, then the naturalizing project of insisting that transcendental structures must be realized in causal structures can proceed on a quite different basis.

Crucial to the strategy pursued by bifurcated intentionality is that it rejects the assumption that intentional content is propositional content. Similarly,

Muller recognizes this assumption as driving much of the debate about whether or not intentionality can be naturalized. Muller notes that Rosenberg's eliminativism turns on this assumption: it is because Rosenberg identifies intentional content with the kind of propositional content found in beliefs that he holds that naturalism rules out intentionality. In reconstructing the resources for non-propositional intentionality, Muller discusses recent work by Gendler, Cunningham, and myself.[45] Previously I suggested that McDowell's own critique of Davidson and Dennett implicitly commits him to a far more demanding conception of animal intentionality than he makes explicit. Instead of denying that non-rational animals are devoid of semantic content entirely, I suggested that we need to explain the difference between the kind of content we attribute to animals as perceivers of environments and the kind of content we attribute to ourselves as 'having the world in view'. Whereas non-rational animals perceive and act, they do not make perceptual judgements or perform actions.

In response, Muller points out that the distinction between non-propositional intentional content and propositional content does not line up neatly with species lines; instead, we should accept 'that there is intentional content to which the sense/reference distinction does not apply, but we should also see that this is true of some of the semantic content of human thought as well'.[46] Not only do I agree, but the appeal to the phenomenology of somatic intentionality used here permits us to characterize precisely such intentional content and its descriptive role in human life. I would add only that, in light of Lance and Kukla's criticism of the declarative fallacy', the point should be made in terms of *discursive* content instead of *propositional* content, if 'propositional' means the content of declarative acts alone.

In light of my agreement with Muller, I should draw attention to one important distinction between how I expressed my views previously and what is presently being entertained. Previously, I took the view that we can happily ascribe conceptual content to non-rational animals so long as it is the kind of content to which the sense/reference distinction does not apply. Here I have defended the view that somatic intentionality is 'non-conceptual' *if and only if* we *identify* conceptual content with the kind of content found in *discursive* activity. It is the discursive/somatic distinction that I want to emphasize; whether we put concepts on one side of that distinction or on both is a separate question, and there are indeed compelling arguments on both sides.

It now seems as if bifurcated intentionality is a promising candidate for any account of intentionality that can be naturalized. However, some caution is in order. The bifurcated account tells us that original intentionality does not consist of individual thoughts, but of social norms and bodily habits. At first blush this is a promising candidate for naturalistic treatment. Unlike our picture of individual thoughts, with its Cartesian hang-over, neither languages nor bodies would seem to be outside of the spatio-temporal causal nexus or inexplicable in terms of entities that are located within that nexus. Unfortunately, things are not quite so simple, because it is far from clear just how easily social norms or bodily habits can be easily integrated into a naturalistic picture.

It is, of course, a fact that somatic intentionality precedes discursive intentionality both phylogenetically (in evolutionary history) and ontogenetically (in psychological development), and a complete account of both kinds of intentionality would have to not only acknowledge this fact but explain the *causal* relation between the two. Such an account would need to explain how both kinds of intentionality are causally realized *in rerum natura*. However, if the distinction between transcendental descriptions and empirical explanations is acceptable, then a model of the causal relation between discursive and somatic intentionality is not necessary for the purposes of transcendental cognitive semantics. Though I do accept deVries's Sellarsian dictum that transcendental structures must be realized in causal structures, specifying the causal structures that realize the transcendental structures I am interested in here is not part of the present project. A salient advantage of closely following Merleau-Ponty's transcendental description of embodiment is that it allows me to place *both* language *and* embodiment on the transcendental side of the story. The causal implementation of both discursive practices and bodily habits is precisely where we would need to take into consideration supra-personal (sociocultural) and sub-personal (neurocomputational) mechanisms, and this is not a task for the philosopher alone, but for interdisciplinary collaboration between philosophers and both social and natural scientists.

Two different naturalistic objections can be raised to bifurcated intentionality, dependent as it is on Brandom and Merleau-Ponty. Against Brandom, one might object that discursive practices simply cannot be reconciled with any naturalism worth having. Turner, for example, argues that Brandom's account of discursive practices is but the latest version of a long tradition that Turner calls 'normativism': the idea that there is such a thing as 'meaning' or 'reason' that cannot be accounted for in any set of natural facts. In a painstaking analysis of the history of this assumption, especially in social science and philosophy of law, Turner argues that normativism fails to explain the very facts it is invoked to explain, because any such explanation turns out to be (viciously) circular.[47] Though bifurcated intentionality might be able to respond adequately to this challenge, largely by using the account developed here to build on Kukla and Lance, Okrent, and Rouse, it cannot be taken for granted that this challenge has been met.

It may seem odd to pose a question as to whether bodily habits can be naturalized, since if anything is located in the natural world, surely it is our animality. The problem arises for bifurcated intentionality because the account of bodily habits depends on phenomenology. It is one thing to argue that phenomenology, at least that of Merleau-Ponty, can be liberated from the Myth of the semantic

Given (see Appendix); it is another to argue that phenomenology can be, in the right sense, 'naturalized'. In a recent book review, Evan Thompson contrasts 'naturalizing phenomenology', which 'seeks to absorb phenomenological analyses of consciousness into some kind of naturalistic framework' with 'phenomenologizing nature', which 'uses phenomenology to enrich our understanding of nature, especially living being and the body, in order to do justice to consciousness as a natural phenomenon.'[48] It is one thing to urge that we ought to pursue one or both of those projects; it is quite another to show that a non-scientific naturalism can accomplish what scientific naturalism cannot, or to show that scientific naturalism should not be permitted to establish the terms of the debate. If non-scientific naturalism is philosophically viable, then bifurcated intentionality is certainly naturalizable. Though this may seem like a disappointing conclusion, it should not be too surprising that the question of whether intentionality can be naturalized should depend as much on how we resolve the term 'naturalized' as it does on the term 'intentionality'.

CONCLUSION

The book began with several inter-related questions concerning what must be done to have a philosophically adequate conception of intentionality. One criterion imposed on that conception was that it must not fall afoul of the Myth of the semantic Given. I also argued that we need such a conception in order to satisfy the demand for transcendental friction. In meeting this demand, I showed that several of the major philosophers considered here – Lewis, Sellars and McDowell – were not able to meet this demand in entirely satisfactory ways. Although Lewis and Sellars adopted from the tradition of American pragmatism an inferentialist and holistic conception of conceptual content, and both were concerned to avoid idealism, neither was able to do so in a wholly adequate way. By contrast, McDowell sought to accommodate 'friction' *within* the conceptual domain rather than outside of it, but in doing so he overlooks the resources in phenomenology of embodiment for a version of nonconceptualism that avoids the Myth of the semantic Given.

By contrast, the account of bifurcated intentionality satisfies the demand for transcendental friction by accepting an account of discursive intentionality drawn from Lewis, Sellars, but especially Brandom, and complementing that account with an account of somatic intentionality drawn from Merleau-Ponty. Since the two kinds of intentionality are correlated with two different kinds of consciousness (apperceptive and non-apperceptive) and normativity (instituted and habitual) we are able to maintain a generically 'Kantian' orientation that insists on tight connections between intentionality, consciousness, and normativity, but while meeting the demand for transcendental friction that, arguably, Kant was unable to meet. In other words, bifurcated intentionality successfully arrests what Sellars called 'the dialectic which leads from Hegel's *Phenomenology* to nineteenth-century idealism'[1] by showing how the norms of discursive practice are constrained, not by qualia (Lewis), sense-impressions (Sellars), or the brute causal transactions between us and our environments (Brandom), but by the teleological normativity of bodily habits.

If the account of bifurcated intentionality is philosophically adequate, or at least coherent, the consequences are worth noting. Firstly, it shows that not all Givens are Mythic; while Sellars is correct to criticize the Myth of the Given (understood here as the Myth of the semantic Given), there is indeed another kind of Given, the perceptuo-practical Given of lived embodiment or what Hanna calls 'the Grip of the Given', which is not a Myth but a genuinely transcendental condition of the possibility of empirical conceptual content. Distinguishing between these different notions of 'Given' is crucial for assessing what analytic pragmatism and existential phenomenology can learn from each other.

Secondly, bifurcated intentionality entails weak inferentialism about empirical content: the socially-instituted norms that govern inferential articulation and language-entry and language-exit transitions are necessary but not sufficient to determine empirical conceptual content, because our cognitive grasp of the particulars that is partially constitutive of those concepts is conditioned by the resolution of the figure/ground structure of embodied perception. Put otherwise, both habitual normativity (the organism-environment relation) and discursive normativity (the dynamic between deontic scorekeepers) are necessary for empirical concepts. On that basis, I conclude that either that weak inferentialism is more attractive and defensible than Brandom supposes, or that the advocate of strong inferentialism must show that weak inferentialism is somehow deficient.

Thirdly, if the argument from the Appendix is correct in showing that transcendental descriptions must be mediated by empirical explanations in order to avoid the Myth of the Given, then further work is required to show that bifurcated intentionality – developed here as transcendental cognitive semantics – can be successfully brought into productive conversation with empirical explanations, especially (though not only) neuroscience, and also by taking seriously the historical processes that account for our cognitive grasp of transcendental descriptions. Fourthly, as a theory of empirical content that takes language and embodiment with equal seriousness, the account of bifurcated intentionality bears directly on debates in philosophy of mind, epistemology and philosophy of language. Finally, the use of existential phenomenology in conjunction with analytic neo-pragmatismshould re-frame the debate between defenders of classical pragmatism and analytic neo-pragmatism in light of the close affinities between existential phenomenology and classical pragmatism – especially, in my view, between Merleau-Ponty and Dewey – as well as the family quarrel between 'analytic' and 'Continental' philosophy.

It would be beyond presumption for me to say that bifurcated intentionality is the correct view to have about intentionality, or that it resolves all the questions and debates considered here. In the long run, we are all dead and all theories are refuted. No one can hope to be right; the most anyone can hope for is to be wrong in an interesting way. I hope that, if I have been wrong, at least I have been wrong in interesting ways.

APPENDIX: IS PHENOMENOLOGY COMMITTED TO THE MYTH OF THE GIVEN?

In Chapter 1, I noted that the Myth of the Given is often treated as having a fairly narrow scope, as if it were a problem only for empiricist theories of knowledge. Considerably less attention has been given to Sellars's insistence on rejecting 'the entire framework of givenness' that must be rejected, and along with it, any attempt to ground a language-game outside of all language-games.[1] When the Myth of the Given is understood in such broad terms, however, we must inquire into whether or not phenomenology is a version of the Myth. Brassier correctly notes that 'empiricism and Cartesianism are not the only tributaries of the myth of the given'[2] and thereby raises the challenge that '[t]he claim that meaning is rooted in the originary 'sense-bestowing' acts of consciousness renders phenomenology, at least its transcendental variants, directly subservient to the myth'.[3] In the terms I use here to characterize the Myth of the semantic Given, Brassier is correct to claim that phenomenology is a version of the Myth if phenomenology holds that epistemic and semantic roles can be constituted independently of, and prior to, language or any other kind of conceptual consciousness. Here I shall argue that, while this does indeed appear to be true of Husserl, it is not true of Merleau-Ponty. However, Merleau-Ponty's rejection of the phenomenological version of the Myth does not depend on abandoning transcendental phenomenology, but rather on the dialectical relation between transcendental phenomenology and empirical psychology.

To see why Brassier is correct to claim that phenomenology - at least in some versions – is a version of the Myth of the Given, I shall begin by considering what has gone wrong in an argument that it is not. In her 'Revisiting the Myth: Husserl and Sellars on the Given', Soffer notes that Husserl might be thought vulnerable to this critique due to his influence on Chisholm, given a certain reading of the Sellars-Chisholm correspondence.[4] Additionally, it might be thought that Husserl's taxonomy of different modes of givenness in different kinds of consciousness raises Sellarsian suspicions. Nevertheless, she argues not only that the Myth of the Given is irrelevant to phenomenology, but that phenomenology offers insights obscured by Sellars's excessive emphasis on language.

To begin with, Soffer notes that there is little, if any disagreement between Husserl and Sellars about whether conceptual consciousness is required for empirical knowledge. Husserl, like Sellars, points out that empirical knowledge is a sophisticated achievement that requires concepts and language. But this does not mean that the Myth is not lurking elsewhere in Husserl's phenomenology. This concern is obscured by Soffer's inadequate appreciation of Sellars's challenge. On her reading, Sellars holds that 'the essence of the Myth of the Given is to think that there is nonlinguistic, nonconceptual, noninferential awareness which can either serve as evidence for or itself constitutes empirical knowledge.'[5] But this construal of the Myth of the Given misses the point; Sellars is not concerned so much with *non-inferential* knowledge as with *presuppositionless* knowledge.[6] The Myth, then, is *not* the assumption that non-inferential knowledge can play some epistemic role, such as serving as premises in inference, but rather the assumption that all knowledge must rest on some foundation of 'presuppositionless knowledge', and it is but one more episode of the Myth to confuse non-inferential with presuppositionless knowledge. Yet given that emphasis on presuppositionless knowledge, then phenomenology, with its emphasis on pure descriptions of experience once all presuppositions have been suspended, might be an episode in the Myth after all.

Soffer maintains not only that phenomenology evades the attack on the Myth of the Given but also highlights deficiencies of Sellars's 'psychological nominalism': that '*all* awareness of *sorts, resemblances, facts*, etc., in short all awareness of abstract entities – indeed, all awareness even of particulars – is a linguistic affair'.[7] Psychological nominalism allows Sellars to insist that all categorical frameworks – the framework of categories such as 'sort', 'fact' 'abstract entity', 'particular' – are re-acquired (with modification) from generation to generation, and so are not antecedent to the acquisition of natural language. To believe that categorical framework *is* antecedent to the acquisition of natural language is to fall prey to the 'Augustinian' picture of language, as criticized in the opening sections of *Philosophical Investigations*. As Sellars puts it, 'the primary connotation of 'psychological nominalism' is the denial that there is any awareness of logical space prior to, or independent of, language'.[8] By contrast, Soffer attributes to Husserl the view that 'the noticing of individuals and their individual features occurs prior to and as a condition of the formation of general concepts'.[9] If this requires an *awareness* of a logical space *as* a logical space in the absence of an acquired language, then it we are indeed dealing with a version of the Myth.

Yet this depends on how exactly we understand 'noticing.' If this noticing amounts to the claim simply that 'Husserl holds that there is some form of perception which is not predicatively shaped and does not presuppose socially transmitted verbal language',[10] then it not at all clear whether Sellars would disagree. Certainly Sellars acknowledges that there are *aspects* of perception which are not predicatively shaped, a point he stresses as when he says, '*something, somehow* a cube of pink in physical space is present in the perception other than as merely believed in'.[11] As shown in Chapter 3, all Sellars holds is that, *however* one distinguishes between perception and judgment, the nonconceptual aspects of perception do not contribute to the justificatory or semantic role of perceptual episodes, although those aspects do (and indeed must) play other explanatory tasks. Furthermore, whereas Soffer concludes that 'Sellars's arguments for psychological nominalism do not show that there are no concepts or perceptions without language but only that there cannot be conceptions and perceptions of a certain epistemic sophistication without language'[12] it must be pointed out that that is precisely what Sellars does claim, on any reasonable interpretation, esp. one that takes into account his remarks on animal thoughts.[13]

If, as per the traditional interpretation, the Myth of the Given is just a commitment to epistemological foundationalism in general and of sense-data theories in particular, then it is relatively straightforward: Husserl does not commit himself to the Myth, since he is not committed to epistemological foundationalism, and certainly not to phenomenalism. But this hardly settles the matter in the case of Husserl any more than it does in C. I. Lewis, who also is not committed to epistemological foundationalism and yet who does accept a certain kind of Myth of the Given with regard to cognitive semantics. Unfortunately, Soffer does not fully appreciate that the Myth is more protean than the specifically empiricist version that Sellars examines in 'Empiricism and the Philosophy of Mind' and 'Phenomenalism', the primary Sellarsian texts she uses. But in light of Sellars's idea that it is only specific versions of the Myth that are attacked, and not the Myth in its full generality, I shall now argue that just as there could be distinctively Kantian (and even Hegelian!) versions of the Myth, so too that there is a distinctively phenomenological version of the Myth.

More specifically, my concern here is with 'static phenomenology', the project that finds expression in *Logical Investigations* and *Ideas I*; I leave it as future work whether genetic phenomenology and generative phenomenology are vulnerable to the criticisms I will raise here about static phenomenology. As Zahavi describes it, static phenomenology aims

> to account for the relations between the act and the object. It usually takes its point of departure from a certain region of objects (say, ideal objects or physical objects) and then investigates the intentional acts that these objects are correlated to and constituted by. This investigation must be characterized as static since both the types of objects and the intentional structures are taken to be readily available.[14]

A further distinction concerns Husserl's transition from phenomenology to *transcendental* phenomenology between *Logical Investigations* and *Ideas* I. To unpack this conception of static transcendental phenomenology (STP), I now turn to its presentation in *Cartesian Meditations*.[15]

The central idea of STP is the infamous 'phenomenological reduction' arrived at by the *epochē*, the 'bracketing' or 'suspending' of one's presuppositions, posits, ontological commitments, explanatory procedures, etc. to yield a pure description of lived experience. The *epochē* does not dispute the reality of the world, but rather re-inscribes our taking-the-world-to-be-real as a taking-to-be-real-for-consciousness. This is why Husserl says that the '*epochē* with respect to all worldly being does not at all change the fact that the manifold *cogitationes* relating to what is worldly bear this relation *within themselves*'.[16] Central to the descriptive project here is the act-object model of intentionality, or to use Husserl's terms, *noesis* and *noema*. Of particular interest here is how Husserl articulates the attitude of phenomenological reduction itself:

> The phenomenologically altered – and, as so altered, continually maintained – attitude consists in a *splitting of the Ego*: in that the phenomenological Ego establishes himself as 'disinterested on-looker', above the naively interested Ego. That this takes place is then itself accessible by means of a new reflection, which, as transcendental, likewise demands the very same attitude of looking on 'disinterestedly' – the Ego's sole remaining interest being to see and describe adequately what he sees, purely as seen, as what is seen, and seen in such and such a manner.[17]

This standpoint of purely disinterested contemplation allows us to describe the correlation between the acts of consciousness (the *noeses*), and the objects of consciousness (the *noemata*). Once we have become aware of '[t]he general descriptions to be made, always on the basis of particular *cogitationes*, with regards to each of the two correlative sides'[18] we will be able to generate both 'noematic descriptions' and 'noetic descriptions' which are 'characterized descriptively as *belonging together inseparably*'.[19] Likewise, 'when phenomenological reduction is consistently executed, there is left us, on the noetic side, the openly endless life of pure consciousness and, as its correlate on the noematic side, the meant world, purely as meant'.[20] It is here that, with a few caveats, we can see the phenomenological version of the Myth.

Husserl is quick to stress that neither the objects of consciousness nor the acts of consciousness, taken separately, are Given; '[t]his sense, the cogitatum qua cogitatum, is never present to actual consciousness as a finished datum; it becomes 'clarified' only through explication of the given horizon and the new horizons continuously awakened'.[21] The senses or meanings that consciousness takes as its objects are continually explicated, and so are not to be conceived as fixed and indubitable as the sense-data of the naïve empiricist. Likewise there is an infinite multiplicity of acts of consciousness that cannot be exhausted. Hence the phenomenological Myth of the Given is neither noetic nor noematic. Rather, the phenomenological Myth is *the noesis-noema correlation* as described from the perspective of the transcendental ego:

> Each type ... is to be asked about its noetic-noematic structure, is to be systematically
> explicated and established in respect of those modes of intentional flux that pertain
> to it, and in respect of their horizons and the intentional processes implicit in their
> horizons, and so forth.[22]

We now need to understand why the noesis-noema correlation is a version of the
Myth of the Given.

In the first of his 1981 Carus lectures, 'The Lever of Archimedes', Sellars provides the following general (and generous) construal of the Myth of the Given:
'If a person is directly aware of an item which has categorial status C, then the
person is aware of it *as* having categorial status C'; conversely, '*To reject the Myth
of the Given is to reject the idea that the categorial structure of the world – if has a
categorial structure – imposes itself on the mind as a seal on melted wax*.'[23] In this
fully general sense of the Myth, we can begin to understand why Sellars says that
versions of the Myth occur just as much in rationalism as in empiricism, and
even why not even Kant or Hegel were entirely free of it. Likewise, in the *specifically phenomenological* version of the Myth, what is Given is precisely givenness
itself, or as Husserl calls it, the noesis-noema correlation.

The key point to notice is that, if we are to faithful to the phenomenological project, it cannot be the case that anything transcendent or real is imposing
a categorical structure on the mind. The world is precisely what is bracketed by
the phenomenological reduction. But there is something imposing itself on the
mind 'as a seal on melted wax': the mind itself, transcendentally considered in
terms of the correlations between noesis and noema. The correlation must be
Given because it results from neither theoretical postulation nor conceptual
explication. It cannot be posited because it is revealed by the *epochē*, and the
epochē just is the rejection or suspension of posits, and indeed of all possible
explanatory items. Nor is the correlation itself the result of conceptual explication, because the correlations between the acts and objects of consciousness
are simply laid out before the disinterested gaze of the transcendental ego. If we
think about the Myth through Sellars's metaphor of 'the seal on melted wax',
then STP is Mythic in the relevant sense. Hence the categorial structure of the
mind, transcendentally conceived as the modalities of correlation or the mode
of givenness, imposes itself on the sustained attention of the practicing phenomenologist in order to yield pure descriptions of transcendentally ideal activities.

What is Mythic about STP, then, is its 'correlationism'.[24] Correlationism
is Mythic due to its foundational role within the total system as the presuppositionless condition of possibility of cognitive experience, just because our
awareness of the correlation is achieved when all presuppositions are suspended,
i.e. when the phenomenological reduction is complete. In short: static transcendental phenomenology, though it does break with the naiveté of previous

philosophies, nevertheless retains a trace of the dogmatism that afflicted both rationalism and empiricism

But if STP is a version of the Myth, what does that portend for phenomenology in general? In his late (and, during his lifetime, largely unpublished) work, Husserl introduced other kinds of phenomenology - in particular, genetic phenomenology and generative phenomenology - which Merleau-Ponty studied carefully. The complexities of Merleau-Ponty's relation to the phenomenological tradition have usually been under-emphasized in the history of Merleau-Ponty scholarship, especially in the Anglophone world, because of insufficient attention given to Merleau-Ponty's debt to the later Husserl. As Zahavi notes, there is some irony in the fact that Merleau-Ponty scholars who are largely ignorant of the later Husserl find it difficult to take Merleau-Ponty at his word when he pulls his own phenomenology out of Husserl.[25] However, recent interpretations of Merleau-Ponty have paid more attention to the fact that Merleau-Ponty was one of the first philosophers to read the unpublished manuscripts. No doubt one should take the time to read the late Husserl as carefully as Merleau-Ponty did before passing judgment as to whether or not his approach to phenomenology is as indebted to Husserl as he claims it is.

I aim to show that Merleau-Ponty's conception of phenomenology does not entail a version of the Myth of the Given for two reasons. Firstly, Merleau-Ponty carefully distinguishes the transcendental descriptions arrived at through the phenomenological method from the characteristically idealist framework in which Husserl presented those descriptions. Secondly, and correlated with this liberation, Merleau-Ponty holds that transcendental descriptions do not directly convey their epistemological and semantic status to our awareness. Rather, precisely because of the difficulty of being able to appreciate the necessary truth of transcendental descriptions, we should work through the contradictions at work in empirical psychological theories when they are unable to fully account for psychological phenomena, and especially for pathological phenomena.

Of crucial importance to us is the augmentation of phenomenological method that Merleau-Ponty finds in the later Husserl and which he remarks upon at length in his essay, 'The Philosophy and His Shadow', which is primarily devoted to presenting, with commentary, the central ideas (as Merleau-Ponty sees them) of *Ideas II*. While one might be tempted to restrict phenomenology to the first-person explication of mental contents, Merleau-Ponty claims that '[i]n the last analysis, philosophy is neither a materialism nor a philosophy of mind. Its proper work is to unveil the pre-theoretical layer on which both of the idealizations find their relative justification and are gone beyond.[26] That is, *both* knowledge of physical law *and* knowledge of mental events epistemologically or methodologically rest upon a deeper layer of lived experience which, however, phenomenology can elucidate. In doing so, opened up to phenomenological description is 'an operating or latent intentionality, like that which animates time, more ancient than the intentionality of human *acts*'.[27] Beyond the limited phenomenology of the early Husserl, Merleau-Ponty points out that

> There must be beings for us which are not yet kept in being by the centrifugal activity of consciousness: significations it does not spontaneously confer upon contents, and contexts which participate obliquely in a meaning in the sense that they indicate a meaning which remains a distant meaning and which is not yet legible in them as the monogram or stamp of thetic consciousness.[28]

In articulating this dimension of lived experience, phenomenology goes beyond the limitations of the work of the early Husserl (not only *Logical Investigations* but also *Ideas I*) by seeking out 'a network of implications beneath the 'objective material thing' in which we no longer sense the pulsations of constituting consciousness'[29] and which yields a new conception of the structure and significance of the sensible dimension of human life.

Thus, far from it being the case that phenomenology is restricted to the subjective side of the subject/object dichotomy, phenomenology now reveals that the subject/object dichotomy is blurred in *both* the lived body *and* the thing perceived. The deeper kind of intentionality at work in the later Husserl and in Merleau-Ponty is 'neither the mental subject's connecting activity nor the ideal connections of the object. It is the transition that as carnal subject I effect from one phase of movement to the other, a transition which as a matter of principle is always possible for me because I am that animal of perceptions and movements called a body'.[30] Though Merleau-Ponty continues to offer transcendental descriptions, with the distinctive features of universality and necessity that attach to *a priori* claims, the content of those descriptions now encompasses embodiment and intersubjectivity as necessary features of lived experience. Intersubjectivity is not based on an argument from analogy or projection; rather, 'it is the man as a whole who is given to me with all the possibilities (whatever they may be) that I *have in my presence to myself* in my incarnate being, the unimpeachable attestation'.[31]

What, then, of the supposedly solipsistic starting-point that defined the phenomenological reduction? Merleau-Ponty suggests that solipsism was never intended as anything more than a methodological starting-point, certainly not a substantive claim, and that as such, methodological solipsism is 'intended more to reveal than to break the links of the intentional web'.[32] What is eventually disclosed through phenomenological description is nothing other than the entanglement of self, others, and world. One's own subjective embodied experience and my experience of others as embodied beings in the world alongside me are co-constituted and inseparable. For this reason, there is no possibility of first apprehending my own embodied experience and then inquiring into the embodied subjectivity of others.

In expanding the scope of phenomenology to include embodiment and intersubjectivity within it, the very idea of the transcendental field indicated by the reduction is also transformed: 'the transcendental field has ceased to be simply the field of our thought and has become the field of the whole of experience' and that latter contains 'both the truths of consciousness and the truths of Nature'.[33] That is, both subjective consciousness and empirical explanations of natural phenomena are grounded in the whole of experience insofar as our lived experience is the necessary condition for the possibility of both sets of precisely delineated conceptual frameworks. Lived experience is not itself a conceptual framework, but the necessary condition for the possibility of any conceptual framework. Far from this being Merleau-Ponty's unique deviation from Husserl, Merleau-Ponty finds this re-orientation in the later Husserl himself, insofar as '[o]riginally a project to gain intellectual possession of the world, constitution becomes increasingly, as Husserl's thought matures, a means of unveiling a back side of things that we have not constituted'.[34] While the reduction initially seemed to culminate in transcendental *idealism*, Merleau-Ponty sketches a trajectory of Husserl's late philosophy as going beyond idealism but without returning to a naïve realism because reflection on the conditions of reflection itself reveals the terrain on which reflection rests. As Merleau-Ponty sees the importance of the later Husserl

> the picture of a well-behaved world left to us by classical philosophy had to be pushed to the limit – in order to reveal all that was left over: these beings beneath our idealizations and objectifications which secretly nourish them and in which we have difficulty recognizing noema.[35]

It is the phenomenological description of those beings that Merleau-Ponty began in *Phenomenology of Perception* and continued up until his untimely death.

Merleau-Ponty's divergence from the early (and better-known) Husserl turns on how he elaborates on embodiment as a transcendental condition of intelligibility as revealed through a transformed phenomenological *epochē*. To that extent I agree with Carman (1999) and Smith (2005) insofar as the *epochē* deployed by Merleau-Ponty discloses our bodily-grounded being in and with the world. Thus, Carman writes,

> For Merleau-Ponty ... getting out from under the cloud of the mind-body problem demands that we come to recognize the body, even purely descriptively, as the place where consciousness and reality in fact come to occupy *the very same conceptual space*.[36]

and that, unlike for (the early?) Husserl, '[t]he body, Merleau-Ponty insists, is not a thing I identify myself with only by recognizing it as the bearer of my sensations; it is a permanent primordial horizon of all my experience'.[37] Along similar lines, Smith argues that '*être au monde* is incompatible with a certain transcendental idealist and internalist reading of the *epochē*, not with the *epochē* itself'[38] and that a suitably transformed *epochē* 'reveals a fundamental, non-cognitive and pre-reflective subject-world relation that is opaque ... ambiguous and inde-terminate'.[39] The transformation of the *epochē*, whether that transformation is attributed to the later Husserl or to Merleau-Ponty himself, works in tandem with a transformation in the understanding of the being of the phenomenolo-gist herself. The *cogito* is not a transcendentally ideal ego, but rather just what it means to be a living body. On this basis Merleau-Ponty can develop a phenom-enologically rigorous description of our lived embodiment with others.

In response to questions about phenomenological method in relation to science, Merleau-Ponty remarks that 'description is not a return to immedi-ate experience; one never returns to immediate experience',[40] since to describe immediate experience is still to employ the mediation of language. In a related point, he observes that '[p]henomenology could have never come about before all the other philosophical efforts of the rationalist tradition, nor prior to the construction of our science. It measures the distance between our experience and this science'[41] and that 'description is not a return to immediate experience; one never returns to immediate experience'[42] since to describe immediate expe-rience is to employ the mediation of language. Thus, though Merleau-Ponty does not abandon the emphasis on immediate experience, he is fully aware that all immediacy is mediated.

Though Merleau-Ponty breaks with Husserl's idealism, he does not relin-quish the transcendental status of the claims being made. What is distinctive of Merleau-Ponty's philosophical method is that he brings the transcendental descriptions of phenomenology into a complex relation with the empirical explanations of psychology. (Today we might say, of neuroscience). Phenome-nological descriptions differ from both causal explanations and from conceptual analyses and explications because those descriptions give priority to explica-tion the structure of lived experience over the introduction of anything that is invoked to explain what causes that experience. This priority is central to how I understand the phenomenological reduction or *epochē*.

However, it need not be the case that the reduction aims at a complete or pure description, shorn of all explanatory vocabulary. Unlike the early Hus-serl, Merleau-Ponty points out 'we must -precisely in order to see the world and to grasp it as a paradox - rupture our familiarity with it, and this rupture can teach us nothing except the unmotivated springing forth of the world. The most important lesson which the reduction teaches us is the impossibility of a complete reduction'.[43] Romdenh-Romluc (2011) provocatively interprets this to mean that 'it is impossible to describe them [worldly entities] in a way that only captures what is given, and is free from assumptions and theories. There is no sharp line between describing something and offering an explanation of it'.[44] By acknowledging the impossibility of a complete reduction, Merleau-Ponty sets for himself the more modest task of calling our attention to the role played by various posits and explanations by noticing how they operate in what we ordinarily take to be mere descriptions. Nor does phenomenology collapse into conceptual analysis, because conceptual analysis is an *intra*-linguistic undertaking - it explicates implicit semantic content - whereas phenomenology describes the basic structures of experience. If Merleau-Ponty can vindicate this claim, we will see that, since he never arrives at a stratum of pure description spread out before a disinterested transcendental Ego, he disavows the cognitive perspective that brings the noesis-noema correlations into view.

To be sure, Merleau-Ponty holds that the reduction shows us that 'the phenomenological world is not pure being, but the sense which is revealed where the paths of my own various experiences intersect, and also where my own and other people's intersect and engage each other like gears'[45] and that this revealed sense disclosed by the reduction is just that 'the preobjective unity of the thing is correlative to the pre-objective unity of the body'.[46] Yet when we examine this sense more precisely, we see that it is not Given, since 'I say that I perceive correctly when my body has a precise hold on the spectacle, but that does not mean that my hold is all-embracing; it would be so only if I had succeeded in reducing to a state of articulate perceptions all the inner and outer horizons of the object, which is impossible'.[47] In so far as non-apperceptive consciousness is described in terms of the entanglement or intertwining of the pre-subjective body and pre-objective thing, what we find here lacks the precisely articulated structure that Husserl located in the pure Givenness of the correlation of *noesis* and *noema*. Since there is nothing here that can be fully displayed before the pure gaze of the transcendental Ego, it cannot be Given in the pernicious sense that Sellars enjoins us to avoid.

Taking the Myth in its most general form, the *Phenomenology of Perception* would run afoul of the Myth if merely having our attention immediately directed towards lived embodiment were necessary and sufficient for having any conceptualization at all. Yet if that were the case, Merleau-Ponty would not have needed to take us into the transcendental phenomenology of perception 'the long way around', going through the antinomies of empirical psychology and the strange case of Schneider, whose non-apperceivable states of consciousness come into view only because of the defects in the bodily ground of self-consciousness that provides 'the junction of sensitivity and significance'.[48] In taking the long way around, and working through the deficiencies of different psychological theories as well as the deficiencies of Schneider, we come to learn something about ourselves that has hitherto gone unnoticed: that there is a fundamentally different kind of organization and intentionality at work in perception than in thought. Likewise, in his analysis of the relationship between perception and movement, Merleau-Ponty works through both empirical psychology and *a priori* epistemology before concluding, 'we cannot, then, regard either the psychologist or the logician as vindicated, or rather both must be considered vindicated and we must find a means of recognizing thesis and antithesis as both true'.[49]

To refine further just how Merleau-Ponty avoids the Myth, I want to examine briefly his philosophical method. I take Merleau-Ponty's method to be dialectical, in a sense roughly following that of Westphal in his *Hegel's Epistemology*. Based on Westphal's explication of dialectical method, we must distinguish between (a) the conception of the object; (b) the experience of the object; (c) the experience of ourselves as cognitive subjects; and (d) our conception of ourselves as cognitive subjects. The dialectical method consists, in its most stripped-down form, of (1) noticing the discrepancy between (a) and (b); (2) a change in (c) as a result of bearing witness to that discrepancy; (3) reflecting on the discrepancy between our experience of ourselves as cognitive subjects and our conception of ourselves as cognitive subjects, and (4) revising our self-conception accordingly.[50]

Merleau-Ponty does this by working through the antinomies of theoretical psychology, thereby inviting the reader to re-orient herself towards a phenomenology of perception and embodiment. We would not have to do this if transcendental descriptions were simply Given to us (in the pernicious sense) - rather we have to engage in the conceptual activity of dialectical critique of empirical theories in order to be in the right cognitive position to appreciate the truth of transcendental descriptions.[51] Hence our awareness of the validity of transcendental description is mediated through our awareness of the contradictions of empirical explanation.

In order to disrupt the grip that the dominant theories of mind, what he calls 'empiricism' and 'intellectualism' have on us, Merleau-Ponty arranges an encounter between these theories and facts of human perception. Regardless of whether we begin with empiricism and attempt to explain experience in terms of causal interactions between atomic components ('sensations'), or with intellectualism and attempt to explain experience in terms of a unified consciousness that acts on what is given to it, we will in either case be driven to contradictions. The entanglement of explanation and description comes through vividly in Merleau-Ponty's dialectical argument for the transcendental status of motor intentionality. The radical, distinctive nature of embodied perception is best clarified by seeing its contrast from, and relation with, scientific knowledge. Merleau-Ponty works through the contradictions within empirical psychology of perception in order to shift our attention from psychology to transcendental reflection on the necessary conditions of any possible perception. Hence Merleau-Ponty's phenomenology of embodiment *neither* plays a direct cognitive semantic role with regard to knowledge *nor* is it entirely independent of sciences; it is neither epistemically or semantically efficacious, nor epistemically or semantically independent. Hence it is not Given in the Mythic sense.

By showing that neither intellectualism nor empiricism can account for the diversity of normal perceptual phenomena nor for pathological cases such as the strange case of Schneider, Merleau-Ponty is able to confront scientific theories with their own limits by showing how (a) the two dominant theories are conceptually opposed to one another; (b) the strengths of each theory are the weakness of the other; (c) neither theory is able to explain adequately all the empirical phenomena in light of its own assumptions. The situation therefore calls for a dialectical critique which exposes the shared and deep assumptions which animate the oscillation between empiricism and intellectualism. In turn, that dialectical critique puts us in the right position to appreciate the validity of the transcendental descriptions brought into view through the phenomenological method. He thereby confirms the importance of dialectics; Merleau-Ponty avoids the Myth of the Given just because the dialectical method is exactly what is required in order to liberate transcendental reflection from the Myth of the Given.

This argument does not show that there is no other version of the Myth of the Given implicit in *Phenomenology of Perception*. It does show, however, that *PP* is not only sufficiently phenomenological to be immune to the empiricist Myth of the Given, but also and sufficiently dialectical and respectful of natural science to be immune to the phenomenological Myth of the Given. On this basis I conclude that those philosophers concerned with the Myth of the Given in all of its various permutations, and who aim 'to reject the entire framework of givenness', need find nothing objectionable about Merleau-Ponty's philosophical method.

WORKS CITED

Baz, A., 'On When Words Are Called For: Cavell, McDowell, and the Wording of the World', *Inquiry*, 46:4 (2003), pp. 473–500.

Berendzen, J. C., 'Coping Without Foundations: On Dreyfus's Use of Merleau-Ponty', *International Journal of Philosophical Studies*, 18:5 (2010), pp. 629–49.

Bonjour, L., 'C. I. Lewis On the Given and Its Interpretation', *Midwest Studies in Philosophy*, 28:1 (2004), pp. 195–208.

Bourgeois, P. and S. Rosenthal, 'Merleau-Ponty, Lewis and Kant', *International Studies in Philosophy*, 15:3 (1983), pp. 13–23.

Brandom, R., *Making It Explicit* (Cambridge, MA: Harvard University Press, 1994).

—, 'Perception and Rational Constraint: McDowell's "Mind and World", *Philosophical Issues*, 7:Perception (1996), pp. 241–59.

—, *Articulating Reasons* (Cambridge, MA: Harvard University Press, 2000).

—, 'The Centrality of Sellars's Two-Ply Account of Observation to the Arguments of "Empiricism and the Philosophy of Mind"', *Tales of the Mighty Dead* (Cambridge, MA: Harvard University Press, 2002), pp. 348–67.

—, 'Overcoming a Dualism of Concepts and Causes: The Basic Argument of "Empiricism and the Philosophy of Mind"', in R. Gale (ed.), *The Blackwell Guide to Metaphysics* (Malden, MA: Blackwell, 2002), pp. 263–81.

—, 'Reply to Lance and Kukla', in B. Weiss and J. Wanderer (eds), *Reading Brandom* (New York: Routledge, 2010), pp. 316–19.

—, 'Reply to Macbeth', in B. Weiss and J. Wanderer (eds), *Reading Brandom* (New York: Routledge, 2010), pp. 338–41.

—, *Perspectives on Pragmatism* (Cambridge, MA: Harvard University Press, 2011).

Brassier, R., *Nihil Unbound* (New York: Palgrave-Macmillan, 2010).

—, 'Nominalism, Naturalism, and Materialism: Sellars's Critical Ontology', in B. Bashour and H. Muller (eds), *Contemporary Philosophical Naturalism and Its Implications* (New York: Routledge, 2014), pp. 101–14

Braver, L., *Groundless Grounds* (Cambridge, MA: The MIT Press, 2012)

Carman, T., 'The Body in Husserl and Merleau-Ponty', *Philosophical Topics*, 27:2 (1999), pp. 205–26.

—, 'Sensation, Judgment and the Phenomenal Field', in T. Carman and M. Hansen (eds),

The Cambridge Companion to Merleau-Ponty (New York: Cambridge University Press, 2004), pp. 50–73.

Churchland, P., *Plato's Camera* (Cambridge, MA: The MIT Press, 2012).

Crowther, T., 'Two Conceptions of Conceptualism and Nonconceptualism', *Erkenntnis,* 65:2 (2006), pp. 245–76.

Dayton, E., 'C. I. Lewis and the Given', *Transactions of the Charles S. Peirce Society,* 31:2 (1995), pp. 254–84.

deVries, W. and T. Triplett, *Knowledge, Mind, and the Given* (Indianapolis, IN: Hackett, 2000).

—, and P. Coates, 'Brandom's Two-Ply Error', in W. deVries (ed.), *Empiricism, Perceptual Knowledge, Normativity, and Realism* (New York: Oxford University Press 2009), pp. 131–46.

—, 'Sellars vs McDowell on the Structure of Sensory Consciousness', *Diametros,* 27 (2011), pp. 47–63.

Dillon, M., *Merleau-Ponty's Ontology* (Evanston, IL: Northwestern University Press, 1997).

Dreyfus, H., 'Overcoming the Myth of the Mental', *Topoi,* 25:1–2 (2006), pp. 43–9.

—, 'Reply to McDowell', *Inquiry,* 50:4 (2007), pp. 371–7.

—, 'The Myth of the Pervasiveness of the Mental', in J. Schear (ed.), *Mind, Reason, and Being-in-the-World* (New York: Routledge, 2013), pp. 15–40.

Evans, G., *Varieties of Reference* (New York: Oxford University Press, 1982).

Fridland, E., 'Skill Learning and Conceptual Thought', in B. Bashour and H. Muller (eds), *Contemporary Philosophical Naturalism and Its Implications* (New York: Routledge, 2014), pp. 77–100.

Gallagher, S. and K. Miyahara, 'Neo-pragmatism and Enactive Intentionality', in J. Schulkin (ed.), *Action, Perception, and the Brain* (New York: Palgrave-Macmillan, 2012), pp. 117–46.

Gaskin, R., *Experience and the World's Own Language* (New York: Oxford University Press, 2006).

Gowans, C., 'C. I. Lewis's Critique of Foundationalism in *Mind and the World Order*', *Transactions of the Charles S. Peirce Society,* 20:3 (1984), pp. 241–52.

—, 'Two Concepts of the Given in C. I. Lewis: Realism and Foundationalism', *Journal of the History of Philosophy,* 27:4 (1989), pp. 573–90.

Gunther, Y., *Essays on Nonconceptual Content* (Cambridge, MA: The MIT Press, 2003).

Hanna, R., *Kant and the Foundations of Analytic Philosophy* (New York: Oxford University Press, 2001).

—, 'Kant and Nonconceptual Content', *European Journal of Philosophy,* 13:2 (2005), pp. 247–90.

—, 'Truth in Virtue of Intentionality, Or, the Return of the Analytic-Synthetic Distinction', August 2008, at www.colorado.edu/philosophy/paper_hanna_truth_in_virtue_of_intentionality_long_version_aug08.pdf [accessed 10 May 2014].

—, 'Beyond the Myth of the Myth: A Kantian Theory of Non-Conceptual Content', *International Journal of Philosophical Studies,* 19:3 (2011), pp. 323–98.

—, 'The Myth of the Given and the Grip of the Given', *Diametros*, 27 (2011), pp. 25–46.

Haugeland, J., 'The Intentionality All-Stars', *Having Thought: Essays in the Metaphysics of Mind* (Cambridge, MA: Harvard University Press, 1998).

Hecks, R., 'Nonconceptual Content and the "Space of Reasons"', *Philosophical Review*, 109:4 (2000), pp. 483–523.

Hildebrand, D., *Beyond Realism and Anti-realism: John Dewey and the Neopragmatists* (Nashville, TN: Vanderbilt University Press, 2003).

Hook, S. (ed.), *John Dewey: Philosopher of Science and Freedom* (New York: Dial, 1950).

Hookway, C., 'Pragmatism and the Given: C. I. Lewis, Quine, and Peirce', in C. Misak (ed.), *The Oxford Handbook of American Philosophy* (New York: Oxford University Press, 2008), pp. 269–89.

Houlgate, S., 'Thought and Experience in Hegel and McDowell', *European Journal of Philosophy*, 14:2 (2006), pp. 242–61.

Husserl, E., *Cartesian Meditations*, trans. D. Cairns (Boston, MA: Kluwer Academic Publishers, 1991).

Jensen, R., 'Motor Intentionality and the Case of Schneider', *Phenomenology and the Cognitive Sciences,* 8:3 (2009), pp. 371–88.

—, 'Merleau-Ponty and McDowell on the Transparency of the Mind', *International Journal of Philosophical Studies,* 21:3 (2013), pp. 470–92.

Kant, I., *Critique of Pure Reason*, trans. P. Guyer and A. Wood (New York: Cambridge University Press, 1999).

Kraut, R., 'Universals, Metaphysical Explanations, and Pragmatism', *Journal of Philosophy*, 107:11 (2010), pp. 590–609.

Kukla, R. and M. Lance, *'Yo!', and 'Lo!'* (Cambridge, MA: Harvard University Press, 2009).

—, 'Intersubjectivity and Receptive Experience', *Southern Journal of Philosophy,* 52:1 (2014), pp. 22–42.

Lance, M., 'The Word Made Flesh: Toward a Neo-Sellarsian View of Concepts and Their Analysis', *Acta Analytica*, 15:25 (2000), pp. 117–35.

— and R. Kukla, 'Perception, Language and the First Person', in B. Weiss and J. Wanderer (eds), *Reading Brandom* (New York: Routledge, 2010), pp. 115–28.

Levine, S., 'Brandom's Pragmatism', *Transactions of the Charles S., Peirce Society* 48:2 (2012), pp. 125–40.

—, 'Norms and Habits: Brandom on the Sociality of Action', *European Journal of Philosophy*, 21:2 (2012), pp. 1–25.

Lewis, C. I., *Mind and the World Order* (New York: Dover, 1929).

—, *An Analysis of Knowledge and Valuation* (La Salle, IL: Open Court, 1946).

—, 'Reply to Hay', in P. Schilpp (ed.), *The Philosophy of C. I. Lewis* (La Salle, IL: Open Court, 1968), pp. 663–4.

—, 'Reply to Roy Wood Sellars', in P. Schilpp (ed.), *The Philosophy of C. I. Lewis* (La Salle, IL: Open Court, 1968), p. 663.

—, 'Logic and Pragmatism', in J. Goheen and J. Mothershead (eds), *Collected Papers of Clarence Irving Lewis* (Stanford, CA: Stanford University Press, 1970), pp. 3–19.

—, 'A Pragmatic Conception of the *A Priori*', in J. Goheen and J. Mothershead (eds), *Collected Papers of Clarence Irving Lewis* (Stanford, CA: Stanford University Press, 1970), pp. 231–9.

—, 'Professor Chisholm and Empiricism', in J. Goheen and J. Mothershead (eds), *Collected Papers of Clarence Irving Lewis* (Stanford, CA: Stanford University Press, 1970), pp. 317–23.

—, 'Review of John Dewey's *The Quest for Certainty*', in J. Goheen and J. Mothershead (eds), *Collected Papers of Clarence Irving Lewis* (Stanford, CA: Stanford University Press, 1970), pp. 66–77.

Macbeth, D., 'Inference, Meaning, and Truth in Brandom, Sellars, and Frege', in B. Weiss and J. Wanderer (eds), *Reading Brandom* (New York: Routledge, 2010), pp. 197–212.

Maher, C., *The Pittsburgh School* (New York: Routledge, 2012).

Matherne, S., 'The Kantian Roots of Merleau-Ponty's Account of Pathology', *British Journal for the History of Philosophy,* 22:1 (2014), pp. 124–49.

McDowell, J., *Mind and World* (Cambridge, MA: Harvard University Press, 1994).

—, 'The Disjunctive Conception of Experience as Material for a Transcendental Argument', *The Engaged Intellect: Philosophical Essays* (Cambridge, MA: Harvard, 2009), pp. 225–40.

—, 'Experiencing the World', *The Engaged Intellect: Philosophical Essays* (Cambridge, MA: Harvard University Press, 2009), pp. 243–56.

—, 'Knowledge and the Internal Revisited', *The Engaged Intellect: Philosophical Essays* (Cambridge, MA: Harvard University Press, 2009), pp. 279–87.

—, 'Naturalism in Philosophy of Mind', *The Engaged Intellect: Philosophical Essays* (Cambridge, MA: Harvard University Press), pp. 257–75.

—, 'Reply to Dreyfus', *Inquiry*, 50:4 (2007), pp. 366–70, reprinted in J. McDowell, *The Engaged Intellect: Philosophical Essays* (Cambridge, MA: Harvard University Press, 2009), pp. 324–8.

—, 'What Myth', *Inquiry,* 50:4 (2007), pp. 338–51, reprinted in J. McDowell, *The Engaged Intellect: Philosophical Essays* (Cambridge, MA: Harvard University Press, 2009), pp. 308–23.

—, 'Avoiding the Myth of the Given', *Having the World In View: Essays on Kant, Hegel and Sellars* (Cambridge, MA: Harvard University Press, 2009), pp. 256–72.

—, 'Hegel's Idealism as Radicalization of Kant', *Having the World in View: Essays on Kant, Hegel and Sellars* (Cambridge, MA: Harvard University Press, 2009), pp. 69–89.

—, 'Intentionality as a Relation', *Having the World In View: Essays on Kant, Hegel and Sellars* (Cambridge, MA: Harvard University Press, 2009), pp. 44–65.

—, 'The Logical Form of an Intuition', *Having the World In View: Essays on Kant, Hegel and Sellars* (Cambridge, MA: Harvard University Press, 2009), pp. 23–43.

—, 'Sellars on Perceptual Experience', *Having the World In View: Essays on Kant, Hegel and Sellars* (Cambridge, MA: Harvard University Press, 2009), pp. 3–22.

—, 'Why is Sellars's Essay called "*Empiricism* and the Philosophy of Mind"', *Having the World In View: Essays on Kant, Hegel and Sellars* (Cambridge, MA: Harvard University

Press, 2009), pp. 221–38.

—, 'Reply to Lovibond', in J. Lindgaard (ed.), *John McDowell: Experience, Norm, and Nature* (Malden, MA: Blackwell, 2009), pp. 234–8.

—, 'Brandom on Observation', in B. Weiss and J. Wanderer (eds), *Reading Brandom* (New York: Routledge, 2010), pp. 129–44.

—, 'The Myth of the Mind as Detached', in J. Schear (ed.), *Mind, Reason, and Being-in-the-World* (New York: Routledge, 2013), pp. 41–58.

Meillassoux, Q., *After Finitude*, trans. R. Brassier (New York: Continuum, 2009).

Merleau-Ponty, M., 'The Philosopher and His Shadow', *Signs*, trans. R. McClerary (Chicago, IL: Northwestern University Press, 1964), pp. 159–81.

—, 'The Primacy of Perception and Its Philosophical Consequences', in J., Edie (trans. and ed.), *The Primacy of Perception* (Chicago, IL: Northwestern University Press, 1964), pp. 12–42.

—, *Phenomenology of Perception*, trans. D. Landes (New York: Routledge, 2012).

Misak, C., *The American Pragmatists* (New York: Oxford, 2013).

Moran, D., 'The Phenomenology of Embodiment: Intertwining and Reflexivity', in R. Jensen and D. Moran (eds), *The Phenomenology of Embodied Subjectivity* (New York: Springer, 2013), pp. 285–304.

Muller, H., 'Naturalism and Intentionality', in B. Bashour and H. Muller (eds), *Contemporary Philosophical Naturalism and Its Implications* (New York: Routledge, 2013), pp. 155–81.

Murphey, M., *C. I. Lewis: The Last Great Pragmatist* (Albany, NY: SUNY Press, 2005).

—, 'C. I. Lewis', in J. Shook and J. Margolis (eds), *A Companion to Pragmatism* (Malden, MA: Blackwell, 2009), pp. 94–100.

Okrent, M., *Rational Animals* (Athens, OH: Ohio University Press, 2007).

—, 'Heidegger's Pragmatism Redux', in A., Malachowski (ed.), *The Cambridge Companion to Pragmatism* (New York: Cambridge University Press, 2013), pp. 124–58.

O'Shea, J., *Wilfrid Sellars: Naturalism with a Normative Turn* (Malden, MA: Polity, 2007).

O'Shea, J., 'Conceptual Thinking and Nonconceptual Content: A Sellarsian Divide', in J. O'Shea and E. Rubinstein (eds), *Self, Language and World* (Atascadero, CA: Ridgeview, 2010), pp. 205–28.

Pihlström, S., *Naturalizing the Transcendental* (New York: Humanity Books, 2003).

Pippin, R., 'What is "Conceptual Activity"?', in J., Schear (ed.), *Mind, Reason, and Being-in-the-World* (New York: Routledge, 2013), pp. 91–109.

Price, H., *Expressivism, Pragmatism, and Representationalism* (New York: Cambridge University Press, 2013).

Redding, P., *Analytic Philosophy and the Return of Hegelian Thought* (New York: Cambridge University Press, 2007).

Reuter, M., 'Merleau-Ponty's Notion of Pre-reflective Intentionality', *Synthese,* 118:1 (1999), pp. 69–88.

Romdenh-Romluc, K., *Merleau-Ponty and the Phenomenology of Perception* (New York:

Routledge, 2010).

—, 'Habit and Attention', in R. Jensen and D. Moran (eds), *The Phenomenology of Embodied Subjectivity* (New York: Springer, 2013), pp. 3–20.

Rorty, R., *Philosophy and the Mirror of Nature* (Princeton, NJ: Princeton University Press, 1979).

—, 'Introduction', *Empiricism and the Philosophy of Mind* (Cambridge, MA: Harvard University Press, 1997), pp. 1–12.

Rosenberg, A., 'Disenchanted Naturalism', in B. Bashour and H. Muller (eds), *Contemporary Philosophical Naturalism and Its Implications* (New York: Routledge, 2014), pp. 17–37.

Rosenberg, J., *The Thinking Self* (Atascadero, CA: Ridgeview, 1986).

—, *Accessing Kant: A Relaxed Introduction* (New York: Oxford University Press, 2005).

Rosenthal, S., 'C. I. Lewis and the Sense of Sense Meaning', *The Southern Journal of Philosophy*, 9:3 (1971), pp. 313–26.

— and P. Bourgeois, 'Merleau-Ponty, Lewis and Ontological Presence', *Philosophical Topics*, 13:2 (1985), pp. 239–46.

—, *C. I. Lewis in Focus: The Pulse of Pragmatism* (Indianapolis, IN: Indiana University Press, 2007).

Rouse, J., 'What is Conceptually Articulated Understanding?', in J. Schear (ed.), *Mind, Reason, and Being-in-the-World* (New York: Routledge, 2013), pp. 250–71.

Sachs, C., 'The Shape of a Good Question: McDowell, Evolution, and Transcendental Philosophy', *The Philosophical Forum*, 42:1 (2011), pp. 61–78.

—, 'Resisting the Disenchantment of Nature: McDowell and the Question of Animal Minds', *Inquiry*, 55:2 (2012), pp. 131–47.

—, 'Discursive and Somatic Intentionality: Merleau-Ponty Contra 'Sellars or McDowell'' *International Journal of Philosophical Studies*, 22:2 (2014), pp. 199–227.

Schear, J. (ed.), *Mind, Reason, and Being-in-the-World* (New York: Routledge, 2013).

Schellenberg, S., 'Sellarsian Perspectives on Perception and Non-Conceptual Content', in M. Wolf and M. Lance (eds), *The Self-Correcting Enterprise* (New York: Rodopi, 2006), pp. 173–96.

Sedgwick, S., 'McDowell's Hegelianism', *European Journal of Philosophy*, 5:1 (1997), pp. 21–38.

Sellars, R., 'Review of *Experience and Nature* by John Dewey', *The Journal of Religion*, 6:1 (1926), pp. 89–91.

—, *The Philosophy of Physical Realism* (New York: The Macmillan Company, 1932).

—, 'Inference and Meaning', *Mind*, 62 (1953), pp. 313–38.

—, 'Some Reflections on Language Games', *Philosophy of Science*, 21:3 (1954), pp. 204–28.

—, 'Sensations as Guides to Perceiving', *Mind*, 68:269 (1959), pp. 2–15.

Sellars, W., 'Physical Realism', *Philosophical Perspectives* (Springfield, IL: Charles C. Thomas, 1959), pp. 185–208.

—, 'Being and Being Known', *Science, Perception and Reality* (Atascadero, CA: Ridgeview, 1963), pp. 41–59.

—, 'Empiricism and the Philosophy of Mind', *Science, Perception and Reality* (Atascadero, CA: Ridgeview, 1963), pp. 127–96.

—, 'Is There a Synthetic "*A Priori*"?', *Science, Perception and Reality* (Atascadero, CA: Ridgeview, 1963), pp. 298–320.

—, 'The Language of Theories', *Science, Perception and Reality* (Atascadero, CA: Ridgeview, 1963), pp. 106–26.

—, 'Philosophy and the Scientific Image of Man', *Science, Perception and Reality* (Atascadero, CA: Ridgeview Press, 1963), pp. 1–40.

—, 'Truth and Correspondence', *Science, Perception and Reality* (Atascadero, CA: Ridgeview, 1963), pp. 197–224.

—, *Science and Metaphysics* (Atascadero, CA: Ridgeview, 1967).

—, 'Autobiographical Reflections', in H. Castañeda (ed.), *Action, Knowledge, and Reality* (Indianapolis, IN: The Bobbs-Merrill Company, 1975), pp. 277–93.

—, 'The Structure of Knowledge" in H. Castañeda (ed.), *Action, Knowledge and Reality* (Indianapolis, IN: The Bobbs-Merrill Company, 1975), pp. 295–347.

—, 'Language, Rules and Behavior', in J. Sicha (ed.), *Pure Pragmatics and Possible Worlds: The Early Essays of Wilfrid Sellars* (Reseda, CA: Ridgeview Publishing Company, 1980), pp. 129–55.

—, 'The Carus Lectures', *The Monist*, 64:1 (1981), pp. 3–90.

—, 'The Role of the Imagination in Kant's Theory of Experience', in J. Sicha (ed.), *Kant's Transcendental Metaphysics* (Atascadero, CA: Ridgeview Press, 2002), pp. 419–30.

—, 'Some Reflections on Perceptual Consciousness', in J. Sicha (ed.), *Kant's Transcendental Metaphysics* (Atascadero, CA: Ridgeview Press, 2002), pp. 431–41.

—, 'Some Remarks on Kant's Theory of Experience', in J. Sicha (ed.), *Kant's Transcendental Metaphysics* (Atascadero, CA: Ridgeview Press, 2002), pp. 269–82.

—, 'The Lever of Archimedes', in K. Scharp and R. Brandom (eds), *In the Space of Reasons* (Cambridge, MA: Harvard University Press, 2007), pp. 229–57.

—, 'Meaning as Functional Classification', in K. Scharp and R. Brandom (eds), *In the Space of Reasons* (Cambridge, MA: Harvard University Press, 2007), pp. 81–100.

—, 'Mental Events', in K. Scharp and R. Brandom (eds), *In the Space of Reasons* (Cambridge, MA: Harvard University Press, 2007), pp. 282–300.

Sinclair, R., 'Quine and Conceptual Pragmatism', *Transactions of the Charles S. Peirce Society*, 48:3 (2013), pp. 335–55.

Smith, J., 'Merleau-Ponty and the Phenomenological Reduction.', *Inquiry*, 48:6 (2005), pp. 553–71.

Soffer, G., 'Revisiting the Myth: Husserl and Sellars on the Given', *Review of Metaphysics*, 57:2 (2003), pp. 301–37.

Speaks, J., 'Is There a Problem About Nonconceptual Content?', *Philosophical Review*, 114:3 (2005), pp. 359–98.

Strawson, P., *Individuals* (New York: Routledge Press, 1959).

—, *The Bounds of Sense* (New York: Routledge Press, 1966).

Talisse, R. and S. Aikin (eds), *The Pragmatism Reader* (Princeton, NJ: Princeton University Press, 2011).

Thompson, E., 'Review of *Phenomenology and Naturalism: Examining the Relationship between Human Experience and Nature*', ed. H. Carel and D. Meacham, *Notre Dame Philosophical Reviews*, 10 July 2014, at http://ndpr.nd.edu/news/49272-phenomenology-and-naturalism-examining-the-relationship-between-human-experience-and-nature/ [accessed 11 July 2014].

Todes, S., *Body and World* (Cambridge, MA: The MIT Press, 2001).

Toribio, J., 'State Versus Content: The Unfair Trial of Perceptual Nonconceptualism', *Erkenntnis*, 69:3 (2008), pp. 351–61.

Turner, S., *Explaining the Normative* (Malden, MA: Polity, 2010).

Westphal, K., *Hegel's Epistemology* (Indianapolis, IN: Hackett, 2003).

—, 'Kant's *Critique of Pure Reason* and Analytic Philosophy', in P. Guyer (ed.), *The Cambridge Companion to Kant's Critique of Pure Reason* (New York: Cambridge University Press, 2010), pp. 401–30.

—, 'Analytic Philosophy and the Long Tail of *Scientia*', *The Owl of Minerva*, 42:1–2 (2010–11), pp. 1–18.

—, 'Self-Consciousness, Anti-Cartesianism, and Cognitive Semantics in Hegel's 1807 *Phenomenology*', in S. Houlgate and M. Baur (eds), *A Companion to Hegel* (Malden, MA: Blackwell, 2011), pp. 68–90.

Wheeler, M., 'Science Friction: Phenomenology, Naturalism, and Cognitive Science', in H. Carel and D. Meacham (eds), *Phenomenology and Naturalism* (New York: Cambridge University Press, 2013), pp 135–68.

Williams, M., *Groundless Belief* (Princeton, NJ: Princeton University Press, 1999).

Wittgenstein, L., *Philosophical Investigations*, trans. G. E. M. Anscombe, P. M. S. Hacker and J. Schulte (Malden, MA: Blackwell, 2009).

Wrathall, M., 'Motives, Reasons, and Causes', in T. Carman and M. Hansen (eds), *The Cambridge Companion to Merleau-Ponty* (New York: Cambridge University Press, 2004), pp. 111–28.

Zack, N., 'Murray Murphey's Work and C., I., Lewis's Epistemology: Problems with Realism and the Context of Logical Positivism', *Transactions of the Charles S. Peirce Society*, 42:1 (2006), pp. 32–44.

Zahavi, D., 'Merleau-Ponty on Husserl: A Reappraisal', in T. Toadvine and L. Embree (eds), *Merleau-Ponty's Reading of Husserl* (New York: Springer, 2002), pp. 3–30.

—, *Husserl's Phenomenology* (Stanford, CA: Stanford University Press, 2003).

—, 'Mindedness, Mindlessness, and First-Person Authority', in J. Schear (ed.), *Mind, Reason, and Being-in-the-World* (New York: Routledge, 2013), pp. 320–43.

NOTES

Introduction: Why a New Account of Intentionality?

1. The idea of 'cognitive semantics' as distinct from epistemology is central to Hanna on Kant and Westphal on Hegel. See R. Hanna, *Kant and the Foundations of Analytic Philosophy* (New York: Oxford University Press, 2001) and K. Westpha, 'Self-Consciousness, Anti-Cartesianism, and Cognitive Semantics in Hegel's 1807 *Phenomenology*', in S. Houlgate and M. Baur (eds), *A Companion to Hegel* (Malden, MA: Blackwell, 2011), pp. 68–90.
2. This use of 'bifurcated' is indebted to Huw Price's 'new bifurcation thesis' about representation, though comparing his account with mine exceeds the scope of the present work. See H. Price, *Expressivism, Pragmatism, and Representationalism* (New York: Cambridge University Press, 2013).
3. W. Sellars, *Science and Metaphysics* (Atascadero, CA: Ridgeview, 1967), p. 1. Conversely, only those committed to a Platonic picture of concepts would be fully entitled to completely separate philosophy from its history; see K. Westphal, 'Analytic Philosophy and the Long Tail of *Scientia*', *The Owl of Minerva*, 42:1–2 (2010/11), pp. 1–18.
4. For 'the eclipse narrative', see R. Talisse and S. Aikin (eds), *The Pragmatism Reader* (Princeton, NJ: Princeton University Press, 2011), pp. 5–8. See also C. Misak, *The American Pragmatists* (New York: Oxford University Press, 2013) for a new history of American pragmatism that explicitly rejects the eclipse narrative.

1 Intentionality and the Problem of Transcendental Friction

1. J. Haugeland, 'The Intentionality All-Stars', *Having Thought: Essays in the Metaphysics of Mind* (Cambridge, MA: Harvard University Press, 1998), p. 128.
2. Haugeland, 'The Intentionality All-Stars', pp. 160–1.
3. For a more detailed explication of transcendental naturalism, see S. Pihlström, *Naturalizing the Transcendental* (New York: Humanity Books, 2003).
4. A. Rosenberg, 'Disenchanted Naturalism', in B. Bashour and H. Muller (eds), *Contemporary Philosophical Naturalism and Its Implications* (New York: Routledge, 2014), pp. 17–37, on p. 27.
5. W. Sellars, 'Empiricism and the Philosophy of Mind', *Science, Perception, and Reality* (Atascadero, CA: Ridgeview Press, 1963), section 1, pp. 127–96, on pp. 127–8.
6. See 'Appendix: Is Phenomenology Committed to the Myth of the Given?' for whether there is a specifically phenomenological version of the myth.

7. See Y. Gunther, *Essays on Nonconceptual Content* (Cambridge, MA: The MIT Press, 2003).

8. See the following: R. Hecks, 'Nonconceptual Content and the "Space of Reasons"', *Philosophical Review*, 109:4 (2000), pp. 483–523; J. Speaks, 'Is There a Problem About Nonconceptual Content?', *Philosophical Review*, 114:3 (2005), pp. 359–98; T. Crowther, 'Two Conceptions of Conceptualism and Nonconceptualism', *Erkenntnis*, 65:2 (2006), pp. 245–76; and J. Toribio, 'State Versus Content: The Unfair Trial of Perceptual Nonconceptualism', *Erkenntnis*, 69:3 (2008), pp. 351–61.

9. Toribio, 'State Versus Content', p. 354.

10. Toribio, 'State Versus Content', p. 354.

11. C. I. Lewis, *Mind and the World Order* (New York: Dover, 1929).

12. Lewis, *Mind and the World Order*, p. 37.

13. Lewis, *Mind and the World Order*, p. 54.

14. The Quinean phrase is not accidental; for Quine's debt to Lewis, see R. Sinclair, 'Quine and Conceptual Pragmatism', *Transactions of the Charles S. Peirce Society*, 48:3 (2013), pp. 335–55.

15. Lewis, *Mind and the World Order*, p. 65.

16. W. Sellars, *Science and Metaphysics* (Atascadero, CA: Ridgeview), 1967.

17. W. Sellars, 'Empiricism and the Philosophy of Mind', *Science, Perception and Reality* (Atascadero, CA: Ridgeview, 1963), section 7, p. 133.

18. W. Sellars, 'The Carus Lectures', *The Monist*, 64:1 (1981), pp. 3–90.

19. For this way of seeing the problem, see D. Macbeth, 'Inference, Meaning, and Truth in Brandom, Sellars, and Frege' in B. Weiss and J. Wanderer (eds), *Reading Brandom* (New York: Routledge, 2010), pp. 197–212. Though this may be thought similar to Davidson's view, Sellars's emphasis on the 'guidance' of receptivity brings him into much closer proximity to existential phenomenology than Davidson– a point that shall be exploited in the contrast between Sellars and Merleau-Ponty in Chapter 5.

20. J. McDowell, *Mind and World* (Cambridge, MA: Harvard University Press, 1994), p. 11.

21. J. McDowell, 'Intentionality as a Relation', *Having the World In View: Essays on Kant, Hegel and Sellars* (Cambridge, MA: Harvard University Press, 2009), pp. 44–65; J. McDowell, 'The Logical Form of an Intuition', *Having the World In View: Essays on Kant, Hegel and Sellars* (Cambridge, MA: Harvard University Press, 2009), pp. 23–43; and J. McDowell, 'Sellars on Perceptual Experience', *Having the World In View: Essays on Kant, Hegel and Sellars* (Cambridge, MA: Harvard University Press, 2009), pp. 3–22.

22. McDowell, 'Sellars on Perceptual Experience', p. 12.

23. J. McDowell, 'Avoiding the Myth of the Given' in *Having the World In View: Essays on Kant, Hegel and Sellars* (Cambridge, MA: Harvard University Press, 2009), pp. 256–72.

24. For further exploration of this difference in 'mode', see R. Pippin, 'What is "Conceptual Activity"?' in J. Schear (ed.), *Mind, Reason, and Being-in-the-World* (New York: Routledge, 2013), pp. 91–109.

2 The Epistemic Given and the Semantic Given in C. I. Lewis

1. C. Misak, *The American Pragmatists* (New York: Oxford, 2013), pp. 218–19.

2. R. Hanna, 'Beyond the Myth of the Myth: A Kantian Theory of Non-Conceptual Content', *International Journal of Philosophical Studies*, 19:3 (2011), pp. 323–98, on pp. 326–7. It should be noted that neither Beck nor Sellars were Lewis's PhD students.

Sellars did take Lewis's theory of knowledge seminar in 1937 but never wrote a dissertation proposal or formed a committee at Harvard University. Beck wrote his MA and
PhD at Duke University.

3. Lewis reports that, upon finishing his dissertation under Royce and Perry, Royce said
to him, 'I thought you were principally influenced by Perry, but I find he thinks you are
principally influenced by me. Between us, we agreed that perhaps this is original'; C. I.
Lewis, 'Logic and Pragmatism', in J. Goheen and J. Mothershead (eds), *Collected Papers of
Clarence Irving Lewis* (Stanford, CA: Stanford University Press, 1970), pp. 3–19, on p. 4.

4. R. Rorty, Richard, 'Introduction', *Empiricism and the Philosophy of Mind* (Cambridge,
MA: Harvard University Press, 1997), p. 3.

5. For a recent and compelling reconstruction of 'analytic Hegelianism' on the route from
Sellars to Brandom and McDowell, see P. Redding, *Analytic Philosophy and the Return
of Hegelian Thought* (New York: Cambridge University Press, 2007).

6. The interpretation of the Given as involving 'epistemic independence' and 'epistemic
efficacy' is based on W. deVries and T. Triplett, *Knowledge, Mind, and the Given* (Indianapolis, IN: Hackett, 2000).

7. C. I. Lewis, 'A Pragmatic Conception of the *A Priori*', in J. Goheen and J. Mothershead
(eds), *Collected Papers of Clarence Irving Lewis* (Stanford, CA: Stanford University
Press, 1970), pp. 231–9.

8. C. I. Lewis, *Mind and the World Order* (New York: Dover, 1929), p. 37.

9. Lewis, *Mind and the World Order*, p. 37.

10. C. Hookway, 'Pragmatism and the Given: C. I. Lewis, Quine, and Peirce' in C. Misak
(ed.), *The Oxford Handbook of American Philosophy* (New York: Oxford University
Press, 2008), pp. 269–89, on p. 274.

11. *Contra* Bonjour, the given does not play a direct epistemic role, though it does play a
semantic role; see L. Bonjour, 'C. I. Lewis On the Given and Its Interpretation', *Midwest
Studies in Philosophy*, 28:1 (2004), pp. 195–208. A similar conflation between 'cognitive experience' and 'knowledge' can be found in M. Williams's criticism of Lewis; see
Williams *Groundless Belief* (Princeton, NJ: Princeton University Press, 1999), p. 27.

12. Lewis, *Mind and the World Order*, pp. 38–9.

13. Lewis, *Mind and the World Order*, pp. 52–3; cf. p. 66.

14. Lewis, *Mind and the World Order*, p. 54.

15. Lewis, *Mind and the World Order*, p. 63.

16. Lewis, *Mind and the World Order*, p. 77.

17. Lewis, *Mind and the World Order*, p. 80.

18. Lewis, *Mind and the World Order*, p. 258.

19. Lewis, *Mind and the World Order*, pp. 262–3.

20. I. Kant, *Critique of Pure Reason*, trans. P. Guyer and A. Wood (New York: Cambridge,
1999) section A 51/B 75.

21. Hookway, 'Pragmatism and the Given', p. 276.

22. Cf. Lewis, *Mind and the World Order*, p. 115: 'the sharing of a common "reality" is, at
some point, the aim and result of social cooperation, not an initial social datum prereq-
uisite to common knowledge'.

23. Lewis, *Mind and the World Order*, pp. 258–9.

24. Lewis, *Mind and the World Order*, p. 120.

25. 'Nothing is real in all categories; everything is real in some category'; Lewis, *Mind and
the World Order*, p. 321.

26. Lewis, *Mind and the World Order*, pp. 130.

27. Lewis, *Mind and the World Order*, p.144.

28. Lewis, *Mind and the World Order*, p. 144. Individual qualia cannot ground conceptual applications, since they have no temporal spread and no names; Lewis, *Mind and the World Order*, p. 61.
29. Lewis, *Mind and the World Order*, p. 310.
30. Lewis, *Mind and the World Order*, p. 131.
31. C. I. Lewis, *An Analysis of Knowledge and Valuation* (La Salle, IL: Open Court, 1946), pp. 171–72.
32. Lewis, *An Analysis of Knowledge and Valuation*, p. 182.
33. Lewis, *An Analysis of Knowledge and Valuation*, p. 183.
34. Lewis, *An Analysis of Knowledge and Valuation*, p. 188.
35. Lewis, *An Analysis of Knowledge and Valuation*, p. 205.
36. Lewis, *An Analysis of Knowledge and Valuation*, p. 184.
37. Lewis, *An Analysis of Knowledge and Valuation*, p. 189.
38. See Lewis, *An Analysis of Knowledge and Valuation*,
39.   pp. 16–20.
40. C. Gowans, 'C. I. Lewis's Critique of Foundationalism in *Mind and the World Order*', *Transactions of the Charles S. Peirce Society*, 20:3 (1984), pp. 241–52; and C. Gowans, 'Two Concepts of the Given in C. I. Lewis: Realism and Foundationalism', *Journal of the History of Philosophy*, 27:4 (1989), pp. 573–90.
41. E. Dayton, 'C. I. Lewis and the Given', *Transactions of the Charles S. Peirce Society*, 31:2 (1995), pp. 254–84; and S. Rosenthal, *C. I. Lewis in Focus: The Pulse of Pragmatism* (Indianapolis, IN: Indiana University Press, 2007).
42. Bonjour notes this shift in L. Bonjour, 'C. I. Lewis On the Given and Its Interpretation', *Midwest Studies in Philosophy*, 28:1 (2004), pp. 195–208, on p. 200, but says little about it, since his foremost concern is defending what he takes to be the epistemological foundationalism of AKV.
43. M. Murphey, *C. I. Lewis: The Last Great Pragmatist* (Albany, NY: SUNY Press, 2005).
44. C. Hookway, 'Pragmatism and the Given: C. I. Lewis, Quine, and Peirce', in C. Misak (ed.), *The Oxford Handbook of American Philosophy* (New York: Oxford University Press, 2008), pp. 269–89, on pp. 287–8.
45. C. I. Lewis, 'Review of John Dewey's *The Quest for Certainty*', in J. Goheen and J. Mothershead (eds), *Collected Papers of Clarence Irving Lewis* (Stanford, CA: Stanford University Press, 1970), pp. 66–77, on pp. 68–9.
46. In what follows, I put 'Augustinian' in quotes to put the focus on Wittgenstein's understanding of Augustine, rather than on what Augustine himself thought.
47. C. I. Lewis, *An Analysis of Knowledge and Valuation*, (La Salle, IL: Open Court, 1946), p. 39.
48. On the central role of sense meanings, see S. Rosenthal, 'C. I. Lewis and the Sense of Sense Meaning', *The Southern Journal of Philosophy*, 9:3 (1971), pp. 313–26.
49. Lewis, *An Analysis of Knowledge and Valuation*, p. 37.
50. Lewis, *An Analysis of Knowledge and Valuation*, p. 141.
51. Lewis, *An Analysis of Knowledge and Valuation*, p. 141.
52. M. Murphey, *C. I. Lewis: The Last Great Pragmatist*, (Albany, NY: SUNY Press, 2005), p. 289.
53. Lewis, *An Analysis of Knowledge and Valuation*, p. 141.
54. Lewis's transcendental argument offers strong historico-textual support for McDowell's claim that the need to avoid the threat of 'frictionless spinning in the void' sustains the Myth of the Given; see Chapter 4.

55. Lewis, *An Analysis of Knowledge and Valuation*, p. 72.
56. Lewis, *An Analysis of Knowledge and Valuation*, p. 134.
57. Rosenthal, 'C. I. Lewis and the Sense of Sense Meaning', p. 319.
58. R. Hanna, 'Truth in Virtue of Intentionality, Or, the Return of the Analytic-Synthetic Distinction', August 2008, at http://www.colorado.edu/philosophy/paper_hanna_truth_in_virtue_of_intentionality_long_version_aug08.pdf [accessed 10 May 2014].
59. L. Wittgenstein, *Philosophical Investigations*, trans. and ed. P. Hacker and J. Schulte (Malden, MA: Blackwell, 2009), p. 5, section 1.
60. L. Braver, *Groundless Grounds* (Cambridge, MA: The MIT Press, 2012), pp. 68–9.
61. N. Zack, 'Murray Murphey's Work and C. I. Lewis's Epistemology: Problems With Realism and the Context of Logical Positivism', *Transactions of the Charles S. Peirce Society*, 42:1 (2006), pp. 32–44, on p. 37. I regard this problem as more pervasive than Zack does, since it holds of the very distinction between 'sense meaning' and 'linguistic meaning', and not just of the pre-linguistically identifiable given.
62. C. I. Lewis, *Mind and the World Order* (New York: Dover, 1929), p. 71.
63. M. Murphey, 'C. I. Lewis', in J. Shook and J. Margolis (eds), *A Companion to Pragmatism* (Malden, MA: Blackwell, 2009), pp. 94–100, on p. 97.

3 Discursive Intentionality and 'Nonconceptual Content' in Sellars

1. I will leave aside the historical-textual questions as to the transmission of Wittgenstein's late thought to Sellars. Suffice it to say that, at least by 1954, when Sellars wrote 'Some Reflections of Language Games', he seems to have been well-acquainted with Wittgenstein's criticism of the 'Augustinian' picture of language, the inconceivability of a private language, and the problem of rule-following.
2. W. deVries, 'Sellars vs McDowell on the Structure of Sensory Consciousness', *Diametros*, 27 (2011), pp. 47–63, on pp. 61–2.
3. R. Sellars, 'Sensations as Guides to Perceiving', *Mind*, 68:269 (1959), pp. 2–15.
4. R. Sellars, 'Review of *Experience and Nature* by John Dewey'. *The Journal of Religion* 6:1 (1926), pp. 89–91. With regard to how both RWS and Lewis misinterpreted Dewey, see D. Hildebrand, *Beyond Realism and Anti-realism: John Dewey and the Neopragmatists* (Nashville, TN: Vanderbilt University Press, 2003).
5. R. Sellars, *The Philosophy of Physical Realism* (New York: The Macmillan Company, 1932), p. 7.
6. Sellars, *The Philosophy of Physical Realism*, p. 151.
7. Sellars, *The Philosophy of Physical Realism*, p. 122.
8. Sellars, *The Philosophy of Physical Realism*, pp. 144–5.
9. Sellars, *The Philosophy of Physical Realism*, p. 146.
10. Sellars, *The Philosophy of Physical Realism*, p. 152.
11. C. I. Lewis, *An Analysis of Knowledge and Valuation* (La Salle, IL: Open Court, 1946), p. 200, n. 5.
12. Lewis, *An Analysis of Knowledge and Valuation*, p. 200.
13. Lewis, *An Analysis of Knowledge and Valuation*, p. 201.
14. Lewis, *An Analysis of Knowledge and Valuation*, p. 201.
15. Lewis, *An Analysis of Knowledge and Valuation*, p. 202.
16. C. I. Lewis, *Mind and the World Order* (New York: Dover, 1929), p. 425.

17. Elsewhere Lewis indicates that he does not think physicalism is correct: 'But I regard physicalism as an unsound metaphysical and epistemological doctrine and – where it touches the valuational and the normative – one which can be demoralizing. I happily conjecture that recent developments in physics itself will soon enforce the conclusion that the physical is altogether too metaphysical to represent any *pou sto* for philosophy'. C. I. Lewis, 'Reply to Hay', in P. Schilpp (ed)., *The Philosophy of C. I. Lewis* (La Salle, IL: Open Court, 1968), p. 664. RWS's invocation of Spinoza and Nietzsche shows that he would not regard physicalism as 'demoralizing' with respect to values and norms.

18. Lewis, 'Reply to Hay', p. 426.

19. Lewis, 'Reply to Hay', p. 426.

20. In his 1968 response to RWS, who insists on the interdependence of metaphysics and epistemology, Lewis remarks, "In those days [the 1920s–1940s] we recognized clearly that one could not discuss epistemology without reference to metaphysics, or metaphysics without reference to epistemology. Sellars has stood sturdily by that conviction, and here re-emphasizes it. I have not done so well. Whenever I make attempt on metaphysics, it always comes out epistemology. But that represents no decision I make or conviction I have; simply I seem unable to do otherwise'; C. I. Lewis, 'Reply to Roy Wood Sellars', in P. Schilpp (ed)., *The Philosophy of C. I. Lewis* (La Salle, IL: Open Court, 1968), p. 663.

21. W. Sellars, 'Autobiographical Reflections', in H. Castañeda (ed.), *Action, Knowledge, and Reality* (Indianapolis, IN: The Bobbs-Merrill Company, 1975), pp. 277–93, on p. 287.

22. W. Sellars, 'Physical Realism', in *Philosophical Perspectives* (Springfield, IL: Charles C. Thomas, 1959), pp. 185–208.

23. Sellars, 'Physical Realism', p. 208.

24. Sellars, 'Physical Realism', p. 193.

25. Sellars, 'Physical Realism', p. 195.

26. Sellars, 'Physical Realism', pp. 202–4.

27. Lewis did not become completely clear that the second conditional is probabilistic until his dialogue with Reichenbach and Chisholm; see C. I. Lewis, 'Professor Chisholm and Empiricism', in J. Goheen and J. Mothershead (eds)., *The Collected Papers of Clarence Irving Lewis* (Stanford, CA: Stanford University Press, 1970), pp. 317–23. Rosenthal stresses the distinction between these implication relations, where the distinction is drawn between 'strict implication' between non-terminating and terminating judgement and the 'real relations' holding within the terminating judgement. See S. Rosenthal, *C. I. Lewis in Focus: The Pulse of Pragmatism* (Indianapolis, IN: Indiana University Press, 2007), p. 82ff.

28. Sellars, 'Physical Realism', p. 205.

29. Sellars, 'Physical Realism', p. 207.

30. W. Sellars, 'Truth and 'Correspondence', *Science, Perception and Reality* (Atascadero, CA: Ridgeview, 1963), pp. 197–224, on p. 216. That 'espousal of principles must be reflected in uniformity of behavior' is what O'Shea calls 'the norm/nature meta-principle'. J. O'Shea, *Wilfrid Sellars: Naturalism with a Normative Turn* (Malden, MA: Polity, 2007), pp. 50, 61–2.

31. Sellars returns to this point in the example of John the neck-tie salesman in W. Sellars, 'Empiricism and the Philosophy of Mind',*Science, Perception and Reality* (Atascadero, CA: Ridgeview, 1963), sections 14–18, p. 47: 'We thus see that "x is red ≡ x looks red to standard observers in standard conditions" is a necessary truth *not* because the

right-hand side is the definition of "x is red", but because "standard conditions" means conditions in which things look like what they are'.

32. W. Sellars, 'Is There a Synthetic "A Priori"?', *Science, Perception and Reality* (Atascadero, CA: Ridgeview, 1963), pp. 298–320.

33. W. Sellars, 'Inference and Meaning', *Mind*, 62 (1953), pp. 313–38.

34. W. Sellars, 'Some Reflections on Language Games', *Philosophy of Science*, 21:3 (1954), pp. 204–28.

35. For the campaign conducted by White, Quine and Goodman against Lewis, see M. Murphey, *C. I. Lewis: The Last Great Pragmatist* (Albany, NY: SUNY Press, 2005), pp. 320–31; see also C. Misak, *The American Pragmatists* (New York: Oxford University Press, 2013), pp. 195–6.

36. S. Hook (ed.), *John Dewey: Philosopher of Science and Freedom* (New York: Dial, 1950). In fact, White's article immediately follows Sellars's.

37. Sellars, 'Is There a Synthetic "*A Priori*"?', p. 309.

38. Sellars, 'Is There a Synthetic "*A Priori*"?', p. 310.

39. Sellars, 'Is There a Synthetic "*A Priori*"?', pp. 310–11.

40. Sellars, 'Is There a Synthetic "*A Priori*"?', pp. 311–12.

41. Sellars, 'Is There a Synthetic "*A Priori*"?', pp. 316–17.

42. R. Brandom, *Articulating Reasons* (Cambridge, MA: Harvard University Press, 2000).

43. For Sellars's account of meaning as functional role, see W. Sellars, 'Meaning as Functional Classification', in K. Scharp and R. Brandom (eds), *In the Space of Reasons* (Cambridge, MA: Harvard University Press, 2007), pp. 81–100.

44. W. deVries, 'Sellars vs McDowell on the Structure of Sensory Consciousness', *Diametros*, 27 (2011), pp. 47–63, on pp. 61–2.

45. J. Rosenberg, *Accessing Kant: A Relaxed Introduction* (New York: Oxford University Press, 2005).

46. On the distinction between 'the manifest image', i.e. ordinary discourse of objects and persons as disclosed in experience and described by reflection, and 'the scientific image', i.e. the metaphysics underlying scientific theories, see W. Sellars, 'Philosophy and the Scientific Image of Man', *Science, Perception and Reality* (Atascadero, CA: Ridgeview, 1963), pp. 1–40.

47. W. Sellars, 'Empiricism and the Philosophy of Mind', *Science, Perception and Reality* (Atascadero, CA: Ridgeview, 1963), p. 131.

48. W. Sellars, 'The Language of Theories', *Science, Perception and Reality* (Atascadero, CA: Ridgeview, 1963), pp.106–26.

49. Sellars, 'Empiricism and the Philosophy of Mind', p. 172.

50. Sellars, 'Empiricism and the Philosophy of Mind', p. 176.

51. Sellars, 'Empiricism and the Philosophy of Mind', pp. 190–6.

52. Sellars, 'Empiricism and the Philosophy of Mind', p. 169.

53. Sellars, 'Empiricism and the Philosophy of Mind', p. 195.

54. W. Sellars, *Science and Metaphysics* (Atascadero, CA: Ridgeview Press, 1967).

55. Sellars, *Science and Metaphysics*, pp. 16–17, sections 39–41.

56. I. Kant, *Critique of Pure Reason*, trans. P. Guyer and A. Wood (New York: Cambridge University Press, 1999), sections A 79, B 104-5; emphasis added.

57. The details of Sellars' understanding of 'this-such's are worked out in W. Sellars, 'Some Remarks on Kant's Theory of Experience', and 'The Role of the Imagination in Kant's Theory of Experience', in J. Sicha (ed.), *Kant's Transcendental Metaphysics* (Atascadero, CA: Ridgeview Press, 2002), pp. 269–82 and pp. 419–41.

58. W. Sellars, *Science and Metaphysics* (Atascadero, CA: Ridgeview, 1967), p. 16, section 40.

59. Sellars, *Science and Metaphysics,* p. 29, section 71.

60. Cf. 'the pattern of Kant's thought stands out far more clearly if we interpret him as clear about the difference between *general* conceptual representings (sortals and attributive), on the one hand, and on the other, *intuition* as a special class of *non-general* conceptual representings, but add to this interpretation that he was *not* clear about the difference between intuitions in this sense and sensations'; Sellars, 'Some Remarks on Kant's Theory of Experience', p. 272.

61. Sellars, *Science and Metaphysics*, pp. 16–17, section 41; emphasis original.

62. See W. deVries and P. Coates, 'Brandom's Two-Ply Error', in W. deVries (ed.), *Empiricism, Perceptual Knowledge, Normativity, and Realism* (New York: Oxford University Press 2009), 131–46.

63. This phrase is important enough to Sellars that he uses it repeatedly; see W. Sellars, 'Some Reflections on Perceptual Consciousness', in J. Sicha (ed.), *Kant's Transcendental Metaphysics* (Atascadero, CA: Ridgeview Press, 2002), p. 437.

64. W. Sellars, 'The Role of the Imagination in Kant's Theory of Experience', in J. Sicha (ed.), *Kant's Transcendental Metaphysics* (Atascadero, CA: Ridgeview Press, 2002), p. 419.

65. Sellars, 'The Role of the Imagination in Kant's Theory of Experience', p. 421.

66. Sellars, 'The Role of the Imagination in Kant's Theory of Experience', pp. 422–3.

67. Sellars, 'The Role of the Imagination in Kant's Theory of Experience', p. 426.

68. Sellars, 'The Role of the Imagination in Kant's Theory of Experience', p. 427.

69. Sellars, 'Some Remarks on Perceptual Consciousness', p. 437.

70. Sellars, *Science and Metaphysics,* section 58, p. 23.

71. W. Sellars, 'Being and Being Known', *Science, Perception and Reality* (Atascadero, CA: Ridgeview, 1963), pp. 41–59, on p. 46.

72. The irony here is central to O'Shea's important analysis of Sellars's doctrine of sense-impressions; see J. O'Shea 'Conceptual Thinking and Nonconceptual Content: A Sellarsian Divide', in J. O'Shea and E. Rubinstein (eds), *Self, Language and World* (Atascadero, CA: Ridgeview, 2010), pp. 205–28. See also S. Schellenberg, 'Sellarsian Perspectives on Perception and Non-Conceptual Content', in M. Wolf and M. Lance (eds), *The Self-Correcting Enterprise* (New York: Rodopi, 2006), pp. 173–96.

4 The Retreat from Nonconceptualism: Discourse and Experience in Brandom and McDowell

1. R. Rorty, *Philosophy and the Mirror of Nature* (Princeton, NJ: Princeton University Press, 1979).

2. R. Brandom, *Making It Explicit* (Cambridge, MA: Harvard University Press, 1994), and J. McDowell, *Mind and World* (Cambridge, MA: Harvard University Press, 1994).

3. R. Brandom, 'Reply to Lance and Kukla', in B. Weiss and J. Wanderer (eds), *Reading Brandom* (New York: Routledge, 2010), pp. 316–19, on p. 317.

4. Brandom has elaborated his interpretation of pragmatism at length in R. Brandom, *Perspectives on Pragmatism* (Cambridge, MA: Harvard, 2011). For excellent criticism of Brandom's pragmatism, see S. Levine, 'Brandom's Pragmatism', *Transactions of the Charles S. Peirce Society,* 48:2 (2012), pp. 125–40 and S. Levine, 'Norms and Habits: Brandom on the Sociality of Action', *European Journal of Philosophy*, 21:2 (2012), pp. 1–25. The view developed here differs from Levine's primarily by finding the necessary

resources to correct Brandom in Merleau-Ponty rather than in Dewey, but I regard this as more of a methodological than substantive difference.

5. R. Brandom, *Making It Explicit*, (Cambridge, MA: Harvard University Press, 1994), pp. 60–1.
6. For "mentalism" and "lingualism," see R. Brandom, *Articulating Reasons* (Cambridge, MA: Harvard University Press, 2000), pp. 5–7.
7. Brandom, *Making It Explicit*, p. 5.
8. Brandom, *Making It Explicit*, p. 143.
9. Brandom, *Making It Explicit*, pp. 141–4, 167ff. For a particularly elegant and concise explanation of deontic scorekeeping, see C. Maher, *The Pittsburgh School* (New York: Routledge, 2012), pp. 67–70.
10. Maher, *The Pittsburgh School*, p. 155.
11. For the 'two-ply' metaphor in Brandom's account of perception, see R. Brandom, 'The Centrality of Sellars's Two-Ply Account of Observation to the Arguments of "Empiricism and the Philosophy of Mind"', *Tales of the Mighty Dead* (Cambridge, MA: Harvard University Press, 2002), pp. 348–67 and R. Brandom, 'Overcoming a Dualism of Concepts and Causes: The Basic Argument of "Empiricism and the Philosophy of Mind"', in R. Gale (ed.), *The Blackwell Guide to Metaphysics* (Malden, MA: Blackwell, 2002), pp. 263–81. As emphasized in Chapter 3, Sellars insists on the concept of sensory consciousness to mediate between physical causes and conceptual judgment; Brandom does not.
12. Brandom, *Making It Explicit*, p. 8.
13. Brandom, *Making It Explicit*, pp. 234–5.
14. Brandom, *Making It Explicit*, p. 234.
15. Brandom, *Making It Explicit*, p. 225.
16. Brandom, *Making It Explicit*, p. 276.
17. R. Brandom, 'Perception and Rational Constraint: McDowell's "Mind and World"', *Philosophical Issues*, 7: Perception (1996), pp. 241–59.
18. J. McDowell, 'Brandom on Observation', in B. Weiss and J. Wanderer (eds), *Reading Brandom* (New York: Routledge, 2010), pp. 129–44.
19. Brandom, *Making It Explicit*, pp. 276–7.
20. Brandom, *Making It Explicit*, p. 295.
21. Brandom, *Making It Explicit*, pp. 614–23. Interestingly, Brandom does remark that 'C.I. Lewis's heroic expository effort in *Mind and the World Order* is probably as clear a setting-out of this way of conceptualizing intuitions about concepts and intuition as can be had', Brandom, *Making It Explicit*, p. 616.
22. D. Macbeth, 'Inference, Meaning, and Truth in Brandom, Sellars, and Frege', in B. Weiss and J. Wanderer (eds), *Reading Brandom* (New York: Routledge, 2010), pp. 197–212, on p. 204.
23. R. Brandom, 'Reply to Macbeth', in B. Weiss and J. Wanderer (eds), *Reading Brandom* (New York: Routledge, 2010), pp. 338–41, on p. 339.
24. Brandom, *Making It Explicit*, p. 48–9.
25. Note that McDowell is less than enthusiastic about being paired with Brandom in this regard; see J. McDowell, 'Knowledge and the Internal Revisited', *The Engaged Intellect: Philosophical Essays* (Cambridge, MA: Harvard University Press, 2009), pp. 279–87, on p.279, n. 3.
26. R. Brandom, *Articulating Reasons*, (Cambridge, MA: Harvard University Press, 2000), p. 205, n. 7.

27. J. McDowell, 'Experiencing the World', *The Engaged Intellect,* pp. 243–56, on p. 243.
28. J. McDowell, *Mind and World* (Cambridge, MA: Harvard University Press, 1994), p. 7.
29. McDowell, *Mind and World,* p. 11.
30. The contrast between (passive) actualizations and (active) exercises is central to McDowell's contrast between experience and thought; see J. McDowell, 'Sellars on Perceptual Experience', *Having the World in View: Essays on Kant, Hegel and Sellars* (Cambridge, MA: Harvard University Press, 2009), p. 12.
31. McDowell, *Mind and World,* p. 9.
32. McDowell, *Mind and World,* p. 83. The McDowell–Hegel relation has been the subject of much discussion. I agree with Houlgate that 'for McDowell, the world exercises authority over thought through perceptual experience. For Hegel, by contrast, the world exercises authority over our perceptual experience through thought. Thought is the authority that ensures our perceptual experience is of the world, not the other way around', S. Houlgate, 'Thought and Experience in Hegel and McDowell', *European Journal of Philosophy,* 14:2 (2006), pp. 242–61, on p. 254. Unlike Houlgate, I construe this point as one in McDowell's favor.
33. J. McDowell, 'Avoiding the Myth of the Given', *Having the World in View,* pp. 256–72.
34. McDowell, 'Avoiding the Myth of the Given', p. 258.
35. McDowell, 'Avoiding the Myth of the Given', p. 264. Similarly, he now writes that 'intuitions immediately reveal things to be as they would be claimed to be in claims that would be no more than a discursive exploitation of some of the content of the intuitions', McDowell, 'Avoiding the Myth of the Given', p. 267.
36. Cf. 'Hegel in other words agrees with Kant that experience requires the cooperation of receptivity and spontaneity, but rejects what he believes is a further assumption Kant associates with our discursivity: namely, that the respective contributions of the two faculties can be isolated'; S. Sedgwick, 'McDowell's Hegelianism', *European Journal of Philosophy,* 5:1 (1997), pp. 21–38, on p. 33.
37. McDowell, 'Avoiding the Myth of the Given', p. 271.
38. J. McDowell, 'Hegel's Idealism as Radicalization of Kant', *Having the World in View,* pp. 69–89.
39. On this specific distinction and its implications for McDowell – and McDowell's relation to Hegel – see R. Pippin, 'What is 'Conceptual Activity?', in J. Schear (ed.), *Mind, Reason, and Being-in-the-World: The McDowell–Dreyfus Debate,* pp. 91–109.
40. Indeed, McDowell thinks it is an error in Sellars's reading of Kant and of Hegel that Sellars finds sheer receptivity necessary at all; see J. McDowell, 'Intentionality as a Relation', *Having the World in View,* pp. 60–5.
41. McDowell, John, 'Avoiding the Myth of the Given', *Having The World in View,* p. 272.
42. J. McDowell, 'Naturalism in Philosophy of Mind', *The Engaged Intellect,* pp. 257–75, on p. 274, n. 36.
43. McDowell, *Mind and World,* pp. 116–18.
44. McDowell, Mind and World, p. 115.
45. McDowell, *Mind and World,* p. 108ff.
46. Gaskin prefers 'enculturation' over 'acculturation' because the latter suggests the acquisition of a second culture by someone who is already at home in his or her native culture, whereas the former is the acquisition of a native culture to begin with; see R. Gaskin, *Experience and the World's Own Language* (New York: Oxford University Press, 2006).
47. J. McDowell, 'What Myth', *Inquiry,* 50:4 (2007), pp. 338–51, on p. 338, reprinted in

J. McDowell, *The Engaged Intellect: Philosophical Essays* (Cambridge, MA: Harvard University Press), pp. 308–23.

48. For one illuminating example of 'responsiveness to reasons as *such*', see J. McDowell, 'Reply to Lovibond', in J. Lindgaard (ed)., *John McDowell: Experience, Norm, and Nature* (Malden, MA: Blackwell, 2009), pp. 234–8.
49. McDowell, Mind and World, p. 111.
50. McDowell, Mind and World, p. viii.
51. P. Strawson, *The Bounds of Sense* (New York: Routledge Press,1966), p. 15.
52. P. Strawson, *Individuals* (New York: Routledge Press, 1959), p. 9.
53. McDowell, *Mind and World*, p. xi.
54. Reprinted as the first three essays of McDowell, *Having the World In View.*
55. Sellars, 'Empiricism and the Philosophy of Mind', section 38, p. 170.
56. J. McDowell, 'The Logical Form of an Intuition', *Having the World In View*, pp. 23–43, on p. 36.
57. McDowell, 'Why is Sellars's Essay called "Empiricism and the Philosophy of Mind"', pp. 221–38.
58. J. McDowell, 'Naturalism in Philosophy of Mind', *The Engaged Intellect*, pp. 257–75, on p. 275.
59. J. McDowell, 'Intentionality as a Relation', *Having the World in View*, pp. 44–65, on p. 46.
60. McDowell 'Intentionality as a Relation', p. 62.
61. W. deVries, 'Sellars vs McDowellMcDowell, John on the Structure of Sensory Consciousness', *Diametros*, 27 (2011), pp. 47–63.
62. deVries, 'Sellars vs McDowell on the Structure of Sensory Consciousness', p. 57.
63. H. Dreyfus, 'Overcoming the Myth of the Mental', *Topoi*, 25:1–2 (2006), p. 43–9, on p. 43.
64. J. McDowell, 'What Myth', *Inquiry*, 50:4 (2007), pp. 338–51, on p. 349, reprinted in J. McDowell, *The Engaged Intellect: Philosophical Essays* (Cambridge, MA: Harvard University Press, 2009), pp. 308–23.
65. Here the vocabulary has shifted slightly: Dreyfus accuses McDowell of holding the 'Myth of the Pervasiveness of the Mental' (H. Dreyfus, 'The Myth of the Pervasiveness of the Mental', in J. Shear (ed.), *Mind, Reason, and Being-in-the-World* (New York: Routledge, 2013), pp. 15–40) whereas McDowell accuses Dreyfus of holding 'the Myth of the Mind as Detached' (J. McDowell, 'The Myth of the Mind as Detached', in J. Shear (ed.), *Mind, Reason, and Being-in-the-World* (New York: Routledge, 2013), pp. 41–58).
66. J. C. Berendzen, 'Coping Without Foundations: On Dreyfus's Use of Merleau-Ponty', *International Journal of Philosophical Studies*, 18:5 (2010), pp. 629–49.
67. S. Todes, *Body and World* (Cambridge, MA: The MIT Press, 2001), p. 100.
68. W. Sellars, 'Empiricism and the Philosophy of Mind', *Science, Perception, and Reality* (Atascadero, CA: Ridgeview, 1963), section 38, p. 170.
69. J. McDowell, 'What Myth?', *Inquiry*, 50:4 (2007), pp. 338–51, on p. 344, reprinted in J. McDowell, *The Engaged Intellect: Philosophical Essays* (Cambridge, MA: Harvard University Press, 2009), pp. 308–23.
70. McDowell, John, 'What Myth?', p. 344.

5 Somatic Intentionality and Habitual Normativity in Merleau-Ponty's Account of Lived Embodiment

1. M. Merleau-Ponty, *Phenomenology of Perception*, trans. D. Landes (New York: Routledge, 2012). All page numbers refer to the English in this edition.
2. T. Carman, 'Sensation, Judgment and the Phenomenal Field', in T. Carman and M. Hansen (eds), *The Cambridge Companion to Merleau-Ponty* (New York: Cambridge University Press, 2004), pp. 50–73; M. Dillon, *Merleau-Ponty's Ontology* (Evanston, IL: Northwestern University Press, 1997); K. Romdenh-Romluc, *Merleau-Ponty and the Phenomenolgy of Perception* (New York: Routledge, 2010); and M. Wrathall, 'Motives, Reasons, and Causes', in Carman and Hansen (eds.) *The Cambridge Companion to Merleau-Ponty*, pp. 111–28.
3. K. Romdenh-Romluc notes that objective thought is best characterized as 'a view of the world as composed of determinate entities that stand in external relations to one another'; see Romdenh-Romluc, *Merleau-Ponty and the Phenomenology of Perception*, p. 19.
4. The Husserl/Merleau-Ponty relationship is complicated, because Merleau-Ponty extensively studied Husserl's unpublished late writings long before they became published. Here I adopt Moran's judicious assessment: 'The great genius of Merleau-Ponty is to bring to manifestation the embodied phenomenology that was obscured by Husserl's own Neo-Cartesian methodology and ponderous terminology' and that 'without Merleau-Ponty's elaboration we would never have seen the theme in the palimpsest left by Husserl'; see D. Moran, 'The Phenomenology of Embodiment: Intertwining and Reflexivity' in R. Jensen and D. Moran (eds), *The Phenomenology of Embodied Subjectivity* (New York: Springer, 2013), pp. 285–304, on p. 292 and p. 300.
5. Merleau-Ponty *Phenomenology of Perception*, pp. lxxx–lxxxi.
6. Merleau-Ponty, *Phenomenology of Perception*, p. lxxxi.
7. M. Reuter, 'Merleau-Ponty's Notion of Pre-reflective Intentionality', *Synthese*, 118:1 (1999), pp. 69–88.
8. Merleau-Ponty, *Phenomenology of Perception*, p. 53.
9. Merleau-Ponty, *Phenomenology of Perception*, p. 101ff.
10. Merleau-Ponty, *Phenomenology of Perception*, p. 137.
11. Merleau-Ponty, *Phenomenology of Perception*, p. 4.
12. The phenomenological project is therefore quite similar to McDowell's distinction between 'constitutive explanations' and 'enabling explanations'; for a recent use of McDowell's distinction to adjudicate the conflict between phenomenology and naturalism, see M. Wheeler, 'Science Friction: Phenomenology, Naturalism, and Cognitive Science', in H. Carel and D. Meacham (eds), *Phenomenology and Naturalism* (New York: Cambridge University Press, 2013), pp 135–68.
13. Merleau-Ponty, *Phenomenology of Perception*, p. 70.
14. Merleau-Ponty, *Phenomenology of Perception*, p. 71.
15. In the chapter 'Others and the Human World', Merleau-Ponty also argues the coexistence of others, or what is usually called 'intersubjectivity' but which is more precisely called 'intercoporeality' (since it is non-apperceptive and pre-subjective) is also constitutive of perceptual consciousness.
16. Merleau-Ponty, *Phenomenology of Perception*, p. 103.
17. Merleau-Ponty, *Phenomenology of Perception*, p. 49.
18. Merleau-Ponty, *Phenomenology of Perception*, p. 84
19. Merleau-Ponty, *Phenomenology of Perception*, p. 113.

20. However, it is crucial to Sellars's theory that these two *must* be disentangled; sense-impressions are non-intentional states of consciousness. One of the theoretical advantages to Merleau-Ponty's distinction between motor intentionality and discursive intentionality is that it retains the tight link between intentionality and consciousness – a link that Sellars explicitly rejects – while acknowledging the distinction between perceptual intentionality and consciousness and discursive or intellectual intentionalitu and consciousness.

21. Merleau-Ponty, *Phenomenology of Perception*, p. 139.

22. Merleau-Ponty, *Phenomenology of Perception*, p. 81.

23. Merleau-Ponty, *Phenomenology of Perception*, p. 216.

24. Merleau-Ponty, *Phenomenology of Perception*, p. 265.

25. As McDowell puts it, 'Now I could put what I urge at the end of "What Myth?" like this: *I* am the only person-like thing (person, actually) that is needed in a description of my bodily activity. If you distinguish me from my body, and give my body that person-like character, you have too many person-like things in the picture when you try to describe my bodily doings'; J. McDowell, 'Reply to Dreyfus', *Inquiry*, 50:4 (2007), pp. 366–70, reprinted in J. McDowell, *The Engaged Intellect: Philosophical Essays* (Cambridge, MA: Harvard University Press, 2009), pp. 324–8, on p. 328.

26. Merleau-Ponty, *Phenomenology of Perception*, p. 328.

27. Merleau-Ponty, *Phenomenology of Perception*, p. 291.

28. Merleau-Ponty, *Phenomenology of Perception*, p. 311.

29. Merleau-Ponty, *Phenomenology of Perception*, p. 316.

30. Merleau-Ponty, *Phenomenology of Perception*, p. 153.

31. Merleau-Ponty, *Phenomenology of Perception*, p. 93.

32. Merleau-Ponty assimilates the natural sciences to mechanistic physics which explains *partes extra partes*, as distinct from the 'internal relations' of intentionality, and so does not think that somatic intentionalityintentionality can be 'naturalized'. I return to this point in Chapter 6.

33. Merleau-Ponty, *Phenomenology of Perception*, p. 144.

34. Merleau-Ponty, *Phenomenology of Perception*, p. 51.

35. Merleau-Ponty, *Phenomenology of Perception*, p. 113.

36. Wrathall, 'Motives, Reasons, and Causes', pp. 111–28.

37. Merleau-Ponty, *Phenomenology of Perception*, p. 451.

38. S. Levine, 'Norms and Habits: Brandom on the Sociality of Action', *European Journal of Philosophy*, 21:2 (2012), pp. 1–25.

39. G. Evans, *Varieties of Reference* (New York: Oxford University Press, 1982).

40. Motor intentionality allows for actions to be both intentional and not informed by reflection; see K. Romdenh-Romluc, 'Habit and Attention', in R. Jensen and D. Moran (eds), *The Phenomenology of Embodied Subjectivity* (New York: Springer, 2013), pp. 3–20.

41. However, E. Fridland notes the distinction between the Generality Constraint (GC) and the Context-Independence Constraint (CIC) and argues that skills do not conform to the CIC. If I am correct, then habits conform to neither, and this marks a distinction between habits and skills; see E. Fridland, 'Skill Learning and Conceptual Thought', in B. Bashour and H. Muller (eds), *Contemporary Philosophical Naturalism and Its Implications* (New York: Routledge, 2014), pp. 77–100.

42. See J. C. Berendzen, 'Coping Without Foundations: On Dreyfus's Use of Merleau-Ponty', *International Journal of Philosophical Studies*, 18:5 (2010), pp. 629–49; R. Jensen, 'Motor Intentionality and the Case of Schneider', *Phenomenology and the Cognitive*

Sciences, 8:3 (2009), pp. 371–88; and S. Matherne, 'The Kantian Roots of Merleau-Ponty's Account of Pathology', *British Journal for the History of Philosophy*, 22:1 (2014), pp. 124–49.

43. Merleau-Ponty, *Phenomenology of Perception*, p. 137.

44. 'The same function that gives unity to the different representations **in a judgement** also gives unity to the mere synthesis of different representations **in an intuition**, which, expressed generally, is called the pure concept of understanding'; I. Kant, *Critique of Pure Reason*, trans. P. Guyer and A. Wood (New York: Cambridge,1997), section B105.

45. See Merleau-Ponty, *Phenomenology of Perception*, pp. 89, 341.

46. I would like to thank Dionysias Christias for suggesting that Sellars's distinction between language-entry transitions and sense-impressions amounts to a "bifurcation" of somatic intentionality – though this is a bifurcation that he defends and that I reject, for the reasons given here.

47. M. Merleau-Ponty, *Phenomenology of Perception*, trans. D. Landes (New York: Routledge, 2012), p. 36.

48. Merleau-Ponty, *Phenomenology of Perception*, p. 34.

49. W. Sellars, 'Some Reflections on Perceptual Consciousness', in J. Sicha (ed.), *Kant's Transcendental Metaphysics* (Atascadero, CA: Ridgeview Press, 2002), pp. 431–41, on p. 438.

50. Merleau-Ponty, *Phenomenology of Perception*, p. 34.

51. Merleau-Ponty, *Phenomenology of Perception*, p. 35.

52. Merleau-Ponty, *Phenomenology of Perception*, p. 210.

53. Merleau-Ponty, *Phenomenology of Perception*, p. 210.

54. Merleau-Ponty, *Phenomenology of Perception*, p. 211.

55. Merleau-Ponty, *Phenomenology of Perception*, p. 211.

56. Merleau-Ponty, *Phenomenology of Perception*, p. 211.

57. Merleau-Ponty, *Phenomenology of Perception*, p. 358. R. Jensen notes that Merleau-Ponty, much like McDowell, uses a negative transcendental argument for the disjunctive account of perception; see R. Jensen, 'Merleau-Ponty and McDowell on the Transparency of the Mind', *International Journal of Philosophical Studies*, 21:3 (2013), pp. 470–92.

58.   Merleau-Ponty, *Phenomenology of Perception*, p. 242.

59.   Merleau-Ponty, *Phenomenology of Perception*, p. 213.

60. Merleau-Ponty, *Phenomenology of Perception*, p. 41. Cf. 'intellectualism's true flaw is precisely in having taken the determinate universe of science as given' (p. 48); 'Intellectualism's error is to make it [Cassirer's 'the symbolic function'] depend upon itself, to separate it from the materials in which it is realized, and to recognize in us, as originary, a direct presence in the world' (p. 126), and that 'Intellectualism can only conceive of the passage from the perspective to the thing itself, or from the sign to the signification, as an interpretation, an apperception, or an epistemic intention' (p. 154).

61. Merleau-Ponty, *Phenomenology of Perception*, pp. 64–5.

62. W. Sellars, *Science and Metaphysics* (Atascadero, CA: Ridgeview, 1967), section 16, p. 7.

63. L. Wittgenstein *Philosophical Investigations*, trans. G. E. M. Anscombe, P. M. S. Hacker and J. Schulte, revised 4th edn (Malden, MA: Blackwell, 2009), section 115.

64. Sellars, *Science and Metaphysics*, sections 39–40, p. 16.

65. Wittgenstein, *Philosophical Investigations*, section 169.

66. Wittgenstein, *Philosophical Investigations*, sections 170–8.

67. Merleau-Ponty, *Phenomenology of Perception*, pp. 145–6.

68. Merleau-Ponty, *Phenomenology of Perception*, p. 334.

69. W. Sellars, 'The Role of Imagination in Kant's Theory of Experience', section 23, p. 423.

70. M. Merleau-Ponty, *Phenomenology of Perception*, trans. D. Landes (New York: Routledge, 2012), p. 251.

71. J. Rosenberg, *The Thinking Self* (Atascadero, CA: Ridgeview, 1986).

72. R. Hanna, 'The Myth of the Given and the Grip of the Given', *Diametros*, 27 (2011), pp. 25–46; and R. Hanna, 'Beyond the Myth of the Myth: A Kantian Theory of Non-Conceptual Content', *International Journal of Philosophical Studies*, 19:3 (2011), pp. 323–98.

73. Rosenberg, *The Thinking Self*, p. 21.

74. Rosenberg, *The Thinking Self*, p. 25.

75. Rosenberg, *The Thinking Self*, p. 27.

76. Rosenberg, *The Thinking Self*, pp. 76–7.

77. Rosenberg, *The Thinking Self*, p. 83.

78. Rosenberg, *The Thinking Self*, p. 84.

79. Rosenberg, *The Thinking Self*, p. 93.

80. Rosenberg, *The Thinking Self*, p. 93.

81. Rosenberg, *The Thinking Self*, p. 95.

82. Rosenberg, *The Thinking Self*, p. 103.

83. Hanna, 'The Myth of the Given and the Grip of the Given' pp. 25–46 and Hanna, 'Beyond the Myth of the Myth', pp. 323–98.

84. Hanna, 'Beyond the Myth of the Myth', p. 326.

85. Hanna, 'Beyond the Myth of the Myth', p. 327.

86. Hanna, 'Beyond the Myth of the Myth', p. 327.

87. Hanna, 'The Myth of the Given and the Grip of the Given', p. 40.

88. Hanna, 'The Myth of the Given and the Grip of the Given', p. 41.

89. R. Hanna, 'Kant and Nonconceptual Content', *European Journal of Philosophy*, 13:2 (2005), pp. 247–90.

90. Merleau-Ponty, *Phenomenology of Perception*, p. 139.

6 The Possibilities and Problems of Bifurcated Intentionality

1. Sellars, 'Empiricism and the Philosophy of Mind' VI.29 in *Science, Perception and Reality*, p. 160.

2. P. Bourgeois and S. Rosenthal, 'Merleau-Ponty, Lewis and Kant', *International Studies in Philosophy*, 15:3 (1983), pp. 13–23; and S. Rosenthal and P. Bourgeois, 'Merleau-Ponty, Lewis and Ontological Presence', *Philosophical Topics*, 13:2 (1985), pp. 239–46.

3. For McDowell's disjunctivism, an important strand in his recent work, see J. McDowell, 'The Disjunctive Conception of Experience as Material for a Transcendental Argument', *The Engaged Intellect: Philosophical Essays* (Cambridge, MA: Harvard University Press, 2009), pp. 225–40.

4. See K. Romdenh-Romluc, *Merleau-Ponty and the Phenomenology of Perception* (New York: Routledge, 2010), p. 164–7; and R. Jensen, 'Merleau-Ponty and McDowell on the Transparency of the Mind', *International Journal of Philosophical Studies*, 21:3 (2013), pp. 470–92.

5. W. Sellars, 'Preface', *Science and Metaphysics* (Atascadero, CA: Ridgeview, 1967), p. ix.

6. R. Kraut, 'Universals, Metaphysical Explanations, and Pragmatism', *Journal of Philosophy*, 107:11 (2012), pp. 590–609, on p. 601.

7. K. Westphal, 'Kant's *Critique of Pure Reason* and Analytic Philosophy', in P. Guyer (ed.), *The Cambridge Companion to Kant's Critique of Pure Reason* (New York: Cambridge University Press, 2010), pp. 401–30, on p. 429.

8. For a related criticism of McDowell's tendency to assimilate perception to language, see

A. Baz, 'On When Words Are Called For: Cavell, McDowell, and the Wording of the World', *Inquiry*, 46:4 (2003), pp. 473–500.

9.   H. Dreyfus, 'Reply to McDowell', *Inquiry*, 50:4 (2007), pp. 371–7, on pp. 376–7. Berendzen observes, 'this is a very unsatisfactory note for Dreyfus to end on, because he does not explain how this change radically affects his view. The change from vertical to horizontal dependency marks a large difference; presumably that latter would include the kind of reciprocal interrelation of which Merleau-Ponty speaks. It should also lead him to give up much of his other rhetoric, such as the talk of a human life that can in principle involve only coping in flow'; J. C. Berendzen, 'Coping Without Foundations: On Dreyfus's Use of Merleau-Ponty', *International Journal of Philosophical Studies*, 18:5 (2010), pp. 629–49, on p. 646. In his contribution to the Schear anthology, Dreyfus gives no indication of following through on this change in metaphor; see H. Dreyfus, 'The Myth of the Pervasiveness of the Mental', in J. Schear (ed.), *Mind, Reason, and Being-in-the-World* (New York: Routledge, 2013), pp. 15–40.

10. E. Fridland, 'Skill Learning and Conceptual Thought', in B. Bashour and H. Muller (eds), *Contemporary Philosophical Naturalism and Its Implications* (New York: Routledge, 2014), pp. 77–100. Fridland conceives of skills as an intermediate step between actions and concepts; how much of a difference there is between her use of actions and my use of habits, and likewise between concepts and norms, is a further question.

11. D. Zahavi, 'Mindedness, Mindlessness, and First-Person Authority', in J. Schear (ed.), *Mind, Reason, and Being-in-the-World* (New York: Routledge, 2013), pp. 320–43, on p. 337.

12. R. Jensen, 'Motor Intentionality and the Case of Schneider', *Phenomenology and the Cognitive Sciences*, 8:3 (2009), pp. 371–88, on p. 387.

13. R. Brandom, *Making It Explicit* (Cambridge, MA: Harvard University Press, 1994), p. 61.

14. For more on the discussion between Brandom and phenomenology, see S. Gallagher and K. Miyahara, 'Neo-pragmatism and Enactive Intentionality', in J. Schulkin (ed.), *Action, Perception, and the Brain* (New York: Palgrave-Macmillan, 2012), pp. 117–46. They develop the relation between Brandom's pragmatics of language and enactive intentionality in considerable detail, but do not squarely face the question of how discursive intentionality and enactive (in my terms, somatic) intentionality can both be original.

15. W. Sellars, 'Language, Rules and Behavior', in J. Sicha (ed.), *Pure Pragmatics and Possible Worlds: The Early Essays of Wilfrid Sellars* (Reseda, CA: Ridgeview Publishing Company, 1980), pp. 129–55, on p. 138.

16. My use of the phrase 'Words Made Flesh (Compare and Contrast)' for the title of this section is inspired by M. Lance, 'The Word Made Flesh: Toward a Neo-Sellarsian View of Concepts and Their Analysis', *Acta Analytica*, 15:25 (2000), pp. 117–35.

17. Since Lance and Kukla share responsibility for their co-authored projects and reverse the order of their names with each publication, I adopt the convention of reversing the order of their names with each mention of their views.

18. R. Kukla and M. Lance, *'Yo!' and 'Lo!'* (Cambridge, MA: Harvard University Press, 2009), p. 11.

19. Kukla and Lance, *'Yo!' and 'Lo!'*, p. 10.

20. Kukla and Lance, *'Yo!' and 'Lo!'*, p. 5.

21. Kukla and M. Lance, *'Yo!' and 'Lo!'*, p. 5.

22. J. Rouse, 'What is Conceptually Articulated Understanding?', in J. Schear (ed.), *Mind, Reason, and Being-in-the-World* (New York: Routledge, 2013), pp. 250–71, on p. 262.

23. Rouse, 'What is Conceptually Articulated Understanding?', p. 267.
24. Rouse, 'What is Conceptually Articulated Understanding?', p. 264.
25. Kukla and Lance, *'Yo!' and 'Lo!'*, pp. 8–9.
26. Kukla and Lance, *'Yo!' and 'Lo!'*, p. 70.
27. Kukla and Lance, *'Yo!' and 'Lo!'*, pp. 70–1.
28. Kukla and Lance, *'Yo!' and 'Lo!'*, p. 72.
29. Kukla and Lance, *'Yo!' and 'Lo!'*, p. 77.
30. Kukla and Lance, *'Yo!' and 'Lo!'*, p. 78.
31. R. Kukla and M. Lance, 'Intersubjectivity and Receptive Experience', *Southern Journal of Philosophy*, 52:1 (2014), pp. 22–42, on p. 29, n. 7.
32. M. Lance and R. Kukla, 'Perception, Language and the First Person', in B. Weiss and J. Wanderer (eds), *Reading Brandom* (New York: Routledge, 2010), pp. 115–28, on p. 124.
33. M. Okrent, *Rational Animals* (Athens, OH: Ohio University Press, 2007), p. 19.
34. Okrent, *Rational Animals*, p. 19.
35. Okrent, *Rational Animals*, p. 39.
36. Okrent, *Rational Animals*, p. 73.
37. For Okrent on the compatibility of teleological explanations with Darwinist conception of species, see Okrent, *Rational Animals*, pp. 89–94; for Okrent's critique of Millikan and why function-attribution logically presupposes goal-attribution, see Okrent, *Rational Animals*, pp. 95–103.
38. Okrent, *Rational Animals*, p. 121.
39. Okrent, Mark, *Rational Animals*, p. 180.
40. Okrent, *Rational Animals*, p. 193.
41. In other words, we can reconcile Kant with Darwin, but only if we partially rehabilitate Aristotle. Further reflection on this point would further bolster Okrent's self-understanding as a pragmatist. His discussion of 'naturalistic pragmatism', in which he includes but not does not discuss in detail Merleau-Ponty, helpfully clarifies the earlier account; see M. Okrent, 'Heidegger's Pragmatism Redux', in A. Malachowski (ed.), *The Cambridge Companion to Pragmatism* (New York: Cambridge University Press, 2013), pp. 124–58, on pp. 133–4.
42. Rouse, 'What is Conceptually Articulated Understanding?', p. 259.
43. Rouse, 'What is Conceptually Articulated Understanding?', p. 259.
44. Paul Churchland's Domain Portrayal semantics is a theory of this type; see P. Churchland, *Plato's Camera* (Cambridge, MA: The MIT Press, 2012).
45. Sachs, 'Resisting the Disenchantment of Nature: McDowell and the Question of Animal Minds', *Inquiry*, 55:2 (2012), pp. 131–47.
46. H. Muller, 'Naturalism and Intentionality', in B. Bashour and H. Muller (eds), *Contemporary Philosophical Naturalism and Its Implications* (New York: Routledge, 2013), pp. 155–81, on p. 178.
47. See S. Turner, *Explaining the Normative* (Malden, MA: Polity, 2010).
48. Thompson points out – correctly, I think – that 'Ultimately, both strategies are necessary and must be pursued in a complementary and mutually supporting way, if phenomenology is not to be reduced to or eliminated in favor of scientific naturalism, and if naturalism is not to be rejected in favor of metaphysically dualist or idealist forms of phenomenology'; see E. Thompson, 'Review of *Phenomenology and Naturalism: Examining the Relationship between Human Experience and Nature*', ed. H. Carel and D. Meacham, *Notre Dame Philosophical Reviews*, 10 July 2014. http://ndpr.nd.edu/news/49272-phenomenology-and-naturalism-examining-the-relationship-between-human-experience-and-nature/ [accessed 11 July 2014].

Conclusion

1. W. Sellars, *Science and Metaphysics*, (Atascadero, CA: Ridgeview, 1967), section 16, p. 16.

Appendix: Is Phenomenology Committed to the Myth of the Given?

1. W. Sellars, 'Empiricism and the Philosophy of Mind', *Science, Perception and Reality*(Atascadero, CA: Ridgeview, 1963), section 1, pp. 127–8. Compare: 'no giving of reasons for adopting a language game can appeal to reasons outside all language games. The *data* of the positivist must join the *illuminatio* of Augustine', W. Sellars, 'Some Reflections on Language Games', *Philosophy of Science*, 1:3 (1954), pp. 204–28, reprinted in W. Sellars, *Science, Perception and Reality*, section 85, p. 356.
2. R. Brassier, 'Nominalism, Naturalism, and Materialism: Sellars's Critical Ontology', in B. Bashour and H. Muller (eds), *Contemporary Philosophical Naturalism and Its Implications* (New York: Routledge, 2014), pp. 101–14, on p. 105.
3. Brassier, 'Nominalism, Naturalism, and Materialism', p. 105.
4. G. Soffer, 'Revisiting the Myth: Husserl and Sellars on the Given', *Review of Metaphysics,* 57:2 (2003), pp. 301–37.
5. Soffer, 'Revisiting the Myth', p. 305.
6. Sellars, 'Empiricism and the Philosophy of Mind', section 32, p. 164.
7. Sellars, 'Empiricism and the Philosophy of Mind', section 29, p. 160.
8. Sellars, 'Empiricism and the Philosophy of Mind', section 31, p. 162.
9. Soffer, 'Revisiting the Myth', p. 311.
10. Soffer, 'Revisiting the Myth', p. 314.
11. W. Sellars, 'Some Reflections on Perceptual Consciousness', in J. Sicha (ed.), *Kant's Transcendental Metaphysics* (Atascadero, CA: Ridgeview, 2002), section 4, p. 35.
12. Soffer, 'Revisiting the Myth', p. 316.
13. W. Sellars, 'The Structure of Knowledge', in H. Castañeda (ed.), *Action, Knowledge and Reality* (Indianapolis, IN: The Bobbs-Merrill Press, 1974), pp. 295–347; and W. Sellars, 'Mental Events', in K. Scharp and R. Brandom (eds), *In the Space of Reasons* (Cambridge, MA: Harvard University Press, 2007), pp. 282–300.
14. D. Zahavi, *Husserl's Phenomenology* (Stanford, CA: Stanford University Press, 2003), p. 94.
15. E. Husserl, *Cartesian Meditations*, trans. D. Cairns (Boston, MA: Kluwer Academic Publishers, 1991). In Sellars, *Science, Perception, and Reality*, p. 148. Sellars's allusion to 'Empiricism and the Philosophy of Mind' as his *'Meditations Hegeliènnes'* suggests that he was familiar with the 1931 French translation: E. Husserl, *Méditations cartésiennes*, trans. G. Peiffer and E. Levinas (Paris: Armand Colin, 1931).
16. Husserl, *Cartesian Meditations*, p. 32.
17. Husserl, *Cartesian Meditations*, p. 35.
18. Husserl, *Cartesian Meditations*, p. 36.
19. Husserl, *Cartesian Meditations*, p. 39.
20. Husserl, *Cartesian Meditations*, p. 37.
21. Husserl, *Cartesian Meditations*, p. 45.
22. Husserl, *Cartesian Meditations*, p. 51. Compare: 'Every object that the ego ever means, thinks of, values, deals with, likewise each that he ever phantasies or can phantasy, indicates its correlative system and exists only as itself the correlate of the system'; Husserl, *Cartesian Meditations*, p. 65.

23. W. Sellars, 'The Lever of Archimedes', in K. Scharp and R. Brandom (eds), *In the Space of Reasons* (Cambridge, MA: Harvard University Press, 2007), pp. 229–57, on p. 237.

24. I borrow this term from Q. Meillassoux, *After Finitude*, trans. R. Brassier (New York: Continuum, 2009); the connection between Meillassoux's critique of phenomenology and Sellars's critique of the Myth of the Given is central to R. Brassier's *Nihil Unbound* (New York: Palgrave-Macmillan, 2010).

25. D. Zahavi, 'Merleau-Ponty on Husserl: A Reappraisal', in T. Toadvine and L. Embree (eds), *Merleau-Ponty's Reading of Husserl* (New York: Springer, 2002), pp. 3–30.

26. 'M. Merleau-Ponty, 'The Philosopher and His Shadow', *Signs*, trans. R. McClerary (Chicago, IL: Northwestern University Press, 1964), pp. 159–81, on p. 165.

27. Merleau-Ponty, 'The Philosopher and His Shadow', p. 165.

28. Merleau-Ponty, 'The Philosopher and His Shadow', p. 165.

29. Merleau-Ponty, 'The Philosopher and His Shadow', p. 165.

30. Merleau-Ponty, 'The Philosopher and His Shadow', p. 167.

31. Merleau-Ponty, 'The Philosopher and His Shadow', p. 169.

32. Merleau-Ponty, 'The Philosopher and His Shadow', p. 173.

33. Merleau-Ponty, 'The Philosopher and His Shadow', p. 177.

34. Merleau-Ponty, 'The Philosopher and His Shadow', p. 180.

35. Merleau-Ponty, Maurice, 'The Philosopher and His Shadow', p. 189.

36. T. Carman, 'The Body in Husserl and Merleau-Ponty', *Philosophical Topics*, 27:2 (1999), pp. 205–26, on p. 209.

37. Carman, 'The Body in Husserl and Merleau-Ponty', p. 214.

38. J. Smith, 'Merleau-Ponty and the Phenomenological Reduction', *Inquiry*, 48:6 (2005), pp. 553–71, on p. 561.

39. Smith, 'Merleau-Ponty and the Phenomenological Reduction', p. 562.

40. M. Merleau-Ponty, 'The Primacy of Perception and Its Philosophical Consequences', in J. Edie (trans. and ed)., *The Primacy of Perception* (Chicago, IL: Northwestern University Press, 1964), pp. 12–42, on p. 30.

41. Merleau-Ponty, 'The Primacy of Perception and Its Philosophical Consequences', p. 29.

42. Merleau-Ponty, 'The Primacy of Perception and Its Philosophical Consequences', p. 30.

43. Merleau-Ponty, *Phenomenology of Perception*, p. xv.

44. K. Romdenh-Romluc, *Merleau-Ponty and the* Phenomenology of Perception, p. 33

45. M. Merleau-Ponty, *Phenomenology of Perception*, trans. D. Landes (New York: Routledge, 2012), p. xxii.

46. Merleau-Ponty, *Phenomenology of Perception*, p. 367.

47. Merleau-Ponty, *Phenomenology of Perception*, p. 346.

48. Merleau-Ponty, *Phenomenology of Perception*, p. 151. The case of Schneider forms the empirical side of M. Merleau–Ponty, 'The Spatiality of One's Own Body and Motility', *Phenomenology of Perception*, pp. 118–61, and also appears in M. Merleau–Ponty, 'The Body in its Sexual Being',*Phenomenology of Perception*, pp. 179–82.

49. Merleau-Ponty, *Phenomenology of Perception*, p. 317.

50. K. Westphal, *Hegel's Epistemology* (Indianapolis, IN: Hackett, 2003), pp. 40–7.

51. Note the contrast with McDowell, who *does* end up treating transcendental descriptions as Given, precisely because he does not explicate the mediation between transcendental description and empirical explanation.

INDEX